R. Gupta's®

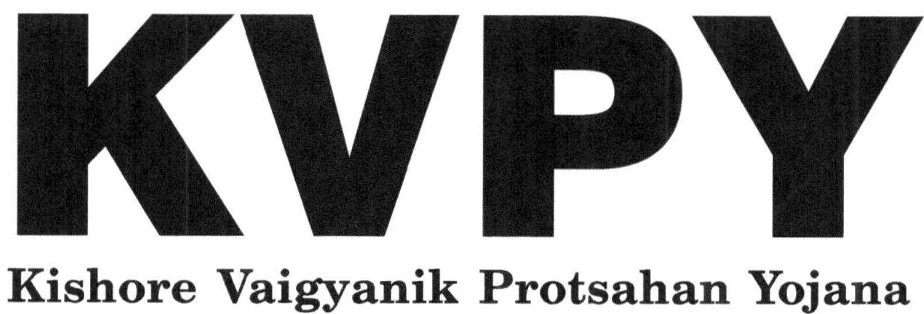

Kishore Vaigyanik Protsahan Yojana

STREAM–SA

Examination

For Class XI

Previous Years' Papers

(Solved)

2020
EDITION

Ramesh Publishing House, New Delhi

Published by
O.P. Gupta *for* Ramesh Publishing House

Admin. Office
12-H, New Daryaganj Road, Opp. Officers' Mess,
New Delhi-110002 ✆ 23261567, 23275224, 23275124

E-mail: info@rameshpublishinghouse.com
Website: www.rameshpublishinghouse.com

Showroom
- Balaji Market, Nai Sarak, Delhi-6 ✆ 23253720, 23282525
- 4457, Nai Sarak, Delhi-6, ✆ 23918938

Book Code: R-2044

ISBN: 978-93-88642-99-6

HSN Code: 49011010

CONTENTS

☆ ☆ ☆ ☆ ☆

FELLOWSHIP ELIGIBILITY

- **The KVPY Fellowships are given to Indian Nationals to Study in India** (Students intending to pursue/pursuing undergraduate program under Distance Education scheme/correspondence course of any university are not eligible to apply).
- **Stream SA:** Students enrolled in XI Standard (Science Subjects) and having secured a minimum of 75% (65% for SC/ST/PWD) marks in aggregate in MATHEMATICS and SCIENCE subjects in the X Standard Board examination immediately in the preceding academic year are eligible to appear for Aptitude test.
- The fellowship of the students selected under this stream will be activated only if they join an undergraduate course in Basic Sciences (B.Sc./B.S./B.Stat./B.Math./Int. M.Sc./Int. M.S.) after having secured a minimum of 60% (50% for SC/ST/PWD) marks in aggregate in Science subjects in the XII standard/(+2) Board Examination. During the interim period of one year they will be invited for the National Science (Vijyoshi) Camp and their travel expenses and local hospitality will be met by KVPY.
- In the Stream-SA all questions are compulsory (Science and Mathematics).

☆ ☆ ☆ ☆

Previous Paper (Solved), 2018

Kishore Vaigyanik Protsahan Yojana (KVPY)

STREAM – SA

Part-I

Mathematics

1. The number of pairs (a, b) of positive real numbers satisfying $a^4 + b^4 < 1$ and $a^2 + b^2 > 1$ is:
A. 0 B. 1
C. 2 D. more than 2

2. The number of real roots of the polynomial equation $x^4 - x^2 + 2x - 1 = 0$ is:
A. 0 B. 2
C. 3 D. 4

3. Suppose the sum of the first m terms of an arithmetic progression is n and the sum of its first n terms is m, where $m \neq n$. Then the sum of the first $(m + n)$ terms of the arithmetic progression is:
A. $1 - mn$ B. $mn - 5$
C. $-(m + n)$ D. $m + n$

4. Consider the following two statements:
I. Any pair of consistent linear equations in two variables must have a unique solution.
II. There do not exist two consecutive integers, the sum of whose squares is 365.
Then,
A. Both I and II are true
B. Both I and II are false
C. I is true and II is false
D. I is false and II is true

5. The number of polynomials $p(x)$ with integer coefficients such that the curve $y = p(x)$ passes through (2, 2) and (4, 5) is:
A. 0
B. 1
C. more than 1 but finite
D. infinite

6. The median of all 4-digit numbers that are divisible by 7 is:
A. 5497 B. 5498.5
C. 5499.5 D. 5490

7. A solid hemisphere is attached to the top of a cylinder, having the same radius as that of the cylinder. If the height of the cylinder were doubled (keeping both radii fixed), the volume of the entire system would have increased by 50%. By what percentage would the volume have increased if the radii of the hemisphere and the cylinder were doubled (keeping the height fixed)?
A. 300% B. 400%
C. 500% D. 600%

8. Consider a triangle PQR in which the relation $QR^2 + PR^2 = 5PQ^2$ holds. Let G be the point of intersection of medians PM and QN. Then $\angle QGM$ is always:
A. less than 45°
B. obtuse
C. a right angle
D. acute and larger than 45°

9. Let a, b, c be the side-lengths of a triangle, and l, m, n be the lengths of its medians. Put $K = \frac{l+m+n}{a+b+c}$. Then, as a, b, c vary, K can assume every value in the interval:
A. $\left(\frac{1}{4}, \frac{2}{3}\right)$ B. $\left(\frac{1}{2}, \frac{4}{5}\right)$
C. $\left(\frac{3}{4}, 1\right)$ D. $\left(\frac{4}{5}, \frac{5}{4}\right)$

10. Let x_0, y_0 be fixed real numbers such that $x_0^2 + y_0^2 > 1$. If x, y are arbitrary real numbers such that $x^2 + y^2 \leq 1$, then the minimum value of $(x - x_0)^2 + (y - y_0)^2$ is:
A. $\left(\sqrt{x_0^2 + y_0^2} - 1\right)^2$ B. $x_0^2 + y_0^2 - 1$
C. $(|x_0| + |y_0| - 1)^2$ D. $(|x_0| + |y_0|)^2 - 1$

11. Let PQR be a triangle in which PQ = 3. From the vertex R, draw the altitude RS to meet PQ at S. Assume that $RS = \sqrt{3}$ and PS = QR. Then PR equals:

A. $\sqrt{5}$ B. $\sqrt{6}$
C. $\sqrt{7}$ D. $\sqrt{8}$

12. A 100 mark examination was administered to a class of 50 students. Despite only integer marks being given, the average score of the class was 47.5. Then, the maximum number of students who could get marks more than the class average is:

A. 25
B. 35
C. 45
D. 49

13. Let s be the sum of the digits of the number $15^2 \times 5^{18}$ in base 10. Then:

A. $s < 6$ B. $6 \leq s < 140$
C. $140 \leq s < 148$ D. $s \geq 148$

14. Let PQR be an acute-angled triangle in which PQ < QR. From the vertex Q draw the altitude QQ_1, the angle bisector QQ_2 and the median QQ_3, with Q_1, Q_2, Q_3 lying on PR. Then:

A. $PQ_1 < PQ_2 < PQ_3$ B. $PQ_2 < PQ_1 < PQ_3$
C. $PQ_1 < PQ_3 < PQ_2$ D. $PQ_3 < PQ_1 < PQ_2$

15. All the vertices of a rectangle are of the form (a, b) with a, b integers satisfying the equation $(a - 8)^2 - (b - 7)^2 = 5$. Then the perimeter of the rectangle is:

A. 20 B. 22
C. 24 D. 26

Physics

16. A block of wood is floating on water at 0°C with volume V_0 above water. When the temperature of water increases from 0 to 10°C, the change in the volume of the block that is above water is best described schematically by the graph:

A.
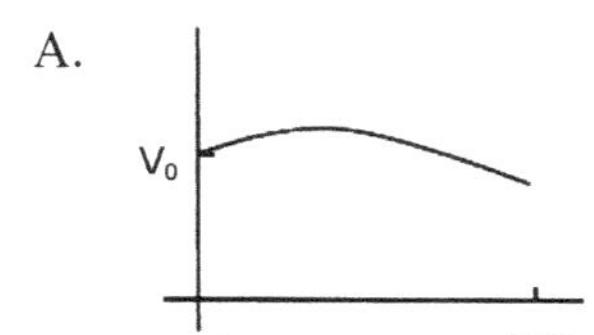

B.
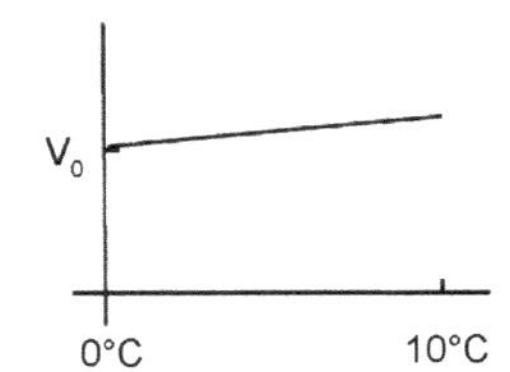

C.
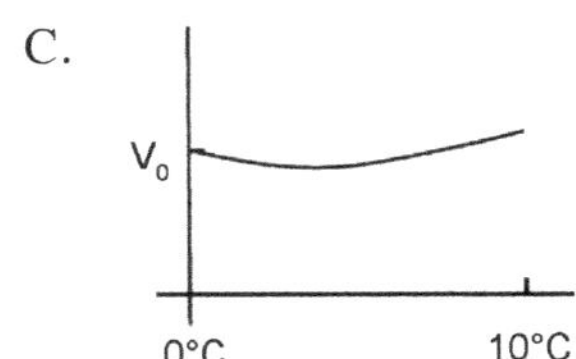

D.
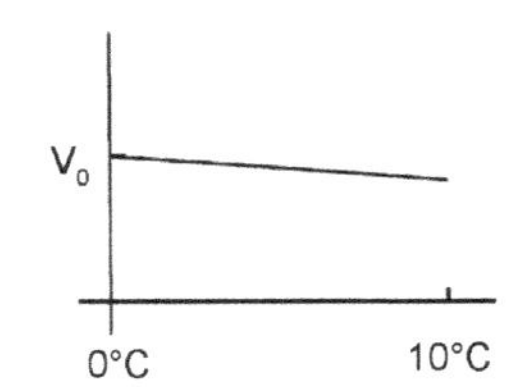

17. A very large block of ice of the size of a volleyball court and of uniform thickness of 8 m is floating on water. A person standing near its edge wishes to fetch a bucketful of water using a rope. The smallest length of rope required for this is about:

A. 3.6 m B. 1.8 m
C. 0.9 m D. 0.4 m

18. A box filled with water has a small hole on its side near the bottom. It is dropped from the top of a tower. As it falls, a camera attached on the side of the box records the shape of the water stream coming out of the hole. The resulting video will show:

A. the water coming down forming a parabolic stream.
B. the water going up forming a parabolic stream.
C. the water coming out in a straight line.
D. no water coming out.

19. An earthen pitcher used in summer cools water in it essentially by evaporation of water from its porous surface. If a pitcher carries 4 kg of water and the rate of evaporation is 20 g per hour, temperature of water in it decreases by ΔT in two hours. The value of ΔT is close to (ratio of latent of evaporation to specific heat of water is 540°C)

A. 2.7°C B. 4.2°C
C. 5.4°C D. 10.8°C

20. Two plane mirrors are kept on a horizontal table making an angle θ with each other as shown schematically in the figure. The angle θ is such that any ray of light reflected after striking both the mirrors returns parallel to its incident path. For this to happen, the value of θ should be:

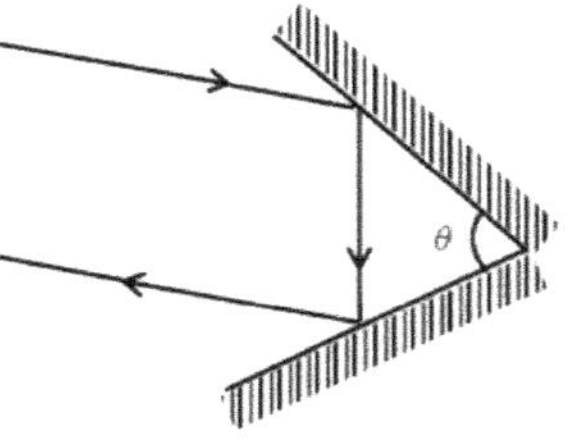

A. 30° B. 45°
C. 60° D. 90°

21. A certain liquid has a melting point of –50°C and a boiling point of 150°C. A thermometer is designed with this liquid and its melting and boiling points are designated as 0°L and 100°L. The melting and boiling points of water on this scale are:

A. 25°L and 75°L, respectively.
B. 0°L and 100°L, respectively.
C. 20°L and 70°L, respectively.
D. 30°L and 80°L, respectively.

22. One can define an alpha-Volt (αV) to be the energy acquired by an α particle when it is accelerated by a potential of 1 Volt. For this problem, you may take a proton to be 2000 times heavier than an electron. Then:

A. 1 αV = 1 eV/4000 B. 1 αV = 2 eV
C. 1 αV = 8000 eV D. 1 αV = 1 eV

23. In a particle accelerator, a current of 500 μA is carried by a proton beam in which each proton has a speed of 3×10^7 m/s. The cross sectional area of the beam is 1.50 mm^2. The charge density in this beam in Coulomb/m^3 is close to:

A. 10^{-8} B. 10^{-7}
C. 10^{-6} D. 10^{-5}

24. Which of the following is NOT true about the total lunar eclipse?

A. A lunar eclipse can occur on a new moon and full moon day.
B. The lunar eclipse would occur roughly every month if the orbits of earth and moon were perfectly coplanar.
C. The moon appears red during the eclipse because the blue light is absorbed in earth's atmosphere and red is transmitted.
D. A lunar eclipse can occur only on a full moon day.

25. Many exoplanets have been discovered by the transit method, wherein one monitors a dip in the intensity of the parent star as the exoplanet moves in front of it. The exoplanet has a radius R and the parent star has radius 100 R. If I_0 is the intensity observed on earth due to the parent star, then as the exoplanet transits:

A. the minimum observed intensity of the parent star is 0.9 I_0.
B. the minimum observed intensity of the parent star is 0.99 I_0.
C. the minimum observed intensity of the parent star is 0.999 I_0.
D. the minimum observed intensity of the parent star is 0.9999 I_0.

26. A steady current I is set up in a wire whose cross-sectional area decreases in the direction of the flow of the current. Then, as we examine the narrowing region:

A. the current density decreases in value.
B. the magnitude of the electric field increases.
C. the current density remains constant.
D. the average speed of the moving charges remains constant.

27. Select the correct statement about rainbow:

A. We can see a rainbow in the western sky in the late afternoon.
B. The double rainbow has red on the inside and violet on the outside.
C. A rainbow has an arc shape since the earth is round.
D. A rainbow on the moon is violet on the inside and red on the outside.

28. Remote sensing satellites move in an orbit that is at an average height of about 500 km from the surface of the earth. The camera onboard one such satellite has a screen of area A on which the images captured by it are formed. If the focal length of the camera lens is 50 cm, then the terrestrial area that can be observed from the satellite is close to:

A. 2×10^3 A B. 10^6 A
C. 10^{12} A D. 4×10^{12} A

29. Letters A, B, C and D are written on a cardboard as shown in the picture.

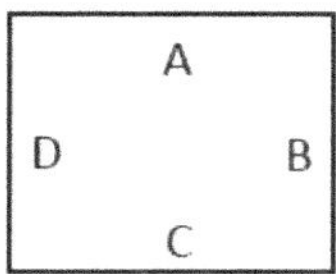

The cardboard is kept at a suitable distance behind a transparent empty glass of cylindrical shape. If the glass is now filled with water, one sees an inverted image of the pattern on the cardboard when looking through the glass. Ignoring magnification effects, the image would appear as:

A. 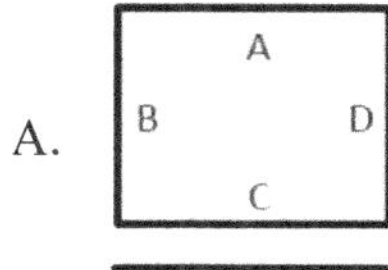

B.

C.

D.

30. If a ball is thrown at a velocity of 45 m/s in vertical upward direction, then what would be the velocity profile as function of height? Assume g = 10 m/s^2.

A.

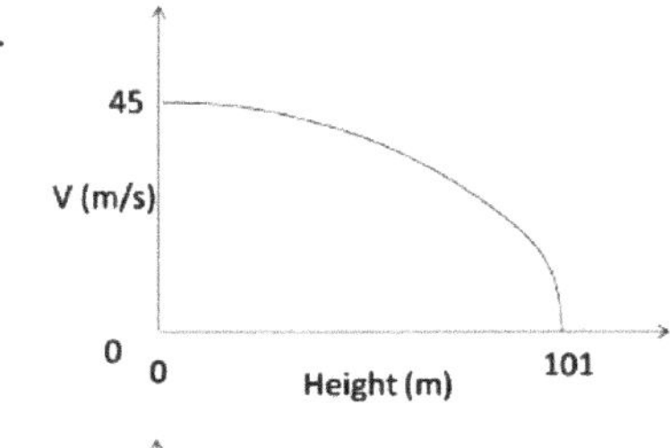

B.

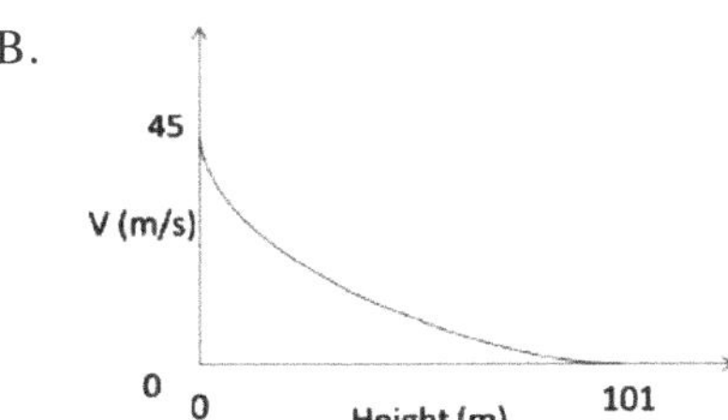

C.

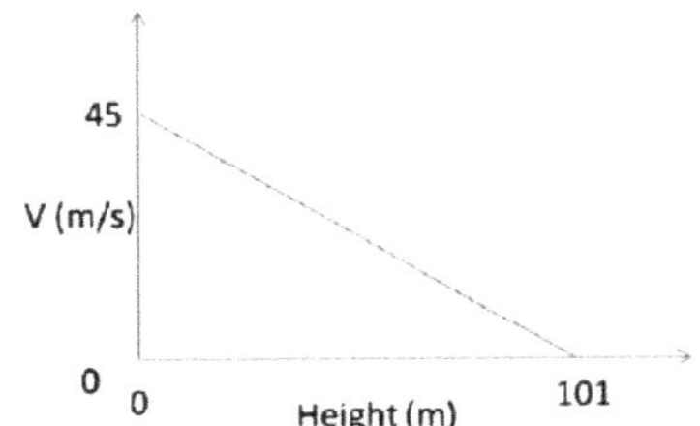

D.

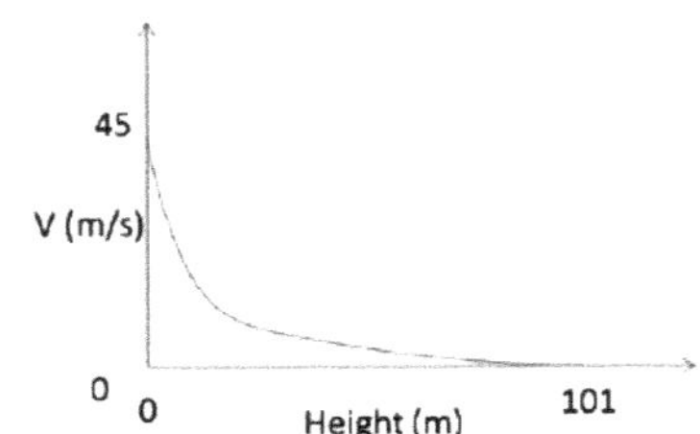

Chemistry

31. The number of water molecules in 250 mL of water is closest to:

[Given: Density of water is 1.0 g mL^{-1}; Avogadro's number = 6.023×10^{23}]

A. 83.6×10^{23} B. 13.9×10^{23}
C. 1.5×10^{23} D. 33.6×10^{23}

32. Among the following, the correct statement is:

A. pH decreases when solid ammonium chloride is added to a dilute aqueous solution of NH_3
B. pH decreases when solid sodium acetate is added to a dilute aqueous solution of acetic acid
C. pH decreases when solid NaCl is added to a dilute aqueous solution of NaOH
D. pH decreases when solid sodium oxalate is added to a dilute aqueous solution of oxalic acid

33. The solubility of $BaSO_4$ in pure water (in g L^{-1}) is closest to:
[Given: K_{sp} for $BaSO_4$ is 1.0×10^{-10} at 25°C. Molecular weight of $BaSO_4$ is 233 g mol^{-1}]

A. 1.0×10^{-5} B. 1.0×10^{-3}
C. 2.3×10^{-5} D. 2.3×10^{-3}

34. Among the following, the INCORRECT statement is:

A. No two electrons in an atom can have the same set of four quantum numbers
B. The maximum number of electrons in the shell with principal quantum number, n, is equal to $n^2 + 2$
C. Electrons in an orbital must have opposite spin
D. In the ground state, atomic orbitals are filled in the order of their increasing energies.

35. A container of volume 2.24 L can withstand a maximum pressure of 2 atm at 298 K before exploding. The maximum amount of nitrogen (in g) that can be safely put in this container at this temperature is closest to:

A. 2.8 B. 5.6
C. 1.4 D. 4.2

36. The compound shown below

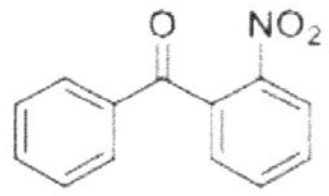

can be readily prepared by Friedel-Crafts reaction between:

A. benzene and 2-nitrobenzoyl chloride
B. benzyl chloride and nitrobenzene
C. nitrobenzene and benzoyl chloride
D. benzene and 2-nitrobenzyl chloride

37. The correct statement about the following compounds

is:

A. Both are chiral
B. Both are achiral
C. X is chiral and Y is achiral
D. X is achiral and Y is chiral

38. The most acidic proton and the strongest nucleophilic nitrogen in the following compound

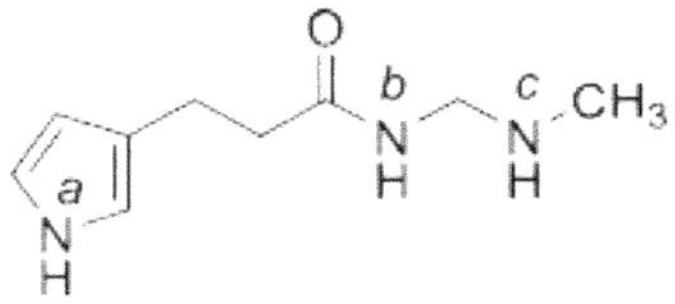

respectively, are:

A. N^a–H; N^b
B. N^b–H; N^c
C. N^a–H; N^c
D. N^c–H; N^a

39. The chlorine atom of the following compound

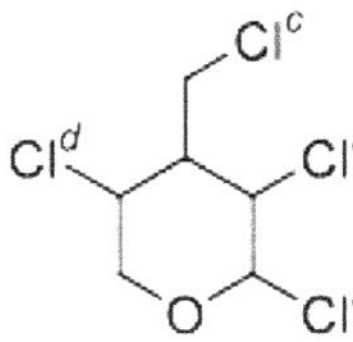

that reacts most readily with $AgNO_3$ to give a precipitate is:

A. Cl^a B. Cl^b
C. Cl^c D. Cl^d

40. Among the following sets, the most stable ionic species are:

A. 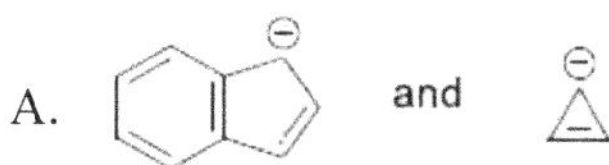

B. 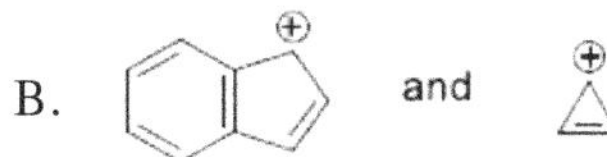

C. 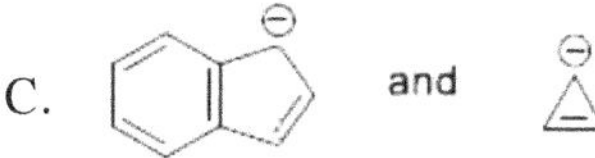

D. 

41. The correct order of energy of 2*s* orbitals in H, Li, Na and K, is:
A. K < Na < Li < H B. Na < Li < K < H
C. Na < K < H < Li D. H < Na < Li < K

42. The hybridization of xenon atom in XeF_4 is
A. sp^3 B. dsp^2
C. sp^3d^2 D. d^2sp^3

43. The formal oxidation numbers of Cr and Cl in the ions $Cr_2O_7^{2-}$ and ClO_3^-, respectively, are:
A. +6 and +7 B. +7 and +5
C. +6 and +5 D. +8 and +7

44. A filter paper soaked in salt X turns brown when exposed to HNO_3 vapour. The salt X is:
A. KCl B. KBr
C. KI D. K_2SO_4

45. The role of haemoglobin is to:
A. store oxygen in muscles
B. transport oxygen to different parts of the body
C. convert CO to CO_2
D. convert CO_2 into carbonic acid

Biology

46. Which ONE of the following molecules is a secondary metabolite?
A. Ethanol B. Lactate
C. Penicillin D. Citric Acid

47. Lecithin is a:
A. Carbohydrate B. Phospholipid
C. Nucleoside D. Protein

48. The water potential (ψ^P) of pure water at standard temperature and atmospheric pressure is:
A. 0 B. 0.5
C. 1.0 D. 2.0

49. Action potential in neurons is generated by a rapid influx of:
A. Chloride ions B. Potassium ions
C. Calcium ions D. Sodium ions

50. Erythropoietin is produced by:
A. Heart B. Kidney
C. Bone marrow D. Adrenal gland

51. Tendrils are modifications of:
A. Stem or leaf B. Stem only
C. Leaf only D. Aerial roots only

52. Which ONE of the following combinations of biomolecules is present in the ribosomes?
A. RNA, DNA and protein
B. RNA, lipids and DNA
C. RNA and protein
D. RNA and DNA

53. Which ONE of the following proteins does NOT play a role in skeletal muscle contraction?
A. Actin B. Myosin
C. Troponin D. Microtubule

54. Which ONE of the following reactions is catalyzed by high-energy ultraviolet radiation in the stratosphere?
A. $O_2 + O \rightarrow O_3$ B. $O_2 \rightarrow O + O$
C. $O_3 + O_3 \rightarrow 3O_2$ D. $O + O \rightarrow O_2$

55. Which ONE of the following statements is TRUE about trypsinogen?
A. It is activated by enterokinase
B. It is activated by renin
C. It is activated by pepsin
D. It does not need activation

56. Which ONE of the following organisms respire through the skin?
A. Blue whale B. Salamander
C. Platypus D. Peacock

57. Which ONE of the following human cells lacks a nucleus?
A. Neutrophil B. Neuron
C. Mature erythrocyte D. Keratinocyte

58. The first enzyme that the food encounters in human digestive system is:
A. Pepsin B. Trypsin
C. Chymotrypsin D. Amylase

59. Glycoproteins are formed in which ONE of the following organelles?
A. Peroxisome B. Lysosome
C. Golgi apparatus D. Mitochondria

60. An example of nastic movement (external stimulus-dependent movement) in plants is:
A. folding-up of the leaves of *Mimosa pudica*
B. climbing of tendrils
C. growth of roots from seeds
D. growth of pollen tube towards the ovule

Part-II

Mathematics

61. What is the sum of all natural numbers n such that the product of the digits of n (in base 10) is equal to $n^2 - 10n - 36$?

A. 12
B. 13
C. 124
D. 2612

62. Let m (respectively, n) be the number of 5-digit integers obtained by using the digits 1, 2, 3, 4, 5 with repetitions (respectively, without repetitions) such that the sum of any two adjacent digits is odd. Then $\frac{m}{n}$ is equal to:

A. 9 B. 12
C. 15 D. 18

63. The number of solid cones with integer radius and integer height each having its volume numerically equal to its total surface area is:

A. 0 B. 1
C. 2 D. infinite

64. Let ABCD be a square. An arc of a circle with A as center and AB as radius is drawn inside the square joining the points B and D. Points P on AB, S on AD, Q and R on arc BD are taken such that PQRS is a square. Further suppose that PQ and RS are parallel to AC. Then $\frac{\text{area PQRS}}{\text{area ABCD}}$ is:

A. $\frac{1}{8}$ B. $\frac{1}{5}$
C. $\frac{1}{4}$ D. $\frac{2}{5}$

65. Suppose ABCD is a trapezium whose sides and height are integers and AB is parallel to CD. If the area of ABCD is 12 and the sides are distinct, then $|AB - CD|$:

A. is 2
B. is 4
C. is 8
D. cannot be determined from the data

Physics

66. A coffee maker makes coffee by passing steam through a mixture of coffee powder, milk and water. If the steam is mixed at the rate of 50 g per minute in a mug containing 500 g of mixture, then it takes about t_0 seconds to make coffee at 70°C when the initial temperature of the mixture is 25°C. The value of t_0 is close to (ratio of latent heat of evaporation to specific heat of water is 540°C and specific heat of the mixture can be taken to be the same as that of water):

A. 30 B. 45
C. 60 D. 90

67. A person in front of a mountain is beating a drum at the rate of 40 per minute and hears no distinct echo. If the person moves 90 m closer to the mountain, he has to beat the drum at 60 per minute to not hear any distinct echo. The speed of sound is:

A. 320 ms^{-1} B. 340 ms^{-1}
C. 360 ms^{-1} D. 380 ms^{-1}

68. A glass beaker is filled with water up to 5 cm. It is kept on top of a 2 cm thick glass slab. When a coin at the bottom of the glass slab is viewed at the normal incidence from above the beaker, its apparent depth from the water surface is d cm. Value of d is close to (the refractive indices of water and glass are 1.33 and 1.50, respectively)

A. 2.5 B. 5.1
C. 3.7 D. 6.0

69. A proton of mass m and charge e is projected from a very large distance towards an α particle with velocity v. Initially, α particle is at rest, but it is free to move. If gravity is neglected, then the minimum separation along the straight line of their motion will be:

A. $e^2/4\pi\varepsilon_0 mv^2$ B. $5e^2/4\pi\varepsilon_0 mv^2$
C. $2e^2/4\pi\varepsilon_0 mv^2$ D. $4e^2/4\pi\varepsilon_0 mv^2$

70. A potential is given by $V(x) = k(x + a)^2/2$ for $x < 0$ and $V(x) = k(x - a)^2/2$ for $x > 0$. The schematic variation of oscillation period (T) for a particle performing periodic motion in this potential as a function of its energy E is:

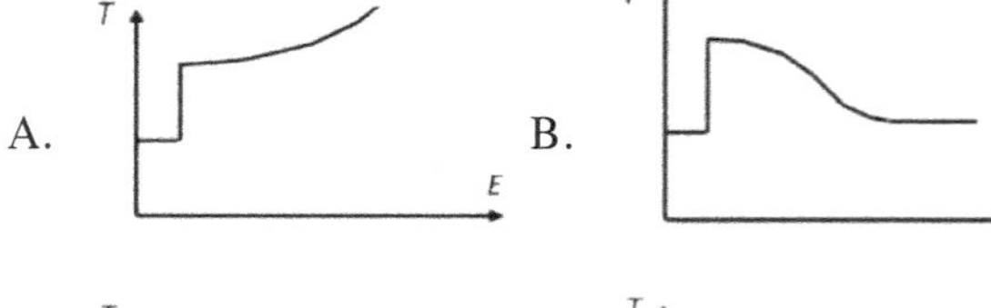

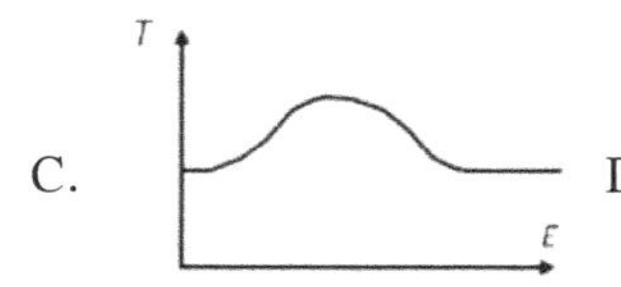

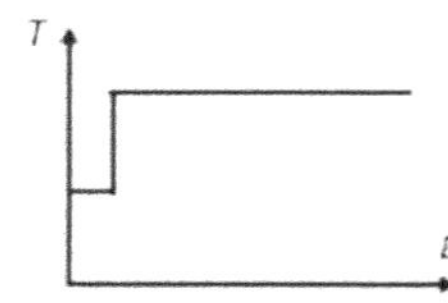

Chemistry

71. Among the following, the species with identical bond order are:

A. CO and O_2^{2-} B. O_2^- and CO
C. O_2^{2-} and B_2 D. CO and N_2^+

72. The quantity of heat (in J) required to raise the temperature of 1.0 kg of ethanol from 293.45 K to the boiling point and then change the liquid to vapour at that temperature is closest to

[Given: Boiling point of ethanol 351.45 K

Specific heat capacity of liquid ethanol 2.44 J g^{-1} K^{-1}

Latent heat of vaporization of ethanol 855 J g^{-1}]

A. 1.42×10^2 B. 9.97×10^2
C. 1.42×10^5 D. 9.97×10^5

73. A solution of 20.2 g of 1, 2-dibromopropane in MeOH upon heating with excess Zn produces 3.58 g of an unsaturated compound X. The yield (%) of X is closest to:

[Atomic weight of Br is 80]

A. 18 B. 85
C. 89 D. 30

74. The lower stability of ethyl anion compared to methyl anion and the higher stability of ethyl radical compared to methyl radical, respectively, are due to:

A. +I effect of the methyl group in ethyl anion and $\sigma \rightarrow$ p-orbital conjugation in ethyl radical
B. –I effect of the methyl group in ethyl anion and $\sigma \rightarrow \sigma^*$ conjugation in ethyl radical
C. +I effect of the methyl group in both cases
D. +I effect of the methyl group in ethyl anion and $\sigma \rightarrow \sigma^*$ conjugation in ethyl radical

75. The F-Br-F bond angles in BrF_5 and the Cl-P-Cl bond angles in PCl_5 respectively, are:

A. identical in BrF_5 but non-identical in PCl_5
B. identical in BrF_5 and identical in PCl_5
C. non-identical in BrF_5 but identical in PCl_5
D. non-identical in BrF_5 and non-identical in PCl_5

Biology

76. If the genotypes determining the blood groups of a couple are $I^A I^O$ and $I^A I^B$, then the probability of their first child having type O blood is:

A. 0 B. 0.25
C. 0.50 D. 0.75

77. A cross was carried out between two individuals heterozygous for two pairs of genes was carried out. Assuming segregation and independent assortment, the number of different genotypes and phenotypes obtained respectively would be:

A. 4 and 9 B. 6 and 3
C. 9 and 4 D. 11 and 4

78. If the H^+ concentration of an aqueous solution is 0.001 M, then the pOH of the solution would be:

A. 0.001 B. 0.999
C. 3 D. 11

79. Consider the following vision defects listed in **Columns I & II** and the corrective measures in **Column III.** Choose the correct combination.

Column I	Column II	Column III
P. Hyper-metropia	(*i*) near-sightedness	(*a*) convex lens
Q. Myopia	(*ii*) far-sightedness	(*b*) concave lens

A. P-(*ii*)-(*b*) B. Q-(*i*)-(*b*)
C. P-(*i*)-(*a*) D. Q-(*i*)-(*a*)

80. Which ONE of the following properties causes the plant tendrils to coil around a bamboo stick?

A. Tendril has spines
B. The base of the tendril grows faster than the tip
C. Part of the tendril in contact with the bamboo stick grows at a slower rate than the part away from it.
D. The tip of the tendril grows faster than the base

ANSWERS

1	2	3	4	5	6	7	8	9	10
D	B	C	B	A	B	C	C	C	A
11	**12**	**13**	**14**	**15**	**16**	**17**	**18**	**19**	**20**
C	D	B	A	A	A	C	D	C	D
21	**22**	**23**	**24**	**25**	**26**	**27**	**28**	**29**	**30**
A	B	D	A	D	B	B	C	D	A
31	**32**	**33**	**34**	**35**	**36**	**37**	**38**	**39**	**40**
A	A	D	B	D	A	C	C	A	D

41	42	43	44	45	46	47	48	49	50
A	C	C	C	B	C	B	A	D	B
51	**52**	**53**	**54**	**55**	**56**	**57**	**58**	**59**	**60**
A	C	D	B	A	B	C	D	C	A
61	**62**	**63**	**64**	**65**	**66**	**67**	**68**	**69**	**70**
B	C	B	D	B	B	C	B	B	B
71	**72**	**73**	**74**	**75**	**76**	**77**	**78**	**79**	**80**
C	D	B	A	D	A	C	D	B	C

EXPLANATORY ANSWERS

1. Let a^2 = M & b^2 = N then M > 0 and N > 0

Now given condition is M + N > 1 and $M^2 + N^2 < 1$

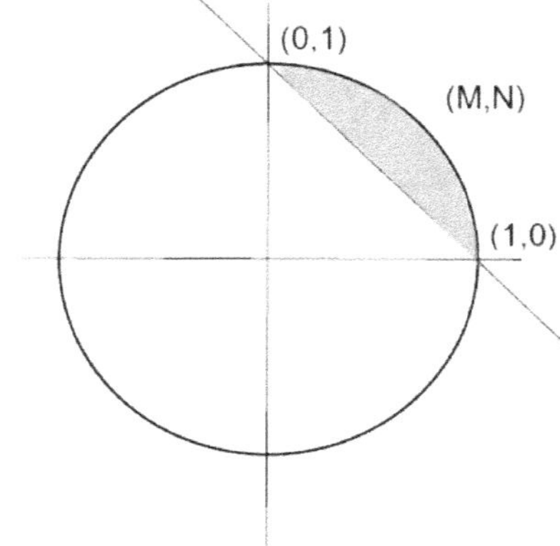

(M, N) lies inside circle $x^2 + y^2 < 1$ and above line $x + y > 1$

$\Rightarrow$ (M, N) lies in shaded region and number of points in shaded region are infinite, so number of pair (a, b) are also infinite.

2.
$$x^4 - x^2 + 2x - 1 = 0$$
$$x^2 - (x - 1)^2 = 0$$
$$\Rightarrow (x^2 + x - 1)(x^2 - x + 1) = 0$$

$x^2 + x - 1 = 0$ has two real roots.

3.
$$S_m = \frac{m}{2}[2a+(m-1)d] = n \quad ...(i)$$
$$S_n = \frac{n}{2}[2a+(n-1)d] = m \quad ...(ii)$$

By (i) and (ii)

$$(m - n)a + (m - n)\{m + n - 1\}\frac{d}{2} = -(m - n)$$

$\Rightarrow 2a + (m + n - 1)d = -2 \ (m \neq n)$

$$\Rightarrow \quad S_{m+n} = \frac{m+n}{2}[2a+(m+n-1)d]$$
$$= -(m + n).$$

4. Clearly statement I is false as they can have infinite solutions.

Statement II is also false as $13^2 + 14^2 = 365$.

5. $y = P(x) = a_0 + a_1x + a_2x^2 + ... + a_nx^n$

$a_0, a_1, a_2, a_3, ...a_n \in I$

$$2 = P(2) \quad ...(i)$$
$$5 = P(4) \quad ...(ii)$$

By (i) & (ii)

$$\Rightarrow \quad 3 = a_1(4 - 2) + a_2(4^2 - 2^2) + a_3(4^3 - 2^3) + ... + a_n(4^n - 2^n)$$

Clearly RHS is even and LHS is odd no polynomial exists.

6. Four digit numbers which are divisible by 7 are: 1001, 1008, 1015, ..., 9996

Hence, total number of such numbers = 1286

$$\Rightarrow \quad \text{Median} = \frac{\left(\frac{N}{2}\right)^{th} \text{value} + \left(\frac{N}{2}+1\right)^{th} \text{value}}{2}$$
$$= \frac{(643)^{th} \text{ value} + (644)^{th} \text{ value}}{2}$$
$$= 1001 + \frac{1285 \times 7}{2}$$
$$= 1001 + 4497.5$$
$$= 5498.5.$$

7. Let height of radius of cylinder are h & r respectively.

Then volume $V_1 = \pi r^2 h + \frac{2}{3}\pi r^3 \quad ...(i)$

When height of cylinder is doubled then volume

$$V_2 = 2\pi r^2 h + \frac{2}{3}\pi r^3 \quad ...(ii)$$

Given that, $\frac{V_2}{V_1} = \frac{3}{2}$

$$\Rightarrow \quad \frac{2h + \frac{2}{3}r}{h + \frac{2}{3}r} = \frac{3}{2}$$

$$\Rightarrow \quad 2h+\frac{2}{3}r = \frac{3}{2}h+r$$

$$\Rightarrow \quad \frac{h}{2} = \frac{r}{3}$$

$$\Rightarrow \quad h = \frac{2}{3}r \qquad ...(iii)$$

When radius is doubled then volume

$$V_2^1 = 4\pi r^2 h+\frac{16}{3}\pi r^3$$

$$\frac{V_2^1}{V_1} = \frac{4h+\frac{16}{3}r}{h+\frac{2}{3}r}$$

By (iii) $\quad \frac{V_2^1}{V_1} = \frac{4h+8h}{h+h} = 6$

Hence volume will be increased by 500%.

8.

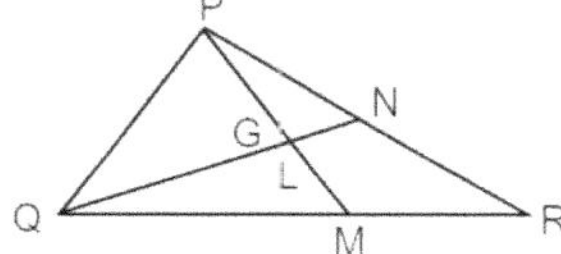

Let, QR = p, PR = q, PQ = r

Given, $\quad p^2 + q^2 = 5r^2$

Now, $\quad QG^2 + GM^2 = \left(\frac{2QN}{3}\right)^2 + \left(\frac{PM}{3}\right)^2$

$$= 4\frac{QN^2}{9}+\frac{PM^2}{9}$$

$$= \frac{1}{9}\left[4.\frac{1}{4}\left(2r^2+2p^2-q^2\right)+\frac{1}{4}\left(2r^2+2q^2-p^2\right)\right]$$

$$= \frac{p^2}{4} = QM^2$$

Hence, Angle QGM is 90°.

9.

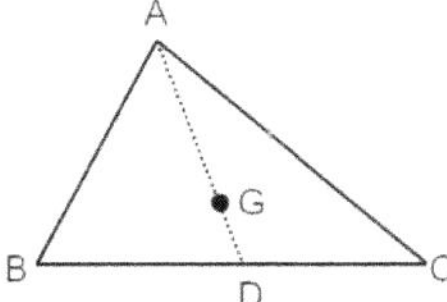

As AD is medium

$$\Rightarrow \quad AD < \frac{AB+AC}{2}$$

$$\Rightarrow \quad \ell < \frac{b+c}{2}$$

Similarly, $\quad m < \frac{c+a}{2}$ and $n < \frac{a+b}{2}$

$$\Rightarrow \quad \ell + m + n < a + b + c$$

$$\Rightarrow \quad \frac{\ell+m+n}{a+b+c} < 1 \qquad ...(i)$$

Also in the ΔBGC

$$BG + GC > BC$$

$$\Rightarrow \quad \frac{2}{3}(m+n) > a$$

Similarly, $\quad \frac{2}{3}(n+\ell) > b$

and, $\quad \frac{2}{3}(\ell+m) > c$

Hence, $\quad \frac{4}{3}(\ell+m+n) > a + b + c$

$$\frac{\ell+m+n}{a+b+c} > \frac{3}{4} \qquad ...(ii)$$

By (i) and (ii) $\quad \frac{\ell+m+n}{a+b+c} \in \left(\frac{3}{4}, 1\right)$.

10. $\quad x_0^2+y_0^2 > 1 \qquad x_0 - y_0$ fixed

$x, y \quad$ arbitrary

$x^2 + y^2 \le 1$, Let $x = \cos\theta$, $y = \sin\theta$

For men, $\quad z = (x - x_0)^2 + (y - y_0)^2$

$$z = x^2 + x_0{}^2 + y^2 + y_0{}^2 - 2(x\,x_0 + y\,y_0)$$

put $x = \cos\theta$, $y = \sin\theta$

$$z = x_0^2 + y_0^2 - 2(x_0\cos\theta + y_0\sin\theta)$$

$$\frac{dz}{d\theta} \Rightarrow 0 - 2\,(-x_0\sin\theta + y_0\cos\theta)$$

$$\frac{dz}{d\theta} = 0$$

$$-x_0\sin\theta = -y_0\cos\theta$$

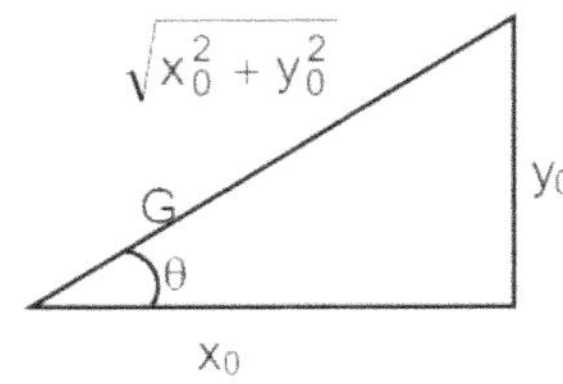

$$\tan\theta = \frac{y_0}{x_0}$$

$$\sin\theta = \frac{y_0}{\sqrt{x_0^2+y_0^2}}$$

$$\cos\theta = \frac{x_0}{\sqrt{x_0^2 + y_0^2}}$$

$$x = \frac{x_0}{\sqrt{x_0^2 + y_0^2}},$$

$$y = \frac{y_0}{\sqrt{x_0^2 + y_0^2}}$$

$$z = \left(\frac{x_0}{\sqrt{x_0^2 + y_0^2}} - x_0\right)^2 + \left(\frac{y_0}{\sqrt{x_0^2 + y_0^2}} - y_0\right)^2$$

$$= x_0^2\left(\frac{1}{\sqrt{x_0^2 + y_0^2}} - 1\right)^2 + y_0^2\left(\frac{1}{\sqrt{x_0^2 + y_0^2}} - 1\right)^2$$

$$= \left(x_0^2 + y_0^2\right)\frac{\left(1 - \sqrt{x_0^2 + y_0^2}\right)^2}{\left(\sqrt{x_0^2 + y_0^2}\right)^2}$$

$$= \left(1 - \sqrt{x_0^2 + y_0^2}\right)^2$$

$$\Rightarrow \left(\sqrt{x_0^2 + y_0^2} - 1\right)^2.$$

11.

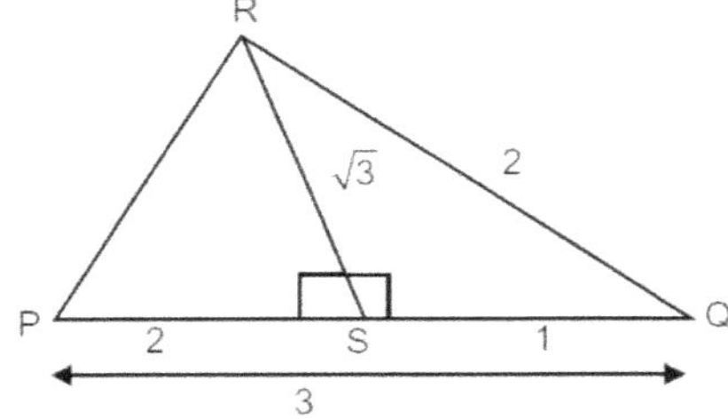

$$PS = QR$$
$$PS + SQ = 3$$
in ΔRSQ, $SQ = 3 - PS = 3 - QR$
$$QR^2 = RS^2 + SQ^2$$
$$QR^2 = 3 + (3 - QR)^2$$
$$QR^2 = 3 + 9 + QR^2 - 6QR$$
$$6QR = 12$$
$$QR = 2$$
$$SQ = 1,$$
$$PS = 2$$
in ΔRSP, $PR^2 = RS^2 + PS^2$
$$= 3 + 4$$
$$PR^2 = 7$$
$$PR = \sqrt{7}.$$

12. Total students = 50

Average = 47.5

Total marks = 2375

Now, student can obtain only integer marks.

Hence for maximum students we will divide total marks by 48

$$\Rightarrow \left[\frac{2375}{48}\right] = 49.$$

13. $15^2 \times 5^{18} = 9 \times 5^{20}$

$$\left[\log_{10}\left(9 \times 5^{20}\right)\right] = \left[2\log_{10} 3 + 20\log_{10} 5\right]$$
$$= [2 \times 0.4771 + 20(1 - 0.3010)]$$
$$= 14 \text{ \{characteristic\}}$$

Hence, the number have 15 digits

At worst all digit can have value 9

Hence, sum should less than 135

And the last digit should be 5

Hence, sum should greater than or equal to 6.

14.

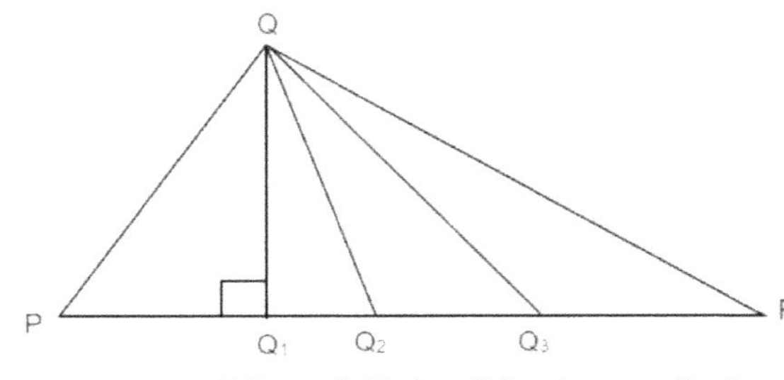

$PQ_3 = Q_3R$ ($\therefore$ QQ_3 *i.e.,* median)

$$PQ_3 = \frac{1}{2}PR$$

$PQ_2 : Q_2R = r : p$ (By property of angle bisector)

$$PQ_2 = \left(\frac{r}{r+P}\right)PR$$

But $r < P$ (Given)

$$PQ_2 < \frac{1}{2}PR$$

Comparison between Altitude and angle bisector

$\Rightarrow \angle QPQ_2 + \angle PQ_2Q + \angle PQQ_2$

$= \angle RQQ_2 + \angle QQ_2R + \angle QRQ_2$

$\therefore$ $\angle PQQ_2 = \angle RQQ_2$ {Since angle bisector}

$\angle QPQ_2 + \angle PQ_2Q = \angle QQ_2R + \angle QRQ_2$

$\therefore$ $PQ < QR$ then $\angle QPQ_2 > \angle QRQ_2$

Hence, $\angle QQ_2P < \angle QQ_2R$

But $\angle QQ_2P + \angle QQ_2R = 180°$

Hence, $\angle QQ_2P < 90°$ & $\angle QQ_2R > 90°$

$\Rightarrow$ Foot from Q to side PR lies inside ΔPQQ_2

$\Rightarrow PQ_1 < PQ_2 < PQ_3$.

15. $(a-8)^2-(b-7)^2=5$

$(a-b-1)(a+b-15)=5$

l_1 l_2

Four cases

l_1	l_2
5	1
1	5
–5	–1
–1	–5

Case-1, $a-b-1=5$ & $a+b-15=1$

$\Rightarrow$ $a=11, b=5$

Case-2, $a-b-1=-5$ & $a+b-15=-1$

$\Rightarrow$ $a=5, b=9$

Case-3, $a-b-1=1$ & $a+b-15=5$

$\Rightarrow$ $a=11, b=9$

Case-4, $a-b-1=-1$ & $a+b-15=-5$

$\Rightarrow$ $a=5, b=5$

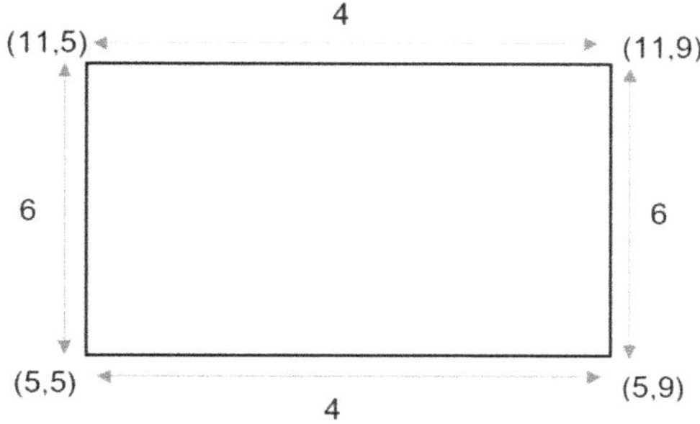

Perimeter = 4 + 4 + 6 + 6 = 20.

16. Since when temperature of water rises from 0°C to 10°C, its density first increases, becomes maximum at 4°C and then decreases, therefore fractional submergence will first decrease and then increase.

17. Since, $\rho_i = 0.9\ \rho_w$

Minimum Length required = 0.8 m.

18. Since bucket and water both are in state of free fall so water will not come out of the hole.

19. Vapourisation rate of water = 20 g/h

Water vapourised in 2 hour = 20 × 2 gm

$$dm = \frac{40}{1000}\text{kg}$$

$$\frac{\text{Latent heat of vapourisation}}{\text{specific heat of water}} = 540 = \frac{L}{C}$$

Heat contain in vapourised vapour = (dm).L.

Heat lost by water in earthen pitcher = $mc.dT$

$$m = 4 \text{ kg}$$

Heat loss by water in earthen pitcher = heat contain in vaporised water

$$dm.L = m.C.dT$$

$$\frac{40}{1000}\left(\frac{L}{C}\right) = 4.dT$$

$$dT = \frac{1}{100}\times 540 = 5.4°C$$

$$dT = 5.4\ °C.$$

20.

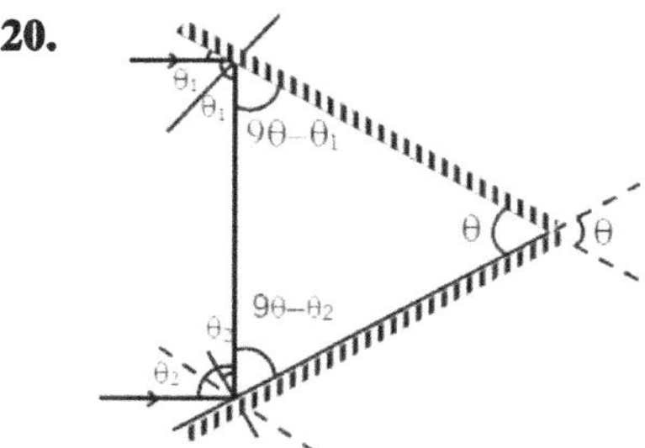

$$90-\theta_1+90-\theta_2+\theta = 180$$

$$2\theta_1+2\theta_2 = 180$$

$$\theta = \theta_1+\theta_2$$

$$\theta_1+\theta_2 = 90$$

$$\theta = 90°.$$

21.

$$100°L = 200°C$$

$$1°L = 2°C$$

$$0°C = 25°L$$

$$100°C = 75°L.$$

22.

$$q = +2e$$

$$1\alpha V = +2\ eV.$$

23.

$$I = neAv$$

$$ne = \frac{I}{Av}$$

$$= \frac{500\times10^{-6}}{15\times10^{-7}\times3\times10^{7}}$$

$$= \frac{100}{9}\times10^{-6}\ \text{c/m}^3 \sim 10^{-5}\ \text{c/m}^3.$$

24. A lunar eclipse can occur on a new moon and full moon day.

25. The minimum observed intensity of the parent star is 0.9999 I_0.

26.

$$I = neAv_d$$

$$J = \frac{I}{A} = \sigma E.$$

27. The double rainbow has red on the inside and violet on the outside.

28. ← 500 km → 50 cm.

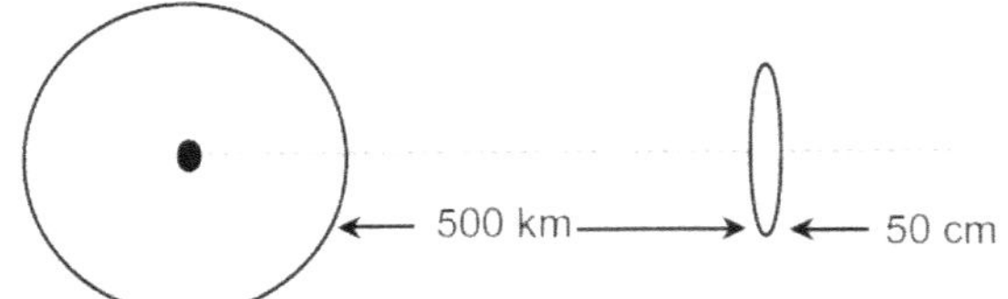

$$\frac{A_0}{A} = \left[\frac{u}{v}\right]^2$$

$\Rightarrow$ $A_0 = 10^{12}$ A.

29. 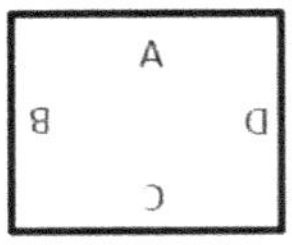 A B D C

30. $v^2 = u^2 - 2gh \rightarrow$ parabola.

31. Volume of H_2O = 250 ml,

Weight of water = 250 gm,

Number of molecule of $H_2O = \frac{250}{18}$

Number of molecule of $H_2O = \frac{250}{18} \times N_A$

$= 83.6 \times 10^{23}$.

32. Dilute aqueous Solution of NH_3 is NH_4OH solution

$$NH_4OH \rightleftharpoons NH_4^+ + \bar{O}H$$

On adding solid ammonium chloride

$$NH_4 \longrightarrow NH_4^+ + Cl^-$$

The reaction moves backward due to common ion effect. The concentration of OH^- decreases and pH decreases.

33. Given, $K_{sp} = 10^{-10}$

For $BaSO_4$, $K_{sp} = S^2$

$S = 10^{-5}$ mol/L

$\Rightarrow$ $= 2.33 \times 10^{-3}$ g/L.

34. The maximum number of electrons in the nth shell is $2n^2$.

35. The maximum amount of nitrogen that can be safely put in this container must, exert a pressure less than 2 atm at 298 K.

i.e., maximum moles in container n

$$= \frac{PV}{RT}$$

$$= \frac{2 \times 2.24}{0.0821 \times 298} = 0.18$$

i.e., maximum weight of N_2 in container

$= 0.183 \times 28 = 5.127$ gm.

The correct answer is, (D) 4.2 grams for safety concern, we can't go for adding more nitrogen.

36. 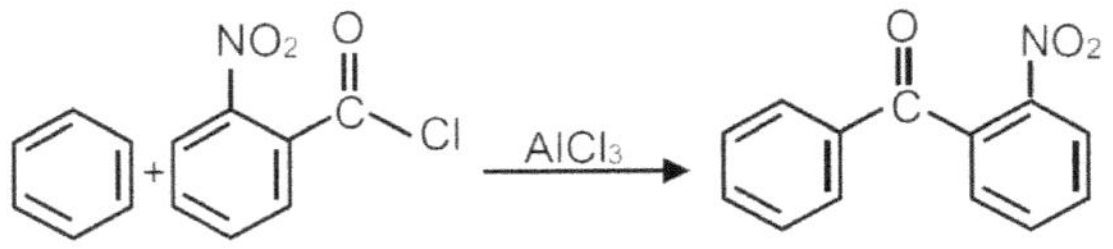 NO_2, Cl, $AlCl_3$, NO_2

37. (X)

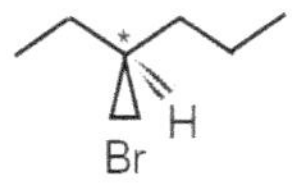

Here the * marked carbon is Chiral, as it has 4 different groups attached.

(Y)

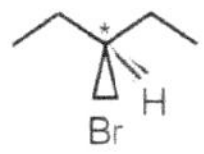

Here the * marked carbon is achiral as it has two identical ethyl group attached.

38.

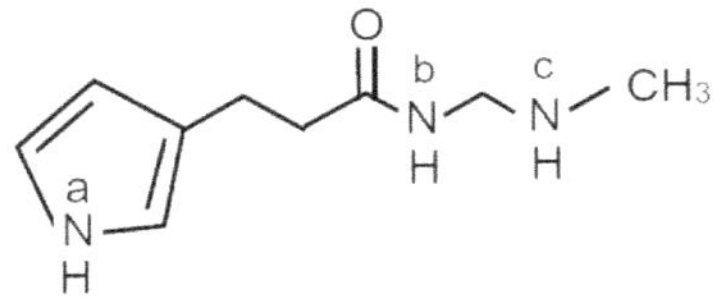

Most acidic proton = "*b*" as the conjugate base is resonance stabilized and the most nucleophilic nitrogen is "*c*" as the lone pair electron on nitrogen is localized in sp^3 hybrid orbital.

39. The resulting carbocation formed by loss of Cl(a) is resonance stabilized.

$AgNO_3$

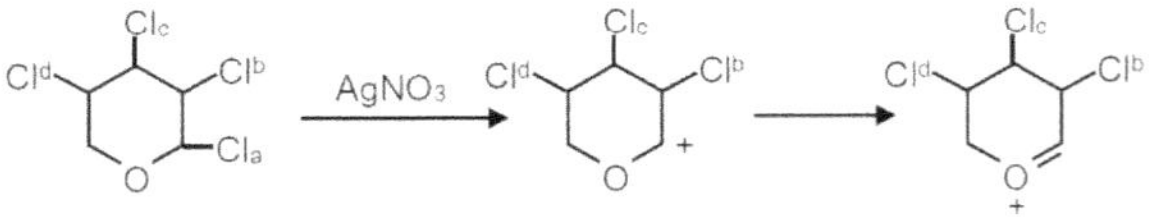

41. As the atomic number increases the energy of orbitals decreases.

42. $\Rightarrow$ 4 bond pair + 2 lone pair.

$\Rightarrow$ Steric Number = 6 = sp^3d^2.

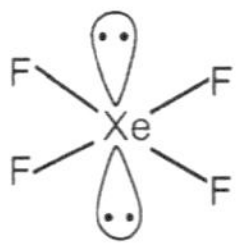

43. Oxidation number of Cr in $Cr_2O_7^{2-}$

$= +2x - 14 = -2 \Rightarrow x = +6$

Oxidation number of Cl in ClO_3^-

$= x - 6 = -1 \Rightarrow x = +5$.

44. $2KI + 4HNO_3 \rightarrow I_2 + 2NO_2 + 2KNO_3 + 2H_2O$

Iodide ion is a strong reducing agent and reduces HNO_3 vapours to NO_2 (Brown gas).

45. Haemoglobin is oxygen carrier.

46. **Secondary metabolism** is a term for pathways and small molecule products of metabolism that are not absolutely required for the survival of the organism.

Examples of the products include antibiotics and pigments. To distinguish non-secondary ("ordinary") metabolism, the term *basic metabolism* is sometimes used. Secondary metabolites are produced by many *microbes*, plants, fungi and animals. Penicillium species are important producers of bioactive secondary metabolites.

47. The carbohydrates present in commercial soybean lecithin consist of two types: free sugars which can be removed by extraction with 55% alcohol, and bound sugars which remain with the phosphatides. The free sugars consist mainly of sucrose and stachyose with a smaller amount of raffinose. Upon extraction of phosphatides with absolute alcohol, the sucrose is found mainly in the absolute alcohol-soluble fraction, the stachyose in the insoluble fraction, and the raffinose in both fractions.

49. Action potentials are generated by special types of voltage-gated ion channels embedded in a cell's plasma membrane. These channels are shut when the membrane potential is near the (negative) resting potential of the cell, but they rapidly begin to open if the membrane potential increases to a precisely defined threshold voltage, depolarising the transmembrane potential. When the channels open, they allow an inward flow of sodium ions, which changes the electrochemical gradient, which in turn produces a further rise in the membrane potential.

50. **Erythropoietin (EPO),** also known as hematopoietin or hemopoietin, is a glycoprotein cytokine secreted by the kidney in response to cellular hypoxia; it stimulates red blood cell production (erythropoiesis) in the bone marrow. Low levels of EPO (around 10 mU/mL) are constantly secreted sufficient to compensate for normal red blood cell turnover. Common causes of cellular hypoxia resulting in elevated levels of EPO (up to 10 000 mU/mL) include any anemia, and hypoxemia due to chronic lung disease.

51. In Botany, a **tendril** is a specialized stem, leaves or petiole with a threadlike shape that is used by climbing plants for support, attachment and cellular invasion by parasitic plants, generally by twining around suitable hosts found by touch. They do not have a lamina or blade, but they can photosynthesize. They can be formed from modified shoots, modified leaves, or auxiliary branches and are sensitive to chemicals, often determining the direction of growth, as in species of *Cuscuta*.

52. **Ribosome:** This was invented by G.E. Palade in 1955 by the help of electron microscope. Ribosome forms nearly 80% part of r-RNA and the diameter of it varies from 150Å–250Å. Chemically, it is composed from RNA and protein and its main function is protein synthesis, so it is also called the factory of the protein. Until all invented cell organelles ribosome is the smallest among all and it was firstly seen by Calede in 1941 and called microsome, later in 1955 it was called ribosome by Palade.

56. Salamanders are amphibians that look like a cross between a frog and a lizard. Their bodies are long and slender; their skin is moist and usually smooth; and they have long tails. Salamanders are very diverse; some have four legs; some have two. Also, some have lungs, some have gills, and some have neither—they breathe through their skin. Salamanders belong to the order Caudata, one of three orders in the Amphibia class, along with Anura (frog and toads) and Gymnophiona (caecilians, which have no legs and resemble large worms).

57. **Red blood cell,** also called **erythrocyte,** cellular component of blood, millions of which in the circulation of vertebrates give the blood its characteristic colour and carry oxygen from the lungs to the tissues. The mature human red blood cell is small, round, and biconcave; it appears dumbbell-shaped in profile. The cell is flexible and assumes a bell shape as it passes through extremely small blood vessels. It is covered with a membrane composed of lipids and proteins, lacks a nucleus, and contains hemoglobin—a red, iron-rich protein that binds oxygen.

58. **Amylase** are enzymes that catalyse the hydrolysis of starch into sugars. Amylase is present in the saliva of humans and some other mammals, where it begins the chemical process of digestion. Foods that contain large amounts of starch but little sugar, such as rice and potatoes, may acquire a slightly sweet taste as they are chewed because amylase degrades some of their starch into sugar. The pancreas and salivary gland make amylase (alpha amylase) to hydrolyse dietary starch into disaccharides and trisaccharides which are converted by other enzymes to glucose to supply the body with energy.

60. Examples of nastic movements are:

1. In the *Mimosa pudica plant,* when we touch the leaves of the plant they fold up. Here the stimulus is touch.
2. In a *dandelion flower,* the opening up of the petals of this flower in the morning in bright light and closing in the evening when light fades. Here, the stimulus is light.

We can say that Nastic movement may or may not be a growth movement because we have seen above that folding up of the leaves of a sensitive plant on touching is not a growth movement but the opening and closing of petals of flowers is a growth movement.

61. Product of digits of natural number will be a non negative integer

so, $n^2 - 10n - 36 \geq 0$

$\Rightarrow \; n \in \left(-\infty, 5-\sqrt{61}\right] \cup \left(5+\sqrt{61}, \infty\right)$

but $n \in$ IN

so $n \geq 13$; where $n \in$ N

case-1 for all 2 digit natural numbers max value of product of digits = 9 × 9 = 81

so $n^2 - 10n - 36 \leq 81$

$\Rightarrow \; n \in \left[5-\sqrt{142}, 5+\sqrt{142}\right]$

but n is taken as a 2 digit natural no.; so $13 \leq n < 17$;

⇒ product of digits = 3, 4, 5 or 6 for 13, 14, 15 and 16 respectively

checking n = 12

product of digits = 1 × 3 = 3

and $13^2 - 10 \times 13 - 36 = 3$

so 13 satisfies the given condition

Hence, it is a solution

checking for n = 14

product = 1 × 4 = 4

142 – 10 × 14 – 36 = 196 – 140 – 36 = 20 > 6

and $n^2 - 10n - 36$ is increasing function for $n > 5$; rest of the 2 digit integers won't satisfy the given condition

case-2 for all 3-digit integers max product

= 9 × 9 × 9 = 729

The smallest 3 digit no. is 100

$f(n) = n^2 - 10n - 36;$

$f(100) = 100^2 - 10 \times 100 - 36$

$= 8964 > 729$

and $f(n)$ is increasing. Hence no 3 digit Integers and similarly any higher integer will not satisfy

⇒ n = 13 is the only answer.

62. Digits are 1, 2, 3, 4, 5

Even digits = 2, 4;

number of Even digits = 2

Total marks = 2375;

number of Odd digits = 3

Sum of any 2 adjacent digits is odd

⇒ Odd and even digits will alternate.

Case-I: For n; Repetition is not allowed

⇒ OEOEO is the only possibility of arrangement of digits.

Where O = Odd digit, E = Even digit.

So number of arrangements n

$$= \frac{3}{O} \times \frac{2}{E} \times \frac{2}{O} \times \frac{1}{E} \times \frac{1}{O} = 12$$

Case-II: For m; Repetition is allowed

⇒ Two possibilities

(a) OEOEO

Number of such arrangements

$$= \frac{3}{O} \times \frac{2}{E} \times \frac{3}{O} \times \frac{2}{E} \times \frac{3}{O} = 108$$

(b) EOEOE

Number of such arrangements

$$= \frac{2}{E} \times \frac{3}{O} \times \frac{2}{E} \times \frac{3}{O} \times \frac{2}{E} = 72$$

So, $m = 108 + 72 = 180$

$$\frac{m}{n} = \frac{180}{12} = 15.$$

63. Let, Height of cone = h

Radius of base = r

And slant height = ℓ; $\ell = \sqrt{r^2 + h^2}$

Given volume = surface area

$$\Rightarrow \quad \frac{1}{3}\pi r^2 h = \pi r\ell + \pi r^2$$

$$\Rightarrow \quad rh = 3\ell + 3r$$

$$\Rightarrow \quad l = \frac{1}{3}(rh - 3r)$$

$$\Rightarrow \quad \sqrt{r^2 + h^2} = \frac{r}{3}(h-3)$$

$$\Rightarrow \quad r^2 + h^2 = \frac{r^2}{9}(h^2 - 6h + 9)$$

$$\Rightarrow \quad h^2 = \frac{r^2h^2}{9} - \frac{2hr^2}{3}$$

$$\Rightarrow \quad h = \frac{6r^2}{r^2 - 9} = 6 + \frac{54}{r^2 - 9}$$

Since h and r must be integers, and $r^2 - g$ must be a factor of 54

$r^2 - 9$ must be divisible by 3

$\Rightarrow \quad r = 3k$

$$h = 6 + \frac{54}{9k^2 - 9} = 6 + \frac{6}{k^2 - 1}$$

since $O < k^2 - 1 < 6$

⇒ k = 2 is only such value; for which h is integer.

So, $r = 2 \times 3 = 6$

$$h = 6 + \frac{6}{3} = 8$$

$$\ell = 10$$

is the only possible values for r and h.

64.

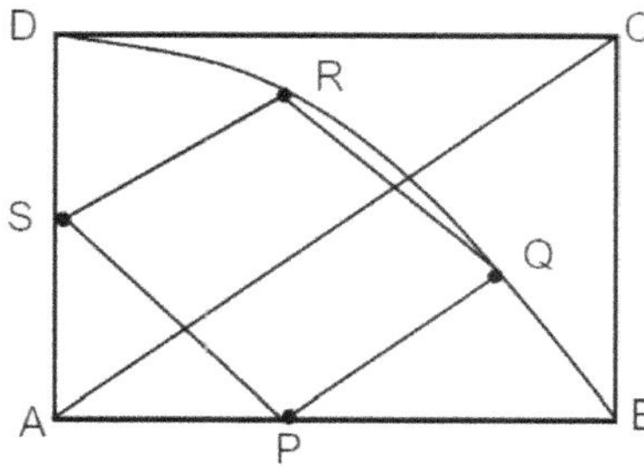

Let, A (0,0), B(1,0), C(1,1) & D(0, 1)

$\Rightarrow$ Area ABCD = 1

Again, let Q $(\cos\alpha, \sin\alpha)$ & R $(\cos\beta, \sin\beta)$

$\Rightarrow$ coordinate of P $(\cos\alpha - \sin\alpha, 0)$ & S $(0, \sin\beta - \cos\beta)$

PQRS is a square $\Rightarrow$ PQ $\perp$ QR

$\Rightarrow$ slope of QR = –1 = slope of SP

$$\Rightarrow \frac{\sin\beta - \sin\alpha}{\cos\beta - \cos\alpha} = -1 = \frac{\sin\beta - \cos\beta}{\sin\alpha - \cos\alpha}$$

$\Rightarrow \sin\beta - \sin\alpha = -\cos\beta + \cos\alpha$

$\Rightarrow \sin\beta - \cos\beta = \sin\alpha + \cos\alpha$ ....(*i*)

and $\sin\alpha + \sin\beta = \cos\alpha + \cos\beta$ ....(*ii*)

$\Rightarrow \cos\alpha = \sin\beta$

$\Rightarrow \cos\alpha = \cos(90 - \beta)$

$\Rightarrow \alpha + \beta = 90°$

Also, PQ = QR

$$\Rightarrow \tan\alpha = \frac{1}{2}$$

Area of PQRS = $2\sin^2\alpha$

$$= 2\left(\frac{1}{5}\right)$$

$$\frac{\text{Area of PQRS}}{\text{Area of ABCD}} = \frac{2/5}{1} = \frac{2}{5}.$$

65.

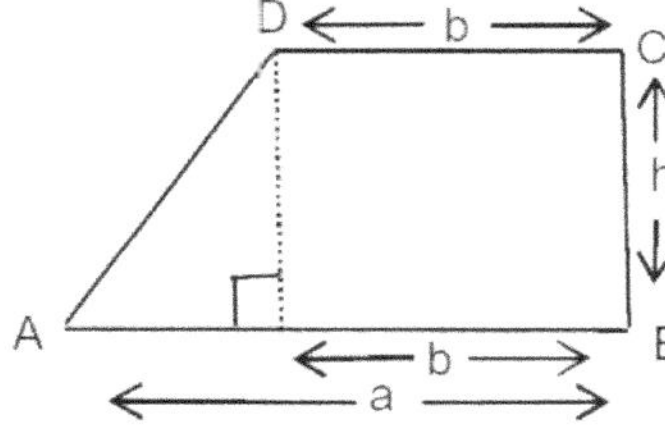

Given: $\frac{1}{2}(a+b) \times h = 12$

$(a + b) \times h = 24$

24×1

12×2

6×4

8×3

In height angle, ΔAED possible height for integer sides.

$h = 4, 3$

Case–I When $h = 4$

Then possible triplet (3, 4, 5)

i.e., DE = 4

AE = 3

AD = 5

if AE = 3

$2b = 3$

$b = 3/2$

(Not possible because $b \in$ I)

Case–II When $h = 3$

Then AE = 4

$2b = 4$

$b = 2$

$\therefore$ CD = 2

AB = 6

$\therefore$ | AB – CD | = 4.

66. $50\, t_0\, (540) + 50\, t_0\, (100 - 70)$

$= 500\,(1)\,(70 - 25)$

$28500\, t_0 = 22500$

$t_0 = 0.789$ min

= 47 sec.

67.

$$\frac{60}{40} = \frac{2d}{v}$$

$$\frac{60}{60} = \frac{2(d-90)}{v}$$

$$= \frac{2d}{v} - \frac{180}{v}$$

$$1 = \frac{3}{2} - \frac{180}{v}$$

$$\Rightarrow \frac{180}{v} = \frac{1}{2}$$

$v = 360$ m/s.

68.

$$d = \frac{5}{4/3} + \frac{2}{3/2}$$

$$= \frac{15}{4} + \frac{4}{3}$$

= 5.08 cm.

69. $$\frac{1}{2}\left(\frac{m.4m}{m+4m}\right)v^2 = \frac{1}{4\pi\varepsilon_0}\frac{2e^2}{r}$$

$$r = \frac{5e^2}{4\pi\varepsilon_0 mv^2}.$$

70.

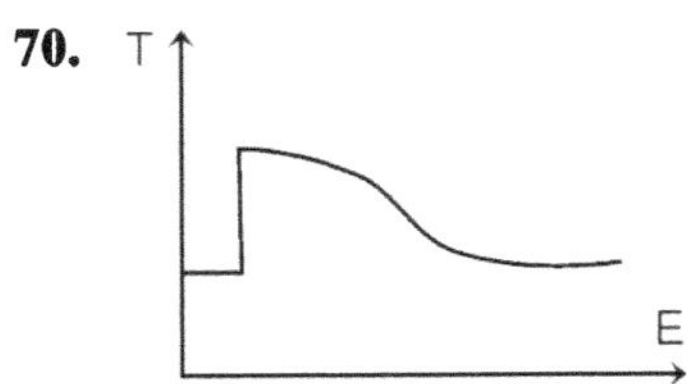

71.

	Number of electron	Bond order
O_2^{2-}	18	$BO = \frac{10-8}{2} = 1$
B_2	10	$BO = \frac{6-4}{2} = 1$

72. $q = mc\,\Delta t$ + heat of vapourisation

$= 1000 \times 2.44\ (351.45 - 293.45) + 855 \times 1000$ J

$= 9.97 \times 10^5$ J.

73. Br, Br (1,2-dibromopropane) $\xrightarrow[\text{NaOH}]{\text{Zn}}$ propene

$$\text{Mole} = \frac{20.2}{202} = 0.1$$

$$\text{Mole} = \frac{3.58}{42} = 0.085$$

$$\%\ \text{yield} = \frac{0.085}{0.1} \times 100$$

$$= 85\%.$$

74. $CH_3-\overline{C}H_2$ is less stable than $\overline{C}H_3$ as the CH_3-group exert +I effect $CH_3-\dot{C}H_2$ radical is more stable than $\dot{C}H_3$, this is due to σ-p conjugation, also known as hyperconjugation.

75.

$BrF_5 \longrightarrow$ = Square pyramidal

The lone pair occupy more space around the central atom and push away the four planar F atom. Here the axial Br–F bond length is 170 pm but equatorial Br–F bond length is 177 pm.

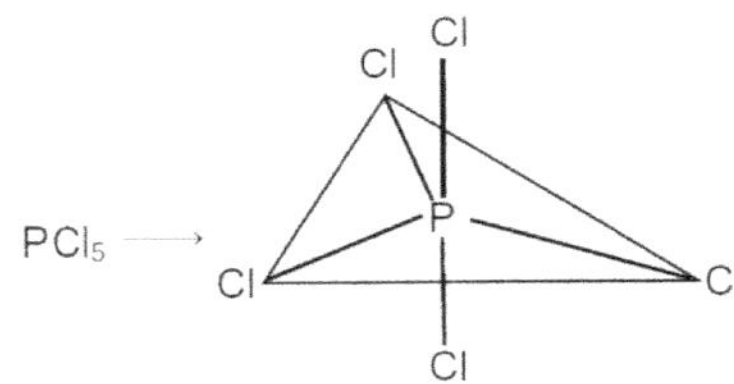

= Triangular pyramidal

Two type of P–Cl bond.

P–Cl axial > P–Cl equatorial.

Previous Paper (Solved), 2017

Kishore Vaigyanik Protsahan Yojana (KVPY)

STREAM – SA

Part-I

Mathematics

1. A quadrilateral has distinct integer side lengths. If the second-largest side has length 10, then the maximum possible length of the largest side is:

A. 25 B. 26
C. 27 D. 28

2. The largest power of 2 that divides $\frac{200!}{100!}$ is:

A. 98 B. 99
C. 100 D. 101

3. Let a_1, a_2, a_3, a_4 be real numbers such that $a_1 + a_2 + a_3 + a_4 = 0$ and $a_1^2 + a_2^2 + a_3^2 + a_4^2 = 1$. Then the smallest possible value of the expression $(a_1 - a_2)^2 + (a_2 - a_3)^2 + (a_3 - a_4)^2 + (a_4 - a_1)^2$ lies in the interval:

A. (0, 1.5) B. (1.5, 2.5)
C. (2.5, 3) D. (3, 3.5)

4. Let S be the set of all ordered pairs (x, y) of positive integers satisfying the condition $x^2 - y^2 = 12345678$. Then:

A. S is an infinite set
B. S is the empty set
C. S has exactly one element
D. S is a finite set and has at least two elements

5. Let $A_1A_2A_3 \dots A_9$ be a nine-sided regular polygon with side length 2 units. The difference between the lengths of the diagonals A_1A_5 and A_2A_4 equals:

A. $2+\sqrt{12}$ B. $\sqrt{12}-2$
C. 6 D. 2

6. Let $a_1, a_2, \dots, a_n$ be n nonzero real numbers, of which p are positive and remaining are negative. The number of ordered pairs (j, k), $j < k$, for which a_ja_k is positive, is 55. Similarly, the number of ordered pairs (j, k), $j < k$, for which a_ja_k is negative, is 50. Then the value of $p^2 + (n - p)^2$ is:

A. 629 B. 325
C. 125 D. 221

7. If a, b, c, d are four distinct numbers chosen from the set {1, 2, 3, ..., 9}, then the minimum value of $\frac{a}{b}+\frac{c}{d}$ is:

A. $\frac{3}{8}$ B. $\frac{1}{3}$
C. $\frac{13}{36}$ D. $\frac{25}{72}$

8. If $72^x \cdot 48^y = 6^{xy}$, where x and y are non-zero rational numbers, then $x + y$ equals

A. 3 B. $\frac{10}{3}$
C. –3 D. $-\frac{10}{3}$

9. Let AB be a line segment of length 2. Construct a semicircle S with AB as diameter. Let C be the midpoint of the arc AB. Construct another semicircle T external to the triangle ABC with chord AC as diameter. The area of the region inside the semicircle T but outside S is:

A. $\frac{\pi}{2}$ B. $\frac{1}{2}$
C. $\frac{\pi}{\sqrt{2}}$ D. $\frac{1}{\sqrt{2}}$

10. Let $r(x)$ be the remainder when the polynomial $x^{135} + x^{125} - x^{115} + x^5 + 1$ is divided by $x^3 - x$. Then:

A. $r(x)$ is the zero polynomial
B. $r(x)$ is a nonzero constant
C. degree of $r(x)$ is one
D. degree of $r(x)$ is two

11. It is given that the number 43361 can be written as a product of two distinct prime numbers p_1, p_2. Further, assume that there are 42900 numbers which are less than 43361 and are co-prime to it. Then, $p_1 + p_2$ is:

A. 462 B. 464
C. 400 D. 402

12. Let ABC be a triangle with ∠C = 90°. Draw CD perpendicular to AB. Choose points M and N on sides AC and BC respectively such that DM is parallel to BC and DN is parallel to AC. If DM = 5, DN = 4, then AC and BC are respectively equal to:

A. $\frac{41}{4}, \frac{41}{5}$ B. $\frac{39}{4}, \frac{39}{5}$

C. $\frac{38}{4}, \frac{38}{5}$ D. $\frac{37}{4}, \frac{37}{5}$

13. Let A, G and H be the arithmetic mean, geometric mean and harmonic mean, respectively of two distinct positive real numbers. If α is the smallest of the two roots of the equation $A(G - H)x^2 + G(H - A)x + H(A - G) = 0$, then:

A. $-2 < \alpha < -1$ B. $0 < \alpha < 1$

C. $-1 < \alpha < 0$ D. $1 < \alpha < 2$

14. In the figure, ABCD is a unit square. A circle is drawn with centre O on the extended line CD and passing through A. If the diagonal AC is tangent to the circle, then the area of the shaded region is:

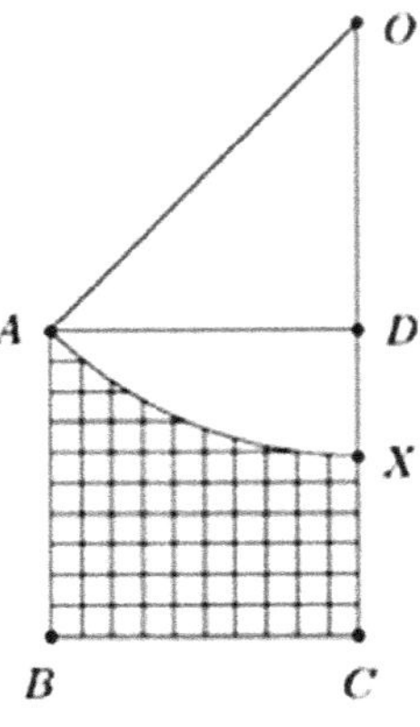

A. $\frac{9-\pi}{6}$ B. $\frac{8-\pi}{6}$

C. $\frac{7-\pi}{4}$ D. $\frac{6-\pi}{4}$

15. The sum of all non-integer roots of the equation $x^5 - 6x^4 + 11x^3 - 5x^2 - 3x + 2 = 0$ is:

A. 6 B. −11

C. −5 D. 3

Physics

16. Consider the following statements (X and Y stand for two different elements)

I. ${}_{32}X^{65}$ and ${}_{33}Y^{65}$ are isotopes.

II. ${}_{42}X^{86}$ and ${}_{42}Y^{85}$ are isotopes.

III. ${}_{85}X^{174}$ and ${}_{88}Y^{177}$ have the same number of neutrons.

IV. ${}_{92}X^{235}$ and ${}_{94}Y^{235}$ are isobars

The correct statements are:

A. II and IV only

B. I, II and IV only

C. II, III and IV only

D. I, II, III and IV

17. A student performs an experiment to determine the acceleration due to gravity g. The student throws a steel ball up with initial velocity u and measures the height h travelled by it at different times t. The graph the student should plot on a graph paper to readily obtain the value of g is:

A. h versus t B. h versus t^2

C. h versus $\sqrt{t}$ D. h/t versus t

18. A person goes from point P to point Q covering 1/3 of the distance with speed 10 km/hr, the next 1/3 of the distance at 20 km/hr and the last 1/3 of the distance at 60 km/hr. The average speed of the person is:

A. 30 km/hr B. 24 km/hr

C. 18 km/hr D. 12 km/hr

19. A person looks at the image of two parallel finite length lines PQ and RS in a convex mirror (see figure).

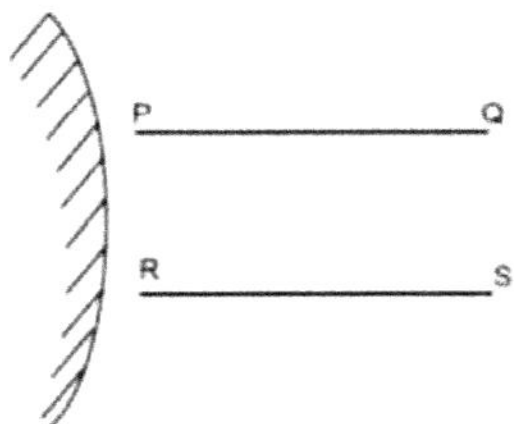

Which of the following represents schematically the image correctly? (Note: Letters P, Q, R and S are used only to denote the endpoints of the lines.)

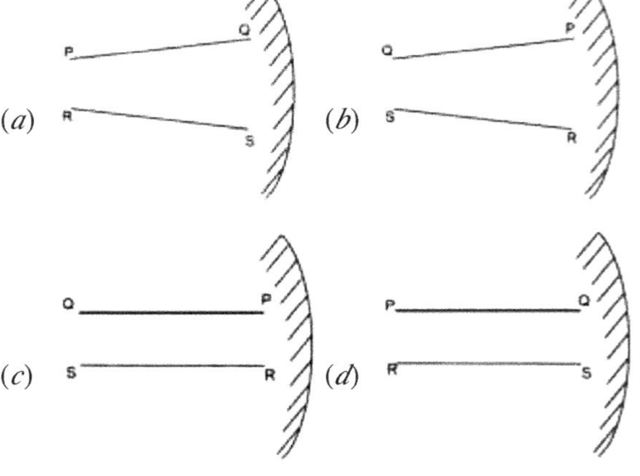

A. (a) B. (b)

C. (c) D. (d)

20. In Guericke's experiment to show the effect of atmospheric pressure, two copper hemispheres were tightly fitted to each other to form a hollow sphere and the air from the sphere was pumped out to create vacuum inside. If the radius of each hemisphere is R and the atmospheric pressure is P, then the minimum force required (when the two hemispheres are pulled apart by the same force) to separate the hemispheres is

A. $2\pi R^2P$ B. $4\pi R^2P$
C. πR^2P D. $\pi R^2P/2$

21. Positive point charges are placed at the vertices of a star shape as shown in the figure. Direction of the electrostatic force on a negative point charge at the centre O of the star is:

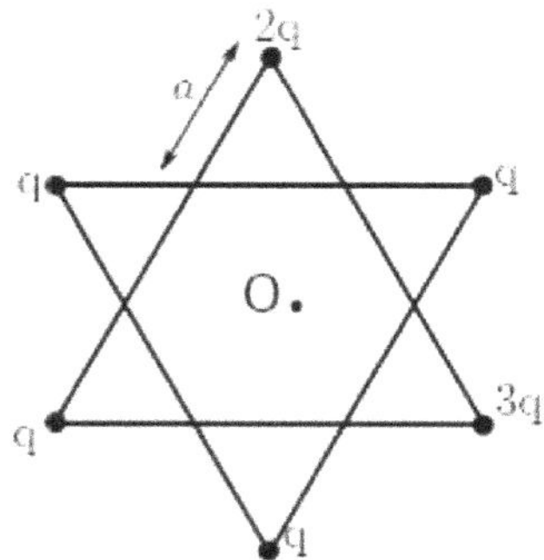

A. towards right B. vertically up
C. towards left D. vertically down

22. A total solar eclipse is observed from the earth. At the same time an observer on the moon views the earth. She is most likely to see (E denotes the earth)

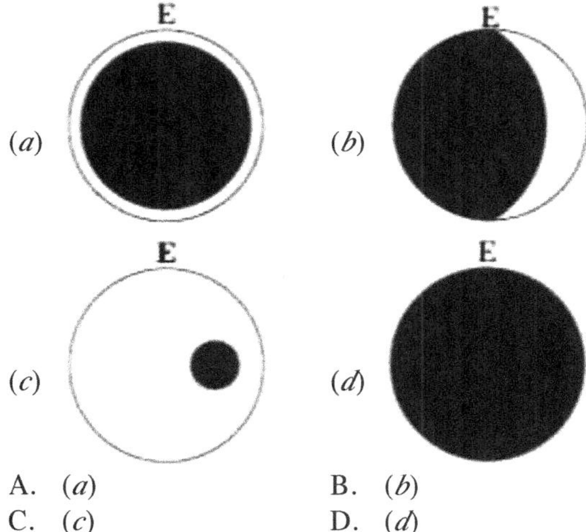

A. (*a*) B. (*b*)
C. (*c*) D. (*d*)

23. Ice in a freezer is at –7°C. 100 g of this ice is mixed with 200 g of water at 15°C. Take the freezing temperature of water to be 0°C, the specific heat of ice equal to 2.2 J/g °C, specific heat of water equal to 4.2 J/g°C, and the latent heat of ice equal to 335 J/g. Assuming no loss of heat to the environment, the mass of ice in the final mixture is closest to:

A. 88 g B. 67 g
C. 54 g D. 45 g

24. A point source of light is placed at $2f$ from a converging lens of focal length f. A flat mirror is placed on the other side of the lens at a distance d such that rays reflected from the mirror are parallel after passing through the lens again. If $f = 30$ cm, then d is equal to:

A. 15 cm B. 30 cm
C. 45 cm D. 75 cm

25. The word "KVPY" is written on a board and viewed through different lenses such that board is at a distance beyond the focal length of the lens.

(*i*)

(*ii*)

Ignoring magnification effects, consider the following statements.

I. Image (*i*) has been viewed from the planar side of a plano-convex lens and image (*ii*) from the convex side of a plano-convex lens.
II. Image (*i*) has been viewed from the concave side of a plano-concave lens and image (*ii*) from the convex side of a plano-convex lens.
III. Image (*i*) has been viewed from the concave side of a plano-concave lens and image (*ii*) from the planar side of a plano-convex lens.
IV. Image (*i*) has been viewed from the planar side of a plano-concave lens and image (*ii*) from the convex side of a plano-convex lens.

Which of the above statements are correct?

A. All four B. Only (III)
C. Only (IV) D. Only (II), (III) and (IV)

26. A ball is dropped vertically from height h and is bouncing elastically on the floor (see figure). Which of the following plots best depicts the acceleration of the ball as a function of time.

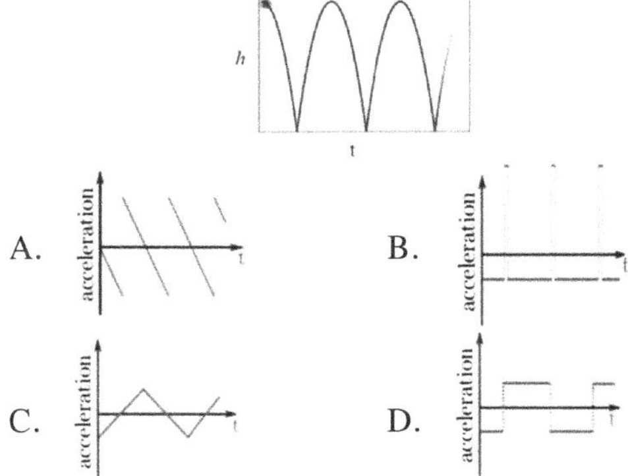

27. A student studying the similarities and differences between a camera and the human eye makes the following observations:

I. Both the eye and the camera have convex lenses.
II. In order to focus, the eye lens expands or contracts while the camera lens moves forward or backward.

III. The camera lens produces upside down real images while the eye lens produces only upright real images.
IV. A screen in camera is equivalent to the retina in the eyes.
V. A camera adjusts the amount of light entering in it by adjusting the aperture of the lens. In the eye the cornea controls the amount of light.

The correct statements are:
A. Only (I), (II), (IV)
B. Only (I), (III), (V)
C. Only (I), (II), (IV), (V)
D. All

28. A particle starts moving along a line from zero initial velocity and comes to rest after moving distance d. During its motion it had a constant acceleration f over 2/3 of the distance, and covered the rest of the distance with constant retardation. The time taken to cover the distance is:

A. $\sqrt{2d/3f}$ B. $2\sqrt{d/3f}$
C. $\sqrt{3d/f}$ D. $\sqrt{3d/2f}$

29. If the image formed by a thin convex lens of power P has magnification m, then image distance v is:

A. $v=\dfrac{1-m}{P}$ B. $v=\dfrac{1+m}{P}$
C. $v=\dfrac{m}{P}$ D. $v=\dfrac{1+2m}{P}$

30. A long cylindrical pipe of radius 20 cm is closed at its upper end and has an airtight piston of negligible mass as shown. When a 50 kg mass is attached to the other end of the piston, it moves down. If the air in the enclosure is cooled from temperature T to T − ΔT, the piston moves back to its original position. Then ΔT/T is close to (Assuming air to be an ideal gas, g = 10 m/s^2, atmospheric pressure is 10^5 Pascal),

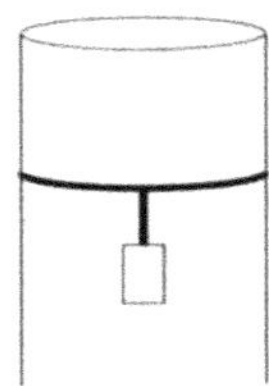

A. 0.01 B. 0.02
C. 0.04 D. 0.09

Chemistry

31. The structure of 3-methylpent-2-ene is:

A. 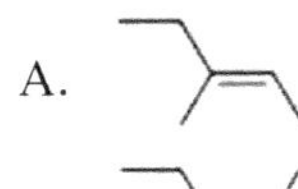 B. 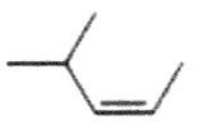
C. 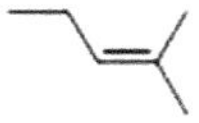 D.

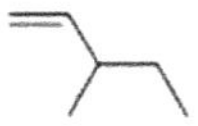

32. The stability of carbanions

I. $CH_3CH_2CH_2\overset{\ominus}{C}H_2$ II. $CH_3\overset{\ominus}{C}HCH_2CH_3$
III. $(CH_3)_3C^{\ominus}$ IV. $CH_3\overset{\ominus}{C}(Ph)CH_2CH_3$

follows the order:
A. III < IV < I < II B. I < II < IV < III
C. III < II < I < IV D. IV < III < II < I

33. In the following reaction

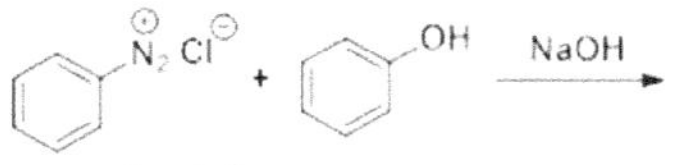

$C_6H_5\overset{\oplus}{N}_2Cl^{\ominus}$ + C_6H_5OH $\xrightarrow{NaOH}$

the major product is:

A. 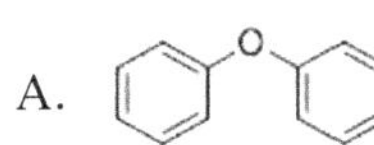 B. 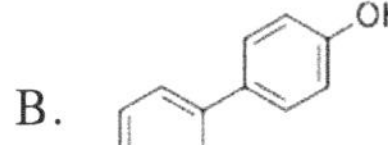

C. 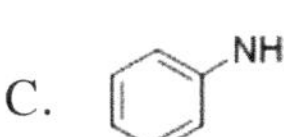 D.

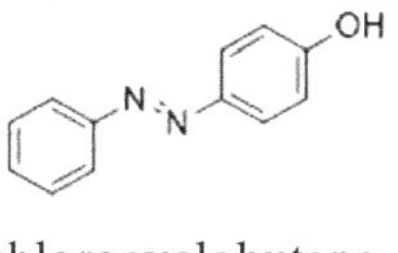

34. In the reaction of 1-bromo-3-chlorocyclobutane with two equivalents of sodium in ether, the major product is:

A. 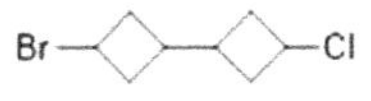 Br—◇—◇—Cl B. 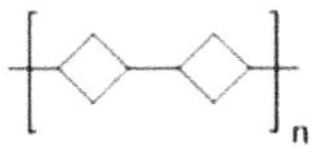 [—◇—◇—]$_n$
C. 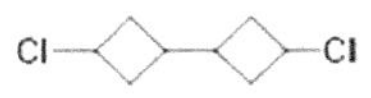 Cl—◇—◇—Cl D.

35. The order of basicity of

I. 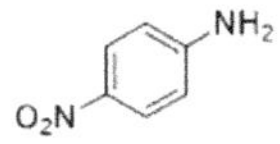 O_2N–C_6H_4–NH_2 II. 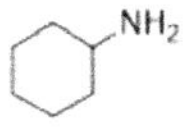 cyclohexyl–NH_2
III. 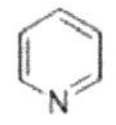 pyridine IV.  pyrrole (N–H)

in water is:
A. IV < III < I < II B. II < I < IV < III
C. IV < I < III < II D. II < III < I < IV

36. The first ionisation energy of Na, B, N and O atoms follows the order:
A. B < Na < O < N B. Na < B < O < N
C. Na < O < B < N D. O < Na < N < B

37. Among P_2O_5, As_2O_3, Sb_2O_3 and Bi_2O_3, the most acidic oxide is:
A. P_2O_5 B. As_2O_3
C. Sb_2O_3 D. Bi_2O_3

38. Among K, Mg, Au and Cu, the one which is extracted by heating its ore in air is:
A. K B. Mg
C. Au D. Cu

39. The metal ion with total number of electrons same as S^{2-} is:
A. Na^+ B. Ca^{2+}
C. Mg^{2+} D. Sr^{2+}

40. X g of Ca [atomic mass = 40] dissolves completely in concentrated HCl solution to produce 5.04 L of H_2 gas at STP. The value of X is closest to:

A. 4.5 B. 8.1
C. 9.0 D. 16.2

41. A 20 g object is moving with velocity 100 m s^{-1}. The de Broglie wavelength (in m) of the object is:

[Planck's constant $h = 6.626 \times 10^{-34}$ J s]

A. 3.313×10^{-34} B. 6.626×10^{-34}
C. 3.313×10^{-31} D. 6.626×10^{-31}

42. In a closed vessel at STP, 50 L of CH_4 is ignited with 750 L of air (containing 20% O_2). The number of moles of O_2 remaining in the vessel on cooling to room temperature is closest to:

A. 5.8 B. 2.2
C. 4.5 D. 6.7

43. CO_2 is passed through lime water. Initially the solution turns milky and then becomes clear upon continued bubbling of CO_2. The clear solution is due to the formation of:

A. $CaCO_3$ B. CaO
C. $Ca(OH)_2$ D. $Ca(HCO_3)_2$

44. The maximum number of electrons that can be filled in the shell with the principal quantum number $n = 3$ is:

A. 18 B. 9
C. 8 D. 2

45. The atomic radii of Li, F, Na and Si follow the order:

A. Si > Li > Na > F B. Li > F > Si > Na
C. Na > Si > F > Li D. Na > Li > Si > F

Biology

46. The major excretory product of birds is:

A. urea B. uric acid
C. nitrates D. ammonia

47. Codon degeneracy means that:

A. several of the amino acids are coded by more than one codon.
B. one codon can code for many amino acids.
C. one amino acid can be coded by only one codon.
D. the codons are triplet nucleotide sequences.

48. In cell cycle, during interphase:

A. two daughter cells are produced.
B. the nucleus is divided into two daughter nuclei.
C. the chromosome condenses.
D. the DNA is replicated.

49. Transfer of genetic material between populations is best defined as:

A. gene flow B. genetic drift
C. genetic shift D. speciation

50. Which ONE of the following statements is CORRECT about the tobacco mosaic virus?

A. It affects all monocotyledonous plants.
B. It affects photosynthetic tissue of the infected plant.
C. It does not infect other species belonging to the *Solanaceae*.
D. It infects gymnosperms.

51. Which ONE of the following statements is CORRECT about placenta?

A. Placenta is permeable to all bacteria.
B. Oxygen and carbon dioxide cannot diffuse through the placenta.
C. Waste products diffuse out of placenta into maternal blood.
D. Placenta does not secrete chorionic gonadotropins.

52. The respiratory quotient of the reaction given below is:

$2(C_{51}H_{98}O_6) + 145\ O_2 \rightarrow 102\ CO_2 + 90\ H_2O$ + energy

A. 0.703 B. 0.725
C. 0.960 D. 1.422

53. Which ONE of the following statements is INCORRECT about nucleosomes?

A. They contain DNA.
B. They contain histones.
C. They are membrane-bound organelle.
D. They are a part of chromosomes.

54. The immediate precursor of thyroxine is:

A. tyrosine B. tryptophan
C. pyridoxine D. thymidine

55. The maximum number of oxygen molecules that can bind to one molecule of haemoglobin is:

A. 8 B. 6
C. 4 D. 2

56. Which ONE of the following biomolecules is synthesized in smooth endoplasmic reticulum?

A. Proteins
B. Lipids
C. Carbohydrates
D. Nucleotides

57. The products of light reaction during photosynthesis include:

A. ATP and NADPH B. O_2 and $NADP^+$
C. O_2 and H_2O D. $NADP^+$ and H_2O

58. Hypothalamus directly controls the production of which of the following hormones?

A. glucocorticoid and insulin
B. insulin and glucagon
C. atrial natriuretic factor and gastrin
D. glucocorticoids and androgens

59. Which ONE of the following drugs is NOT obtained from fungal or plant sources?
A. Penicillin
B. Reserpine
C. Acetaminophen
D. Quinine

60. Jean-Baptiste Lamarck explained evolution based on:
A. natural selection
B. survival of the fittest
C. mutations
D. inheritance of acquired characteristics

Part-II

Mathematics

61. Let S be the circle in *xy*-plane which touches the *x*-axis at point A, the *y*-axis at point B and the unit circle $x^2 + y^2 = 1$ at point C externally. If O denotes the origin, then the angle OCA equals:
A. $\frac{5\pi}{8}$ B. $\frac{\pi}{2}$
C. $\frac{3\pi}{4}$ D. $\frac{3\pi}{5}$

62. In an isosceles trapezium, the length of one of the parallel sides, and the lengths of the non-parallel sides are all equal to 30. In order to maximize the area of the trapezium, the smallest angle should be
A. $\frac{\pi}{6}$ B. $\frac{\pi}{4}$
C. $\frac{\pi}{3}$ D. $\frac{\pi}{2}$

63. Let A_1, A_2, A_3 be regions in the *xy*-plane defined by:
$A_1 = \{(x, y) : x^2 + 2y^2 \leq 1\}$,
$A_2 = \left\{(x, y) : |x|^3 + 2\sqrt{2}\,|y|^3 \leq 1\right\}$,
$A_3 = \left\{(x, y) : \max\left(|x|, \sqrt{2}\,|y|\right) \leq 1\right\}$.
Then
A. $A_1 \supset A_2 \supset A_3$ B. $A_3 \supset A_1 \supset A_2$
C. $A_2 \supset A_3 \supset A_1$ D. $A_3 \supset A_2 \supset A_1$

64. Let ABCD be a square and E be a point outside ABCD such that E, A, C are collinear in that order. Suppose $EB = ED = \sqrt{130}$ and the areas of triangle EAB and square ABCD are equal. Then the area of square ABCD is:
A. 8 B. 10
C. $\sqrt{120}$ D. $\sqrt{125}$

65. Consider the set A = {1, 2, 3, ..., 30}. The number of ways in which one can choose three distinct numbers from A so that the product of the chosen numbers is divisible by 9 is:
A. 1590 B. 1505
C. 1110 D. 1025

Physics

66. Two different liquids of same mass are kept in two identical vessels, which are placed in a freezer that extracts heat from them at the same rate causing each liquid to transform into a solid. The schematic figure below shows the temperature T vs time *t* plot for the two materials. We denote the specific heat in the liquid states to be C_{L1} and C_{L2} for materials 1 and 2 respectively, and latent heats of fusion U_1 and U_2 respectively.

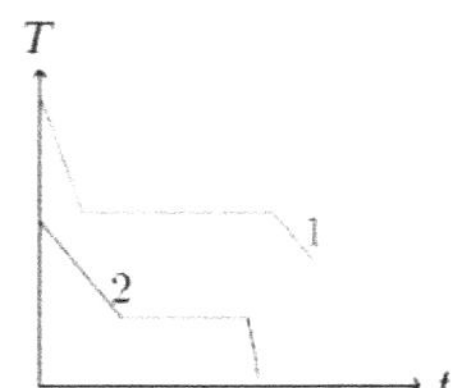

Choose the correct option.
A. $C_{L1} > C_{L2}$ and $U_1 < U_2$
B. $C_{L1} > C_{L2}$ and $U_1 > U_2$
C. $C_{L1} < C_{L2}$ and $U_1 > U_2$
D. $C_{L1} < C_{L2}$ and $U_1 < U_2$

67. A long horizontal mirror is next to a vertical screen (see figure). Parallel light rays are falling on the mirror at an angle α from the vertical. If a vertical object of height *h* is kept on the mirror at a distance $d > h \tan(\alpha)$. The length of the shadow of the object on the screen would be:

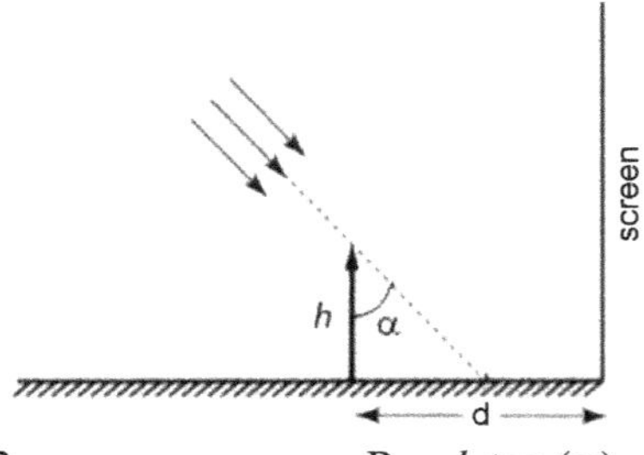

A. $h/2$ B. $h \tan(\alpha)$
C. $2h$ D. $4h$

68. A spherical marble of radius 1 cm is stuck in a circular hole of radius slightly smaller than its own radius (for calculation purpose, both can be taken same) at the bottom of a bucket of height 40 cm and filled with water up to 10 cm. If the mass of the marble is 20 g, the net force on the marble due to water is close to

A. 0.02 N upward B. 0.02 N downward
C. 0.04 N upward D. 0.04 N downward

69. In the circuit shown below (on the left) the resistance and the emf source are both variable. The graph of seven readings of the voltmeter and the ammeter (V and I, respectively) for different settings of resistance and the emf, taken at equal intervals of time Δt, are shown (on the right) by the dots connected by the curve EFGH. Consider the internal resistance of the battery to be negligible and the voltmeter and ammeter to be ideal devices. Take $R_0 \equiv V_0/I_0$.

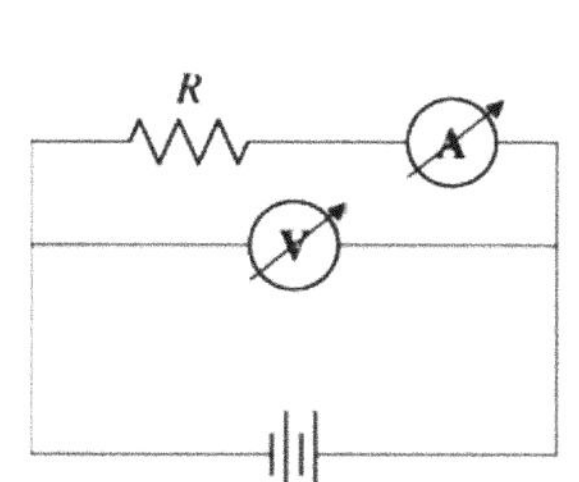

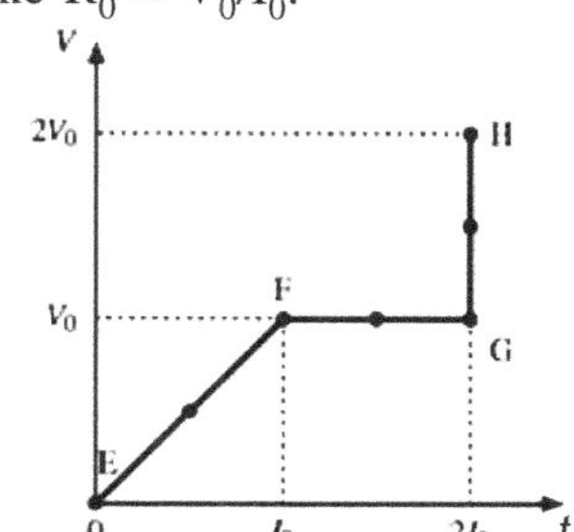

Then the plot of the resistance as a function of time corresponding to the curve EFGH is given by:

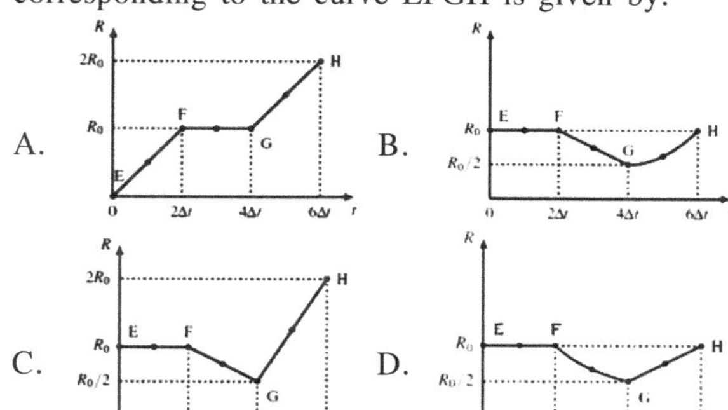

70. Stoke's law states that the viscous drag force F experienced by a sphere of radius *a*, moving with a speed *v* through a fluid with coefficient of viscosity η, is given by F = 6πη*av*.

If this fluid is flowing through a cylindrical pipe of radius *r*, length *l* and a pressure difference of P across its two ends, then the volume of water V which flows through the pipe in time *t* can be written as

$\frac{V}{t} = k\left(\frac{P}{l}\right)^a \eta^b r^c$, where *k* is a dimensional constant.

Correct values of *a*, *b* and *c* are:

A. $a = 1, b = -1, c = 4$ B. $a = -1, b = 1, c = 4$
C. $a = 2, b = -1, c = 3$ D. $a = 1, b = -2, c = -4$

Chemistry

71. The reaction of an alkene X with bromine produces a compound Y, which has 22.22% C, 3.71% H and 74.07% Br. The ozonolysis of alkene X gives only one product. The alkene X is:
[Given: atomic mass of C = 12; H = 1; Br = 80]

A. ethylene B. 1-butene
C. 2-butene D. 3-hexene

72. In the following reaction

$$H_3C-C\equiv C-H \xrightarrow[H_3O^+]{Hg^{2+}} X \xrightarrow[PhCHO]{\text{dil NaOH}} Y$$; X and Y,

respectively, are

A. X = H_3C CHO Y = H_3C CHO Ph

B. X = O H_3C CH_3 Y = O H_3C Ph

C. X = O H_3C CH_3 Y = H_3C Ph CH_3

D. X = H_3C CHO Y = H_3C Ph

73. $KMnO_4$ reacts with H_2O_2 in an acidic medium. The number of moles of oxygen produced per mole of $KMnO_4$ is:

A. 2.5 B. 5
C. 1.25 D. 2

74. The photoelectric behaviour of K, Li, Mg and Ag metals is shown in the plot below. If light of wavelength 400 nm is incident on each of these metals, which of them will emit photoelectrons?

[Planck's constant $h = 6.626 \times 10^{-34}$ J s; velocity of light $c = 3 \times 10^8$ m s^{-1}; 1 eV = 1.6×10^{-19} J]

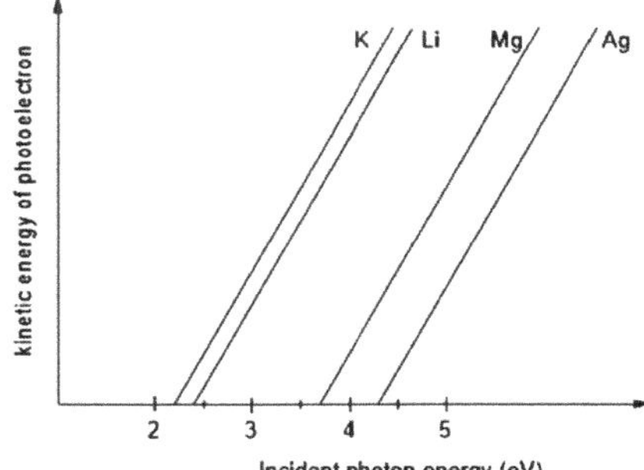

A. K B. K and Li
C. K, Li and Mg D. K, Li, Mg and Ag

75. A piece of metal weighing 100 g is heated to 80°C and dropped into 1 kg of cold water in an insulated container at 15°C. If the final temperature of the water in the container is 15.69°C, the specific heat of the metal in J/g.°C is:

A. 0.38 B. 0.24
C. 0.45 D. 0.13

Biology

76. The nucleus of a diploid organism contains 3 ng of DNA in G_1 phase. Which ONE of the following statements describes the state of the cell at the end of S phase?

A. The nucleus divides into two, and each nucleus contains 3 ng of DNA.

B. The nucleus does not divide, and it contains 3 ng of DNA.

C. The nucleus divides into two, and each nucleus contains 1.5 ng of DNA.

D. The nucleus does not divide, and it contains 6 ng of DNA.

77. Three cellular processes are listed below. Choose the CORRECT combination of processes that involve proton gradient across the membrane.

(*i*) Photosynthesis
(*ii*) Aerobic respiration
(*iii*) Anaerobic respiration

A. (*ii*) and (*iii*) B. (*i*) and (*ii*)
C. (*i*), (*ii*) and (*iii*) D. (*i*) and (*iii*)

78. The concentration of OH^- ions in a solution with the H^+ ions concentration of 1.3×10^{-4} M is:

A. 7.7×10^{-4} M B. 1.3×10^{-4} M
C. 2.6×10^{-8} M D. 7.7×10^{-11} M

79. Given that tidal volume is 600 ml, inspiratory reserve volume is 2500 ml, and expiratory reserve volume is 800 ml, what is the value of vital capacity of lung?

A. 3900 ml B. 3300 ml
C. 3100 ml D. 1400 ml

80. Which of the following organisms produce sperm without involving meiosis?

A. Sand fly and fruit fly
B. House fly and grasshopper
C. Honeybee and ant
D. Zebra fish and frog

ANSWERS

1	2	3	4	5	6	7	8	9	10
B	C	B	B	D	C	D	D	B	C
11	**12**	**13**	**14**	**15**	**16**	**17**	**18**	**19**	**20**
A	A	B	D	D	C	D	C	B	C
21	**22**	**23**	**24**	**25**	**26**	**27**	**28**	**29**	**30**
A	B	B	C	D	B	A	C	A	C
31	**32**	**33**	**34**	**35**	**36**	**37**	**38**	**39**	**40**
A	C	D	D	C	B	A	D	B	C
41	**42**	**43**	**44**	**45**	**46**	**47**	**48**	**49**	**50**
A	B	D	A	D	B	A	D	A	B
51	**52**	**53**	**54**	**55**	**56**	**57**	**58**	**59**	**60**
C	A	C	A	C	B	A	D	C	D
61	**62**	**63**	**64**	**65**	**66**	**67**	**68**	**69**	**70**
A	C	D	B	A	C	C	D	D	A
71	**72**	**73**	**74**	**75**	**76**	**77**	**78**	**79**	**80**
C	B	A	B	C	D	B	D	A	C

EXPLANATORY ANSWERS

1. Let $b = 10$, $c = 9$, $d = 8$

Sum of three sides > IVth side

$$b + c + d > a$$
$$a < 27$$

So the maximum value of $a = 26$.

2. Exponent of 2 in 200! = 197

Exponent of 2 in 100! = 97.

4. $x^2 - y^2 = 12345678$ ($x, y \in I^+$)

R.H.S. is even, so x, y should be odd integer but difference of square of two odd integers is multiple of 8 but R.H.S. is not multiple of 8.

5.

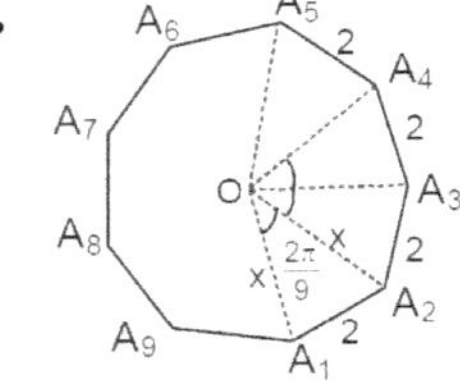

$$\angle A_1OA_2 = \frac{2\pi}{9} = 40°$$

$$\cos\frac{2\pi}{9} = \frac{x^2 + x^2 - 4}{2x^2}$$

$$x^2 \cos 40° = x^2 - 2$$
$$x^2 (1 - \cos 40°) = 2$$
$$x = \frac{1}{\sin 20°} \quad ...(i)$$

Now, $\cos\frac{8\pi}{9} = \frac{x^2 + x^2 - (A_1A_5)^2}{2x^2}$ (in ΔA_1OA_5)

$$(A_1A_5)^2 = 2x^2\left(1 - \cos\frac{8\pi}{9}\right)$$
$$= 2x^2 (1 - \cos 160°)$$
$$= 4x^2 \sin^2 80°$$
$$A_1A_5 = 2x \sin 80° \quad ...(ii)$$

Similarly in ΔA_2OA_4

$$A_2A_4 = 2x \sin 40° \quad ...(iii)$$

(*ii*) – (*iii*)

$$A_1A_5 - A_2A_4 = 2x(\sin 80° - \sin 40°)$$
$$= 2 \text{ (using } (i)).$$

6. $${}^pC_2 + {}^{n-p}C_2 = 55$$

$$\frac{p(p-1)}{2} + \frac{(n-p)(n-p-1)}{2} = 55 \quad ...(i)$$

Also, $p(n - p) = 50 \quad ...(ii)$

Put in (*i*), $p(p-1) + \frac{50}{p}\left(\frac{50}{p} - 1\right) = 110$

$$p^2 - p + \left(\frac{50}{p}\right)^2 - \frac{50}{p} = 110$$
$$\left(p + \frac{50}{p}\right)^2 - 100 - \left(p + \frac{50}{p}\right) = 110$$
$$t^2 - t - 210 = 0$$

$t = 15$ or -14 (not true)

$\therefore \quad p + \frac{50}{p} = 15$

$\therefore$ To find $p^2 + (n - p)^2$

$$= p^2 + \left(\frac{50}{p}\right)^2 = \left(p + \frac{50}{p}\right)^2 - 100 = 125 \text{ (using } (i))$$

7. $\frac{2}{9} + \frac{1}{8} = \frac{25}{72}.$

8. $$72^x . 48^y = 6^{xy}$$
$$3^{2x+y} . 2^{3x+4y} = 2^{xy} . 3^{xy}$$

Compare $2x + y = xy \quad ...(i)$

and $3x + 4y = xy \quad ...(ii)$

From (*i*) and (*ii*) $x = -3y$

put in (*i*) $-5y = -3y^2 \Rightarrow y = \frac{5}{3}$

So, $x + y = -2y = -\frac{10}{3}.$

9.

$\angle ACB = 90°$; $AC = \sqrt{2}$

Required area = Area of semicircle having AC as diameter – Area under arc OAC but outside triangle AOC

$$= \frac{1}{2}\left(\pi\left(\frac{\sqrt{2}}{2}\right)^2\right) - \left(\frac{\pi}{4} - \frac{1}{2}\right) = \frac{\pi}{4} - \frac{\pi}{4} + \frac{1}{2} = \frac{1}{2}.$$

10. $x^{135} + x^{125} - x^{115} + x^5 + 1 = k(x^3 - x) + Ax^2 + Bx + C$

put $x = 0$, $\boxed{C = 1}$

put $x = 1$, $\quad 3 = A + B + 1$

$$A + B = 2 \quad ...(i)$$

put $x = -1$, $\quad -1 = A - B + 1$

$$A - B = -2 \quad ...(ii)$$

(*i*) + (*ii*), $\quad A = 0, B = 2.$

11. $43361 = 131 \times 331.$

12.

$$CD = \sqrt{41}$$
$$\Delta AMD \sim \Delta DNB$$
$$\frac{y}{5} = \frac{4}{x} = \frac{z}{t}$$
$$\boxed{xy = 20} \quad ...(i)$$

In ΔBCD $\quad (y + 5)^2 = 41 + z^2 \quad ...(ii)$

In ΔADC $\quad (x + 4)^2 = 41 + t^2 \quad ...(iii)$

$$\Rightarrow \frac{(y+5)^2 - 41}{(x+4)^2 - 41} = \left(\frac{z}{t}\right)^2$$
$$\Rightarrow \frac{\left(\frac{20}{x} + 5\right)^2 - 41}{(x+4)^2 - 41} = \left(\frac{4}{x}\right)^2 \text{ (use } (i))$$
$$\Rightarrow \frac{(20 + 5x)^2 - 41x^2}{(x+4)^2 - 41} = 16$$
$$\Rightarrow \frac{400 + 25x^2 + 200x - 41x^2}{x^2 + 16 + 8x - 41} = 16$$
$$\Rightarrow -16x^2 + 200x + 400 = 16x^2 + 128x - 400$$
$$\Rightarrow 32x^2 - 72x - 800 = 0$$
$$\Rightarrow 4x^2 - 9x - 100 = 0$$
$$\boxed{x = \frac{25}{4}}$$

So, $y = \frac{20 \times 4}{25} = \frac{16}{5}.$

13. $x = 1$ is a root as sum of coefficient = 0

Now, $\alpha\beta = \dfrac{H(A-G)}{A(G+H)}$

Put $\beta = 1$, $\alpha = \dfrac{HA-HG}{AG-AH} = \dfrac{G^2-HG}{AG-AH}$

$= \dfrac{G(G-H)}{A(G-H)} = \dfrac{G}{A} < 1$

[as A.M. > G.M.]

14. $\therefore$ $\angle OAC = 90°$ as AC is tangent and OA is radius

as $\angle CAD = 45°$

So $\angle OAD = 45°$

$= \angle AOD$

$\therefore$ $OA = \sqrt{2}$

Area of shaded region

= 1 – (area of sector OAX – area of ΔOAD)

$= 1-\left[\dfrac{1}{2}\times 2\times\dfrac{\pi}{4}-\dfrac{1}{2}\right] = 1-\left[\dfrac{\pi}{4}-\dfrac{1}{2}\right] = \dfrac{3}{2}-\dfrac{\pi}{4}.$

15. $(x-1)(x-2)(x^3-3x+1) = 0$

$\therefore$ Required sum of roots = 3.

16. **Isotopes :** Molecules having same number of proton.

Isobars : Molecules having same number of nucleons.

17. $h = ut+\dfrac{1}{2}at^2$

$h = ut-\dfrac{1}{2}gt^2$

$\dfrac{h}{t} = u-\dfrac{1}{2}gt$

$y = mx + c$

slope will define the value gravity.

18. $V_{avg} = \dfrac{\text{Total distance}}{\text{Total time}} = \dfrac{S}{\dfrac{S/3}{10}+\dfrac{S/3}{20}+\dfrac{S/3}{60}}$

V_{avg} = 18 km/hr.

19. Object placed infront of mirror. For all position of object infront of mirror, image in virtual, erect, smaller in size. As object is moved away from pole magnification decreases.

20.

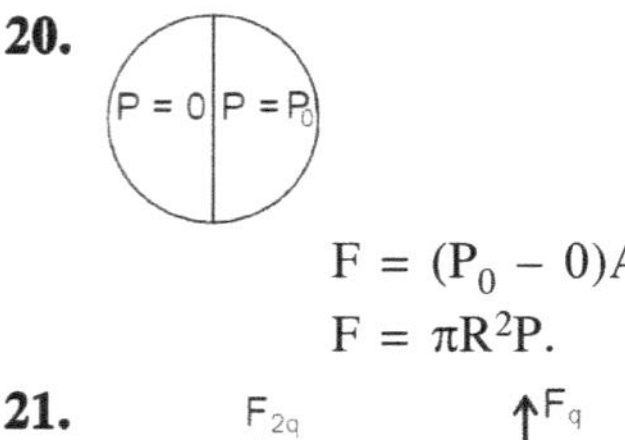

$F = (P_0 - 0)A$

$F = \pi R^2 P.$

21.

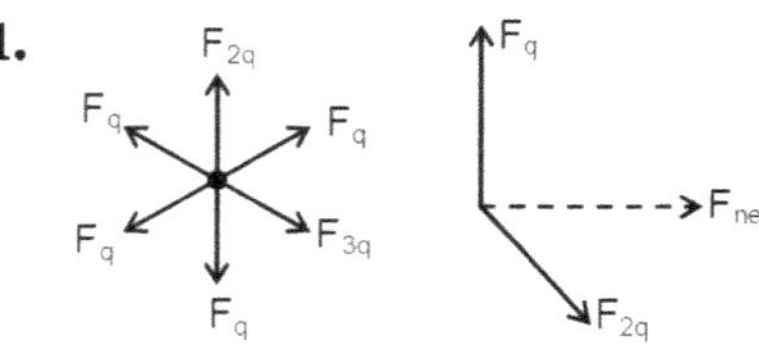

23.

–7°C 15°C

100 gm (ice) 200 gm (water)

Let mgm of ice melted

Mixture will be at 0°C

Heat given = 200 × (4.2) (15) J

Heat absorbed = 100 × 2.2 × (7) + m(335)

by solving m = 33 gm

So ice remain = 100 – 33 = 67 g.

24.

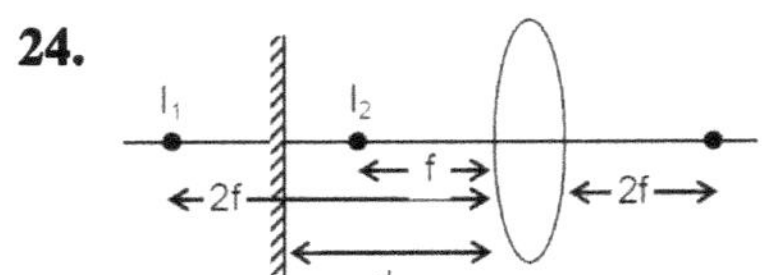

at $2f$– object then image will also be at '$2f$'. Finally image is at ∞ therefore after reflection from mirror, image must be formed at focus.

$d = \dfrac{f+2f}{2} = 45$ cm.

25. (*i*) For plano-concave lens or concave lens if object is placed beyond focus image is erected.

(*ii*) For convex lens if object is placed beyond focus image is inverted.

26. Acceleration is all the time $(-g)$ except at the time of collision it is impulsive force in (+)ve decrease.

28. $a_1 t_1 = a_2 t_2$

by equation of motion

Retardation = $2f$

$t = t_1 + t_2$

$= \sqrt{\dfrac{4d}{3f}}+\sqrt{\dfrac{2d}{2f}} = \sqrt{\dfrac{3d}{f}}.$

30. Initially pressure = P_0

When 50 kg mass is suspended

Pressure = $P_0 - \dfrac{mg}{A}$ (temp. = constant)

$P_0 V_i = \left(V_0 - \dfrac{mg}{A}\right) V_f$

$\left(P_0 - \dfrac{mg}{A}\right) V_f = nRT$

$\left(P_0 - \dfrac{mg}{A}\right) V_i = nR(T - \Delta T)$

$\dfrac{V_f}{V_i} = \dfrac{T}{T-\Delta T}$

$\dfrac{T-\Delta T}{T} = \dfrac{V_i}{V_f}$

$1-\dfrac{\Delta T}{T} = \left(P_0 - \dfrac{mg}{A}\right)\dfrac{1}{P_0}$

$\dfrac{\Delta T}{T} = \dfrac{mg}{AP_0}$

$$= \frac{50 \times 10}{3.14 \times (0.2)^2 \times 10^5}$$

$$= \frac{500}{12.56 \times 10^3} = \frac{5}{125.6} = \frac{1}{25} = 0.04.$$

31. $H_3C - CH_2 - \underset{\underset{CH_3}{|}}{C} = CH - CH_3$

32. (IV) is stabilized by Resonance and

$1° > 2° > 3° \rightarrow$ stability order of carbanion.

33. Coupling reaction

$C_6H_5-\overset{+}{N_2}\overset{(-)}{Cl}$ + H–C_6H_4–OH $\downarrow$ C_6H_5–N=N–C_6H_4–OH

34. Wurtz Reaction

Cl–◇–Br $\xrightarrow{2Na, Ether}$ bicyclic product

35. (II) is most basic because its lone pair is not participating in resonance & attached to sp^3 hyb. carbon.

36. N has half filled stable configuration and Na is most electropositive element.

37. Top to down, Basic strength increases.

39. S^{-2} has 18 electrons & so Ca^{+2} ion are having.

40. $Ca + 2HCl \rightarrow CaCl_2 + H_2(g)$

$\frac{x}{40}$ $\qquad \frac{5.04}{22.4}$

$\Rightarrow \frac{x}{40} = \frac{5.04}{22.4} \Rightarrow \boxed{x = 9.}$

41. $\lambda = \frac{h}{mv} = \frac{6.626 \times 10^{-34}}{20 \times 10^{-3} \times 100} = 3.313 \times 10^{-34}.$

42. $CH_4 + 2O_2 \longrightarrow CO_2 + 2H_2O$

50 L 150 L

CH_4 is limiting reagent

Moles of O_2 remaining $= \frac{50}{22.4} = 2.2$ moles.

43. $Ca(OH)_2 + CO_2 \longrightarrow CaCO_3 + H_2O$

$CaCO_3 + H_2O \xrightarrow{CO_2} Ca(HCO_3)_2$

Clear solution

44. $3s$, $3p$ and $3d$ contains total 18 electrons.

46. For water conservation.

47. Wobbling phenomenon degeneracy occurs at 3rd base of codon.

48. DNA replicates in S-phase of interphase.

49. Definition of gene flow - transfer of gene or allele from one population to another.

51. Because it is permeable for ammonia and other Nitrogenous wastes.

52. $RQ = \frac{CO_2}{O_2} = \frac{102}{145} = 0.703.$

53. Nucleosome - DNA wrapped around histone during DNA packaging.

54. Tyrosine with Iodine form Thyroxine.

55. Due to presence of four hememolecule.

56. SER functions for lipid synthesis.

57. ATP & NADPH is assimilatory power produced in light reaction *i.e.* used in dark reaction.

58. By ACTH-RH which act on adenohypophysis for release of ACTH, ACTH than stimulate adrenal cortex for production of glucocorticoids and androgens.

59. Acetaminophen is paracetamol not produced by plant or fungi, it is artificially formed.

60. Inheritance of acquired character.

61. $\therefore$ Slope of OM = 1

$\therefore \angle COA = 45°$

$C\left(\frac{1}{\sqrt{2}}, \frac{1}{\sqrt{2}}\right)$

Now $\quad OM = OC + CM$

$\sqrt{2}h = 1 + h$

Squaring $\quad 2h^2 = h^2 + 1 + 2h$

$h^2 - 2h - 1 = 0$

$h = \frac{2 \pm \sqrt{8}}{2}$

$\Rightarrow \quad h = 1 \pm \sqrt{2}$

$A\left(1 + \sqrt{2}, 0\right)$

Slope of AC

$$= \frac{0 - \frac{1}{\sqrt{2}}}{1 + \sqrt{2} - \frac{1}{\sqrt{2}}} = -\frac{1}{\sqrt{2}+1} = -\left(\sqrt{2} - 1\right)$$

$$= -\tan 22\frac{1}{2}° = \tan\left(180 - 22\frac{1}{2}\right)° = \tan 157\frac{1}{2}°$$

$\therefore \quad \angle CAX = 157\frac{1}{2}°$

$\therefore \quad \angle OCA = 157\frac{1}{2}° - 45° = 112\frac{1}{2}° = \frac{5\pi}{8}.$

62.

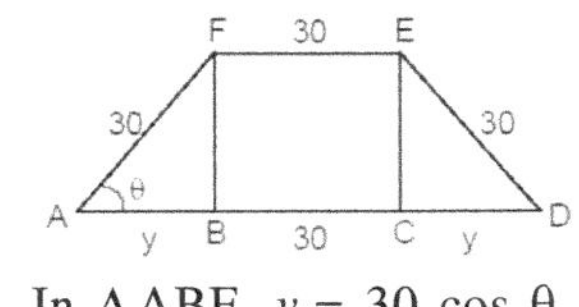

In ΔABF, $y = 30 \cos \theta$

Area is $A = \frac{1}{2}[60 + 60\cos\theta](30\sin\theta)$

$= 30\ (1 + \cos\theta)\ (30 \sin\theta)$

$= 900\ (\sin\theta + \sin\theta\cos\theta)$

For maximum or minimum

$$\frac{dA}{d\theta} = 900\ [\cos\theta + (-\sin^2\theta + \cos^2\theta)] = 0$$

$$\cos\theta - 1 + \cos^2\theta + \cos^2\theta = 0$$

$$2\cos^2\theta + \cos\theta - 1 = 0$$

$$(2\cos\theta - 1)(\cos\theta + 1) = 0$$

$$\cos\theta = \frac{1}{2} \text{ or } \cos\theta = -1 \text{ (not possible)}$$

$$\theta = 60°.$$

64. Given : ar ΔEAB = ar square ABCD

$$EB = ED = \sqrt{130}$$

Let side of square $= x$

$$BM = \frac{x}{\sqrt{2}} = AM$$

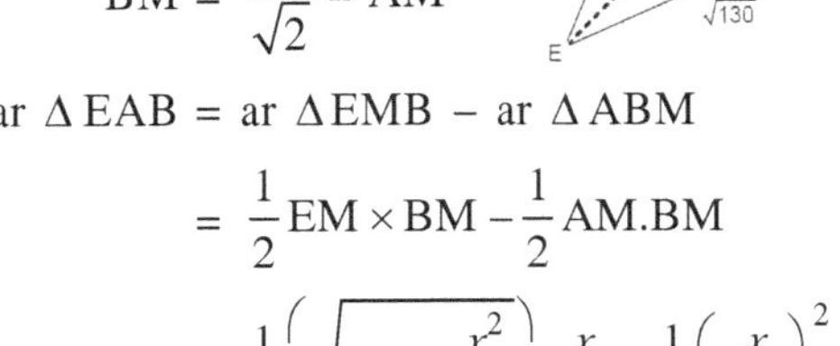

$$\text{ar } \Delta EAB = \text{ar } \Delta EMB - \text{ar } \Delta ABM$$

$$= \frac{1}{2} EM \times BM - \frac{1}{2} AM.BM$$

$$= \frac{1}{2}\left(\sqrt{130 - \frac{x^2}{2}}\right)\frac{x}{\sqrt{2}} - \frac{1}{2}\left(\frac{x}{\sqrt{2}}\right)^2$$

Area of square $= x^2$

Using (*i*) $\frac{1}{2}\frac{x}{\sqrt{2}}\sqrt{130 - \frac{x^2}{2}} - \frac{1}{2}\frac{x^2}{2} = x^2$

$$\frac{x}{2\sqrt{2}}\sqrt{130 - \frac{x^2}{2}} = \frac{5x^2}{4}$$

solve $x = \sqrt{10}$

$\therefore$ $x^2 = 10.$

66. Let Refrigerater extract Q Joul/per second

Q.t $\Rightarrow$ *ms* $(T_f - T)$

Higher the specific heat, Higher the slope.

67.

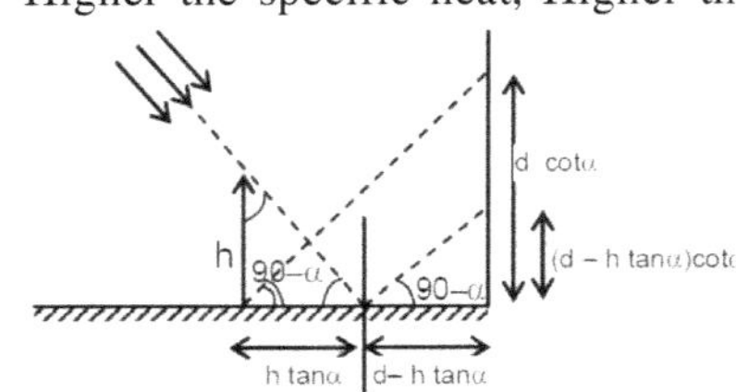

68. F_{net} = weight of water over it

10 cm

$$= (\rho g h)A - \left(\frac{2}{3}\pi R^3\right)\rho g$$

$$= A(10^3 \times 10 \times 10 \times 10^{-2}) - \frac{2}{3}\pi \times 10^{-2} \times 10^3 \times 10$$

= Area = 0.04 N downward.

69. From E $\rightarrow$ F

Slope is constant, $V = IR$

Thus, R must be constant

$$R_0 = V_0/I_0$$

From F $\rightarrow$ G, V = constant

I is increase thus R must be decrease.

$$\text{at G, } R = \frac{V_0}{2I_0} = \frac{R_0}{2}$$

From G $\rightarrow$ H

I = constant, V = increase, thus R must be increase

$$R_H = \frac{2V_0}{2I_0} = R_0.$$

70.
$$\frac{V}{t} = k\left(\frac{P}{\ell}\right)^a.\eta^b.\gamma^c$$

$[r] = L$; $[l] = L$

$[P] = ML^{-1}T^{-2}$; $[\eta] = ML^{-1}T^{-1}$

$[V] = L^3$

$[t] = T$

By calculation, $a = 1$; $b = -1$; $c = 4$.

71. From the data given,

X will be $CH_3 - CH = CH–Ch_3$ which on ozonolysis gives ethanal.

72.

$$CH_3-C\equiv C-H \xrightarrow[H_3O^+]{Hg^{+2}} CH_3-\overset{O}{\overset{\|}{C}}-CH_3$$

$\downarrow$ PhCHO, dil.NaoH

$$CH_3-\overset{O}{\overset{\|}{C}}-CH=CH-Ph$$

(aldol condensation)

73. $(\text{no. of eq.})_{KMnO_4} = (\text{No. of eq.})_{H_2O_2}$

$\Rightarrow$ $1 \times 5 = x \times 2 \Rightarrow \boxed{x = 2.5.}$

74. If energy of incident light $\geq$ work function light, then photoelectrons will be ejected.

76. In S-phase DNA replication occurs.

77. In photosynthesis - photophosphorylation & in aerobic respiration - oxidative phosphorylation occurs that requires proton gradient.

78. $[H^+]\ [OH^-] = 10^{-14}$

$1.3 \times 10^{-4} \times [OH] = 10^{-14}$

$$[OH^-] = \frac{1}{1.3} \times 10^{-10}$$

$$= 0.769 \times 10^{-10} = 7.7 \times 10^{-11}.$$

79. VC = TV + IRV + ERV

Forcefully inspiration after forcefully expiration.

80. Because they are haploid organism.

Kishore Vaigyanik Protsahan Yojana (KVPY)

STREAM – SA

Part-I

Mathematics

1. Suppose the quadratic polynomial $P(x) = ax^2 + bx + c$ has positive coefficients a, b, c in arithmetic progression in that order. If $P(x) = 0$ has integer roots α and β, then $\alpha + \beta + \alpha\beta$ equals:

A. 3 B. 5
C. 7 D. 14

2. The number of digits in the decimal expansion of $16^5 5^{16}$ is:

A. 16 B. 17
C. 18 D. 19

3. Let t be real number such that $t^2 = at + b$ for some positive integers a and b. Then for any choice of positive integers a and b, t^3 is never equal to:

A. $4t + 3$ B. $8t + 5$
C. $10t + 3$ D. $6t + 5$

4. Consider the equation $(1 + a + b)^2 = 3(1 + a^2 + b^2)$, where a, b are real numbers. Then:

A. there is no solution pair (a, b)
B. there are infinitely many solution pairs (a, b)
C. there are exactly two solution pairs (a, b)
D. there is exactly one solution pair (a, b)

5. Let $a_1, a_2, ..., a_{100}$ be non-zero real numbers such that $a_1 + a_2 + ... + a_{100} = 0$. Then:

A. $\sum_{i=1}^{100} a_i 2^{a_i} > 0$ and $\sum_{i=1}^{100} a_i 2^{-a_i} < 0$

B. $\sum_{i=1}^{100} a_i 2^{a_i} \geq 0$ and $\sum_{i=1}^{100} a_i 2^{-a_i} \geq 0$

C. $\sum_{i=1}^{100} a_i 2^{a_i} \leq 0$ and $\sum_{i=1}^{100} a_i 2^{-a_i} \leq 0$

D. the sign of $\sum_{i=1}^{100} a_i 2^{a_i}$ or $\sum_{i=1}^{100} a_i 2^{-a_i}$ depends on the choice of a_i's

6. Let ABCD be a trapezium, in which AB is parallel to CD, AB = 11, BC = 4, CD = 6 and DA = 3. The distance between AB and CD is:

A. 2
B. 2.4
C. 2.8
D. not determinable with the data

7. The points A, B, C, D, E are marked on the circumference of a circle in clockwise direction such that $\angle ABC = 130°$ and $\angle CDE = 110°$. The measure of $\angle ACE$ in degrees is:

A. 50° B. 60°
C. 70° D. 80°

8. Three circles of radii 1, 2 and 3 units respectively touch each other externally in the plane. The circumradius of the triangle formed by joining the centres of the circles is:

A. 1.5 B. 2
C. 2.5 D. 3

9. Let P be a point inside a triangle ABC with $\angle ABC = 90°$. Let P_1 and P_2 be the images of P under reflection in AB and BC respectively. The distance between the circumcenters of triangles ABC and P_1PP_2 is:

A. $\frac{AB}{2}$ B. $\frac{AP + BP + CP}{3}$

C. $\frac{AC}{2}$ D. $\frac{AB + BC + AC}{2}$

10. Let a and b be two positive real numbers such that $a + 2b \leq 1$. Let A_1 and A_2 be, respectively, the areas of circles with radii ab^3 and b^3. Then the maximum possible value of $\frac{A_1}{A_2}$ is:

A. $\frac{1}{16}$ B. $\frac{1}{64}$

C. $\frac{1}{16\sqrt{2}}$ D. $\frac{1}{32}$

11. There are two candles of same length and same size. Both of them burn at uniform rate. The first one burns in 5 hours and the second one burns in 3 hours. Both the candles are lit together. After how many minutes the length of the first candle is 3 times that of the other?

A. 90 B. 120
C. 135 D. 150

12. Consider a cuboid all of whose edges are integers and whose base is a square. Suppose the sum of all its edges is numerically equal to the sum of the areas of all its six faces. Then the sum of all its edges is:

A. 12 B. 18
C. 24 D. 36

13. Let $A_1, A_2, ..., A_m$ be non-empty subsets of {1, 2, 3, ..., 100} satisfying the following conditions:

1. the numbers $|A_1|, |A_2|, ..., |A_m|$ are distinct;
2. $A_1, A_2, ..., A_m$ are pairwise disjoint.

(Here $|A|$ denotes the number of elements in the set A.) Then the maximum possible value of m is:

A. 13 B. 14
C. 15 D. 16

14. The number of all 2-digit numbers n such that n is equal to the sum of the square of digit in its tens place and the cube of the digit in units place is:

A. 0 B. 1
C. 2 D. 4

15. Let f be a function defined on the set of all positive integers such that $f(xy) = f(x) + f(y)$ for all positive integers x, y. If $f(12) = 24$ and $f(8) = 15$, the value of $f(48)$ is:

A. 31 B. 32
C. 33 D. 34

Physics

16. A person walks 25.0° north of east for 3.18 km. How far would she have to walk due north and then due east to arrive at the same location?

A. towards north 2.88 km and towards east 1.34 km.
B. towards north 2.11 km and towards east 2.11 km.
C. towards north 1.25 km and towards east 1.93 km.
D. towards north 1.34 km and towards east 2.88 km.

17. The length and width of a rectangular room are measured to be 3.95 ± 0.05 m and 3.05 ± 0.05 m, respectively. The area of the floor is:

A. 12.05 ± 0.01 m^2 B. 12.05 ± 0.005 m^2
C. 12.05 ± 0.34 m^2 D. 12.05 ± 0.40 m^2

18. A car goes around uniform circular track of radius R at a uniform speed v once in every T seconds. The magnitude of the centripetal acceleration is a_c. If the car now goes uniformly around a larger circular track of radius 2R and experiences a centripetal acceleration of magnitude $8a_c$, then its time period is:

A. 2T B. 3T
C. T/2 D. 3/2T

19. The primary and the secondary coils of a transformer contain 10 and 100 turns, respectively. The primary coil is connected to a battery that supplies a constant voltage of 1.5 volts. The voltage across the secondary coil is:

A. 1.5 V B. 0.15 V
C. 0.0 V D. 15 V

20. Water falls down a 500.0 m shaft to reach a turbine which generates electricity. How much water must fall per second in order to generate 1.00×10^9 Watts of power? (Assume 50% efficiency of conversion and $g = 10$ m/s^2)

A. 250 m^3 B. 400 m^3
C. 500 m^3 D. 200 m^3

21. The diagram below shows two circular loops of wire (A and B) centred on and perpendicular to the x-axis, and oriented with their planes parallel to each other. The y-axis passes vertically through loop A (dashed line). There is a current I_B in loop B as shown. Possible actions which we might perform on loop A are:

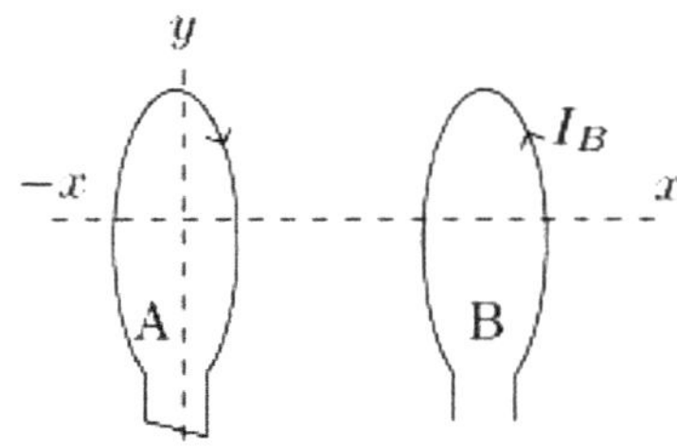

(i) Move A to right along x axis closer to B.
(ii) Move A to the left along x axis away from B.
(iii) As viewed from above, rotate A clockwise about y axis.
(iv) As viewed from above, rotate A anticlockwise about y axis.

Which of these actions will induce a current in A only in the direction shown.

A. Only (i) B. Only (ii)
C. Only (i) and (iv) D. Only (ii) and (iii)

22. A rigid ball rolls without slipping on a surface shown below.

Which one of the following is the most likely representation of the distance travelled by the ball vs time graph?

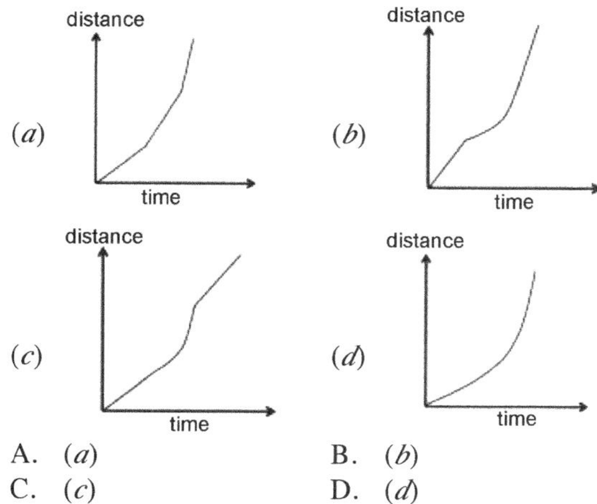

A. (*a*) B. (*b*)
C. (*c*) D. (*d*)

23. In an experiment, setup A consists of two parallel wires which carry currents in opposite directions as shown in the figure. A second setup B is identical to setup A, except that there is a metal plate between the wires.

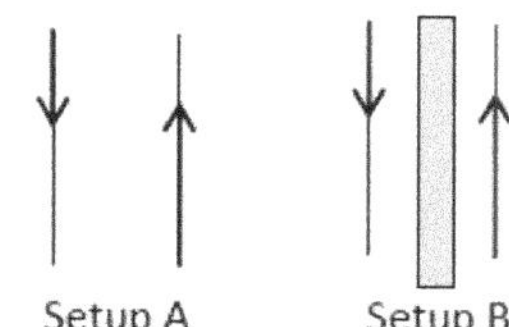

Let F_A and F_B be the magnitude of the force between the two wires in setup A and setup B, respectively.

A. $F_A > F_B \neq 0$ B. $F_A < F_B$
C. $F_A = F_B \neq 0$ D. $F_A > F_B = 0$

24. In the circuit, wire 1 is negligible resistance. Then:

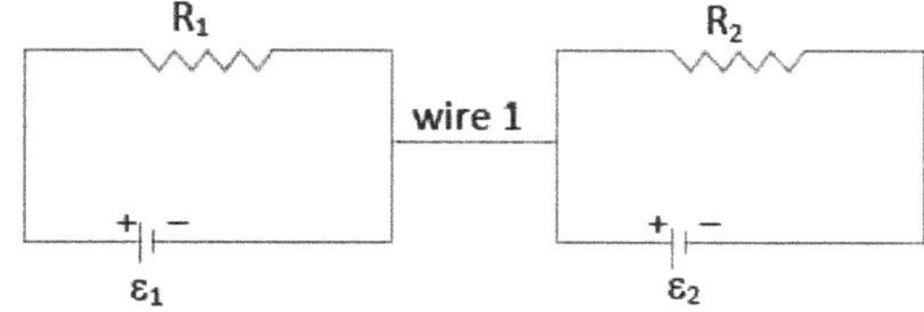

A. Current will flow through wire 1 if $\varepsilon_1 \neq \varepsilon_2$
B. Current will flow through wire 1 if $\varepsilon_1/R_1 \neq \varepsilon_2/R_2$
C. Current will flow through wire 1 if $(\varepsilon_1 + \varepsilon_2)/(R_1 + R_2) \neq (\varepsilon_1 - \varepsilon_2)/(R_1 - R_2)$
D. No current will flow through wire 1

25. The radius of a nucleus is given by $r_0A^{1/3}$ where $r_0 = 1.3 \times 10^{-15}$ m and A is the mass number of the nucleus. The Lead nucleus has A = 206. The electrostatic force between two protons in this nucleus is approximately:

A. 10^2 N B. 10^7 N
C. 10^{12} N D. 10^{17} N

26. A hollow lens is made of thin glass and in the shape of a double concave lens. It can be filled with air, water of refractive index 1.33 or CS_2 of refractive index 1.6. It will act as a diverging lens if it is:

A. filled with air and immersed in water
B. filled with water and immersed in CS_2
C. filled with air and immersed in CS_2
D. filled with CS_2 and immersed in water

27. A stone thrown down with a speed u takes a time t_1 to reach the ground, while another stone, thrown upwards from the same point with the same speed, takes time t_2. The maximum height the second stone reaches from the ground is:

A. $\frac{1}{2} g t_1 t_2$ B. $g/8(t_1 + t_2)^2$
C. $g/8(t_1 - t_2)^2$ D. $\frac{1}{2} g t_2^2$

28. An electric field due to positively charged long straight wire at a distance r from it is proportional to r^{-1} in magnitude. Two electrons are orbiting such a long straight wire in circular orbits of radii 1 Å and 2 Å. The ratio of their respective time peridos is:

A. 1 : 1 B. 1 : 2
C. 2 : 1 D. 4 : 1

29. Two particles of identical mass are moving in circular orbits under a potential given by $V(r) = Kr^{-n}$, where K is a constant. If the radii of their orbits are r_1, r_2 and their speeds are v_1, v_2, respectively, then:

A. $v_1^2 r_1^n = v_2^2 r_2^n$ B. $v_1^2 r_1^{-n} = v_2^2 r_2^{-n}$
C. $v_1^2 r_1 = v_2^2 r_2$ D. $v_1^2 r_1^{2-n} = v_2^2 r_2^{2-n}$

30. Mercury is often used in clinical thermometers. Which one of the following properties of mercury is not a reason for this?

A. The coefficient of the thermal expansion is large.
B. It is shiny.
C. It is a liquid at room temperature.
D. It has high density.

Chemistry

31. One mole of one of the sodium salts listed below, having carbon content close to 14.3%, produces 1 mole of carbon dioxide upon heating (atomic mass Na = 23, H = 1, C = 12, O = 16). The salt is:

A. C_2H_5COONa B. $NaHCO_3$
C. $HCOONa$ D. CH_3COONa

32. Among formic acid, acetic acid, propanoic acid and phenol, the strongest acid in water is:

A. formic acid
B. acetic acid
C. propanoic acid
D. phenol

33. According to Graham's Law, the rate of diffusion of CO, O_2, N_2 and CO_2 follows the order:

A. $CO = N_2 > O_2 > CO_2$
B. $CO = N_2 > CO_2 > O_2$
C. $O_2 > CO = N_2 > CO_2$
D. $CO_2 > O_2 > CO = N_2$

34. The major product formed when 2-butene is reacted with O_3 followed by treatment with Zn/H_2O is:

A. CH_3COOH B. CH_3CHO
C. CH_3CH_2OH D. $CH_2 = CH_2$

35. The IUPAC name for the following compound is:

$$CH_3-CH_2-CH_2-CH_2-\underset{\underset{\displaystyle CH_2}{||}}{C}-CH_2-CH_2-CH_3$$

A. 2-propylhex-1-ene
B. 2-butylpent-1-ene
C. 2-propyl-2-butylethene
D. propyl-1-butylethene

36. The major products obtained in the reaction of oxalic acid with conc. H_2SO_4 upon heating are:

A. CO, CO_2, H_2O B. CO, SO_2, H_2O
C. H_2S, CO, H_2O D. HCOOH, H_2S, CO

37. LiOH reacts with CO_2 to form Li_2CO_3 (atomic mass of Li = 7). The amount of CO_2 (in g) consumed by 1 g of LiOH is closest to:

A. 0.916 B. 1.832
C. 0.544 D. 1.088

38. The oxidation number of sulphur is +4 in:

A. H_2S B. CS_2
C. Na_2SO_4 D. Na_2SO_3

39. Al_2O_3 reacts with:

A. only water B. only acids
C. only alkalis D. both acids and alkalis

40. The major product formed in the oxidation of acetylene by alkaline $KMnO_4$ is:

A. ethanol B. acetic acid
C. formic acid D. oxalic acid

41. In a closed vessel, an ideal gas at 1 atm is heated from 27°C to 327°C. The final pressure of the gas will approximately be:

A. 3 atm B. 0.5 atm
C. 2 atm D. 12 atm

42. Among the elements Li, N, C and Be, one with the largest atomic radius is:

A. Li B. N
C. C D. Be

43. A redox reaction among the following is:

(*i*) $CdCl_2 + 2\,KOH \rightarrow Cd(OH)_2 + 2\,KCl$
(*ii*) $BaCl_2 + K_2SO_4 \rightarrow BaSO_4 + 2\,KCl$
(*iii*) $CaCO_3 \rightarrow CaO + CO_2$
(*iv*) $2\,Ca + O_2 \rightarrow 2\,CaO$

A. (*i*) B. (*ii*)
C. (*iii*) D. (*iv*)

44. The electronic configuration which obeys Hund's rule for the ground state of carbon atom is:

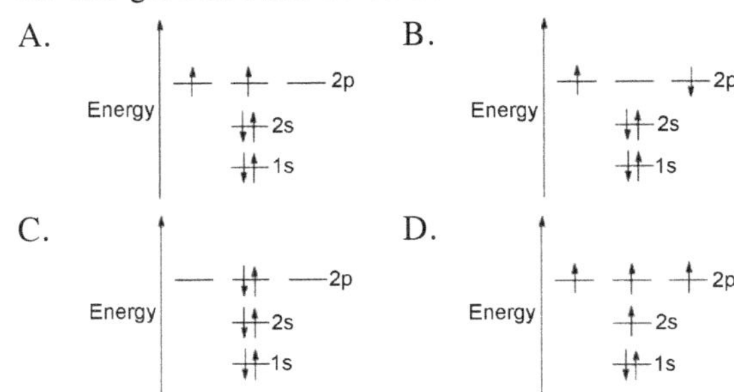

45. The graph that depicts Einstein's photoelectric effect for a monochromatic source of frequency above the threshold frequency is:

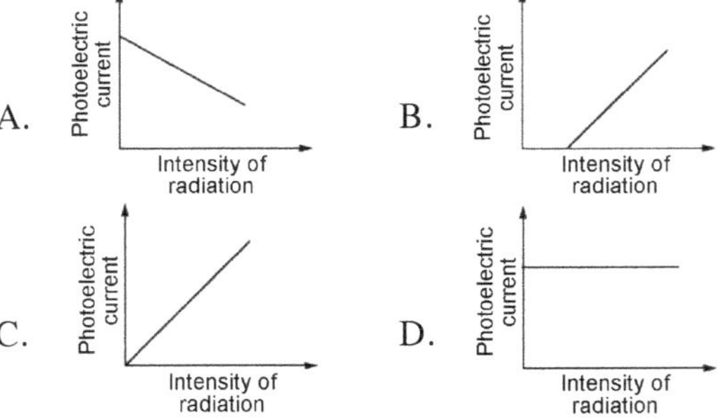

Biology

46. What is the length of human DNA containing 6.6×10^9 bp?

A. 22 nm B. 0.22 mm
C. 2.2 m D. 22 m

47. The *Diptheria, Pertussis, Tetanus* (DPT) vaccine consists of:

A. live attenuated strains of *Diptheria, Pertussis, Tetanus*
B. toxoid of *Diptheria, Tetanus* and heat killed whole cells of *Pertussis*
C. whole cell lysate of *Diptheria, Pertussis, Tetanus*
D. heat killed strains of *Diptheria, Pertussis, Tetanus*

48. Which of the following is NOT an enzyme?

A. Lipase B. Amylase
C. Trypsin D. Bilirubin

49. The pH of the avian blood is maintained by:

A. HCO_3^- B. $H_2PO_4^-$
C. CH_3COO^- D. Cl^-

50. Podocyte layer that provides outer lining to the surface of glomerular capillaries are found in:
A. Bowman's capsule B. Loop of Henle
C. Renal artery D. Ureter

51. If a dsDNA has 20% adenine, what would be its cytosine content?
A. 20% B. 30%
C. 40% D. 80%

52. Which one of the following is incapable of curing Pellagra?
A. Niacine B. Nicotine
C. Nicotinamide D. Tryptophan

53. In *Escherichia coli,* how many codons code for the standard amino-acids?
A. 64 B. 60
C. 61 D. 20

54. *Bombyx mori* (silk worm) belongs to the order:
A. Lepidoptera B. Diptera
C. Hymenoptera D. Coleoptera

55. The source of mammalian hormone "Relaxin" is:
A. ovary B. stomach
C. intestine D. pancreas

56. Which one of the following animals is a connecting link between reptiles and mammals?
A. Platypus B. Bat
C. Armadillo D. Frog

57. What is the number of chromosomes in an individual with Turner's syndrome?
A. 44 B. 45
C. 46 D. 47

58. Chipko movement in the year 1974 in Garhwal Himalayas involved:
A. protecting tigers
B. preventing soil erosion by planting trees
C. preventing pollution by closing down industries
D. hugging trees to prevent the contractors from felling them

59. Which of the following amino acids is NOT involved in gluconeogenesis?
A. Alanine B. Lysine
C. Glutamate D. Arginine

60. Which of the following entities causes syphilis?
A. *Treponema pallidum* B. *Neisseria gonorrhoea*
C. *HIV* D. *Hepatitis B*

Part-II

Mathematics

61. Suppose a is a positive real number such that $a^5 - a^3 + a = 2$. Then:
A. $a^6 < 2$ B. $2 < a^6 < 3$
C. $3 < a^6 < 4$ D. $4 \leq a^6$

62. Consider the quadratic equation $nx^2 + 7\sqrt{nx} + n = 0$, where n is a positive integer. Which of the following statements are necessarily correct?
I. For any n, the roots are distinct.
II. There are infinitely many values of n for which both roots are real.
III. The product of the roots is necessarily an integer.
A. III only B. I and III only
C. II and III only D. I, II and III

63. Consider a semicircle of radius 1 unit constructed on the diameter AB, and let O be its centre. Let C be a point on AO such that AC : CO = 2 : 1. Draw CD perpendicular to AO with D on the semicircle. Draw OE perpendicular to AD with E on AD. Let OE and CD intersect at H. Then DH equals:
A. $\frac{1}{\sqrt{5}}$ B. $\frac{1}{\sqrt{3}}$
C. $\frac{1}{\sqrt{2}}$ D. $\frac{\sqrt{5}-1}{2}$

64. Let S_1 be the sum of areas of the squares whose sides are parallel to coordinate axes. Let S_2 be the sum of areas of the slanted squares as shown in the figure. Then S_1/S_2 is:

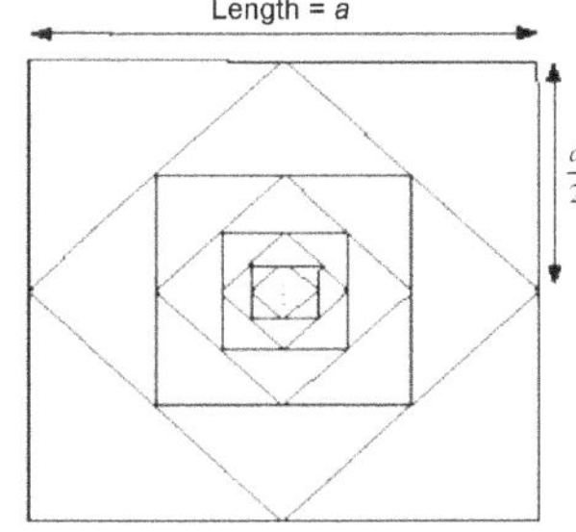

A. 2 B. $\sqrt{2}$
C. 1 D. $\frac{1}{\sqrt{2}}$

65. If a 3-digit number is randomly chosen, what is the probability that either the number itself or some permutation of the number (which is a 3-digit number) is divisible by 4 and 5?
A. $\frac{1}{45}$ B. $\frac{29}{180}$
C. $\frac{11}{60}$ D. $\frac{1}{4}$

Physics

66. Which one of the following four graphs best depict the variation with x of the moment of inertia I of a uniform triangular lamina about an axis parallel to its base at a distance x from it:

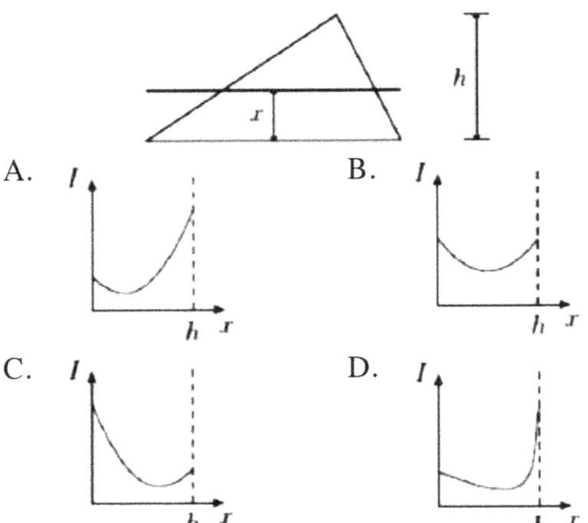

67. A rectangular block is composed of three different glass prisms (with refractive indices μ_1, μ_2 and μ_3) as shown in the figure below. A ray of light incident normal to the left face emerges normal to the right face. Then the refractive indices are related by:

A. $\mu_1^2 + \mu_2^2 = 2\mu_3^2$ B. $\mu_1^2 + \mu_2^2 = \mu_3^2$

C. $\mu_1^2 + \mu_3^2 = 2\mu_2^2$ D. $\mu_2^2 + \mu_3^2 = 2\mu_1^2$

68. A uniform metal plate shaped like a triangle ABC has a mass of 540 gm. The length of the sides AB, BC and CA are 3 cm, 5 cm and 4 cm, respectively. The plate is pivoted freely about the point A. What mass must be added to a vertex, so that the plate can hang with the long edge horizontal?

A. 140 gm at C

B. 540 gm at C

C. 140 gm at B

D. 540 gm at B

69. A 20 gm bullet whose specific heat is 5000 J/(kg-°C) and moving at 2000 m/s plunges into a 1.0 kg block of wax whose specific heat is 3000 J/(kg-°C). Both bullet and wax are at 25°C and assume that (i) the bullet comes to rest in the wax and (ii) all its kinetic energy goes into heating the wax. Thermal temperature of the wax in °C is close to:

A. 28.1 B. 31.5

C. 37.9 D. 42.1

70. A "V" shaped rigid body has two identical uniform arms. What must be the angle between the two arms so that when the body is hung from one end, the other arm is horizontal?

A. $\cos^{-1}$ (1/3) B. $\cos^{-1}$ (1/2)

C. $\cos^{-1}$ (1/4) D. $\cos^{-1}$ (1/6)

Chemistry

71. In the following reactions, X, Y and Z are:

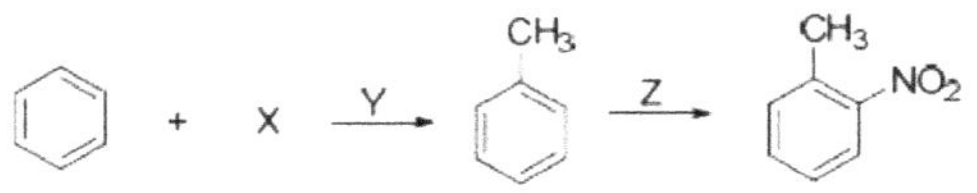

+ X $\xrightarrow{Y}$ (CH_3) $\xrightarrow{Z}$ (CH_3, NO_2)

A. X = CH_3Cl; Y = anhydrous $AlCl_3$;
Z = $HNO_3 + H_2SO_4$

B. X = CH_3COCl; Y = anhydrous $AlCl_3$;
Z = $HNO_3 + H_2SO_4$

C. X = CH_3Cl; Y = conc. H_2SO_4;
Z = $HNO_3 + H_2SO_4$

D. X = CH_3Cl; Y = dil. H_2SO_4; Z = HNO_3

72. 2,3-Dibromobutane can be converted to 2-butyne in a two-step reaction using:

A. (*i*) HCl and (*ii*) NaH

B. (*i*) alcoholic KOH and (*ii*) $NaNH_2$

C. (*i*) Na and (*ii*) NaOH

D. (*i*) Br_2 and (*ii*) NaH

73. Given:

$NO\ (g) + O_3\ (g) \rightarrow NO_2\ (g) + O_2\ (g)$ $\Delta H = -198.9$ kJ/mol

$O_3\ (g) \rightarrow 3/2\ O_2\ (g)$ $\Delta H = -142.3$ kJ/mol

$O_2\ (g) \rightarrow 2\ O\ (g)$ $\Delta H = +495.0$ kJ/mol

The enthalpy change (ΔH) for the following reaction is:

$NO\ (g) + O\ (g) \rightarrow NO_2\ (g)$

A. –304.1 kJ/mol B. +304.1 kJ/mol

C. –403.1 kJ/mol D. +403.1 kJ/mol

74. A 1.85 g sample of an arsenic-containing pesticide was chemically converted to AsO_4^{3-} (atomic mass of As = 74.9) and titrated with Pb^{2+} to form $Pb_3(AsO_4)_2$. If 20 mL of 0.1 M Pb^{2+} is required to reach the equivalence point, the mass percentage of arsenic in the pesticide sample is closest to:

A. 8.1 B. 2.3

C. 5.4 D. 3.6

Biology

75. When treated with conc. HCl, MnO_2 yields a gas (X) which further reacts with $Ca(OH)_2$ to generate a white solid (Y). The solid Y reacts with dil. HCl to produce the same gas X. The solid Y is:

A. CaO B. $CaCl_2$
C. Ca(OCl)Cl D. $CaCO_3$

76. The atmospheric pressure is 760 mm Hg at the sea level. Which of the following ranges is nearest to the partial pressure of CO_2 in mm Hg?

A. 0.30 – 0.31 B. 0.60 – 0.61
C. 3.0 – 3.1 D. 6.0 – 6.1

77. A breeder crossed a pure bred tall plant having white flowers to a pure bred short plant having blue flowers. He obtained 202 F_1 progeny and found that they are all tall having white flowers. Upon selfing these F_1 plants, he obtained a progeny of 2160 plants. Approximately, how many of these are likely to be short and having blue flowers?

A. 1215 B. 405
C. 540 D. 135

78. Match the different types of heart given in column A with organisms given in the column B. Choose the correct combination.

	Column A		***Column B***
P.	Neurogenic heart	(*i*)	Human
Q.	Bronchial heart	(*ii*)	King crab
R.	Pulmonary heart	(*iii*)	Shark

A. P-(*ii*), Q-(*iii*), R-(*i*)
B. P-(*iii*), Q-(*ii*), R-(*i*)
C. P-(*i*), Q-(*iii*), R-(*ii*)
D. P-(*ii*), Q-(*i*), R-(*iii*)

79. Given below are the four schematics that describe the dependence of the rate of an enzymatic reaction on temperature. Which of the following combinations is true for thermophilic and psychrophilic organisms?

P. 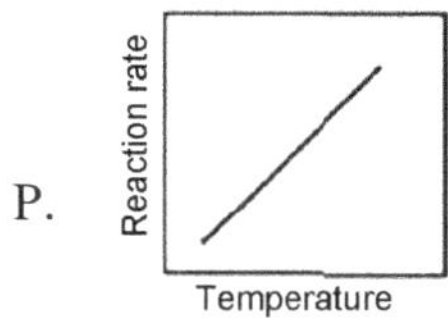

Q. 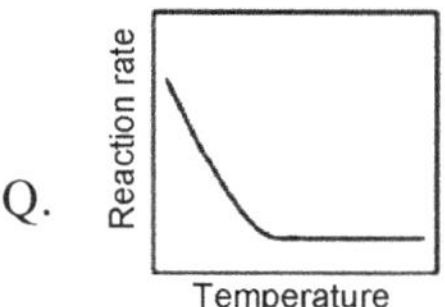

R. 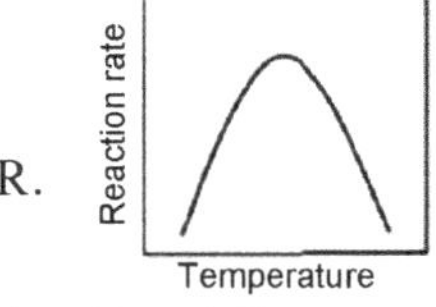

S. Reaction rate / Temperature

A. P and P B. P and S
C. P and R D. R and R

80. Match the enzymes in Group I with the reactions in Group II. Select the correct combination.

Group-I		***Group-II***
P. Hydrolase	(*i*)	Inter-conversion of optical isomers
Q. Lyase	(*ii*)	Oxidation and reduction of two substrates
R. Isomerase	(*iii*)	Joining of two compounds
S. Ligase	(*iv*)	Removal of a chemical group from a substrate
	(*v*)	Transfer of a chemical group from one substrate to another.

A. P-(*iv*), Q-(*ii*), R-(*iii*), S-(*i*)
B. P-(*v*), Q-(*iv*), R-(*i*), S-(*iii*)
C. P-(*iv*), Q-(*i*), R-(*iii*), S-(*v*)
D. P-(*i*), Q-(*iv*), R-(*v*), S-(*ii*)

ANSWERS

1	**2**	**3**	**4**	**5**	**6**	**7**	**8**	**9**	**10**
C	C	B	D	A	B	B	C	C	B
11	**12**	**13**	**14**	**15**	**16**	**17**	**18**	**19**	**20**
D	C	A	C	D	D	C	C	C	B
21	**22**	**23**	**24**	**25**	**26**	**27**	**28**	**29**	**30**
A	D	C	D	A	D	B	B	A	D
31	**32**	**33**	**34**	**35**	**36**	**37**	**38**	**39**	**40**
B	A	A	B	A	A	A	D	D	D
41	**42**	**43**	**44**	**45**	**46**	**47**	**48**	**49**	**50**
C	A	D	A	C	C	B	D	A	A
51	**52**	**53**	**54**	**55**	**56**	**57**	**58**	**59**	**60**
B	B	C	A	A	A	B	D	B	A
61	**62**	**63**	**64**	**65**	**66**	**67**	**68**	**69**	**70**
C	B	C	A	B	A	C	C	C	A
71	**72**	**73**	**74**	**75**	**76**	**77**	**78**	**79**	**80**
A	B	A	C	C	A	D	A	D	B

EXPLANATORY ANSWERS

1. $P(x) = ax^2 + bx + c = a(x - \alpha)(x - \beta)$

and $\alpha + \beta + \alpha\beta + 1 - 1 = (\alpha + 1)(\beta + 1) - 1$

$$= \frac{a-b+c}{a} - 1$$

$\Rightarrow \quad \alpha + \beta + \alpha\beta = \frac{b}{a} - 1 = \lambda_1 - 1$

i.e., $\frac{b}{a}$, is integer $= \lambda_1$

if $b = a\lambda_1$

then, $c = a(2\lambda_1 - 1)$ {because a, b, c are in AP}

$\therefore \quad P(x) = ax^2 + a\lambda_1 x + a(2\lambda_1 - 1)$

$= a[x^2 + \lambda_1 x + (2\lambda_1 - 1)]$

$D = \lambda_1^2 - 4(2\lambda_1 - 1)$ is perfect square for integral roots

$\Rightarrow \quad D = \lambda_1^2 - 8\lambda_1 + 4$ is perfect square

Let $\quad D = (\lambda_1 - 4)^2 - 12 = k^2$ {where $k \in I$}

$\Rightarrow \quad (\lambda_1 - 4 - k)(\lambda_1 - 4 + k) = 12$

This gives, $\quad \lambda_1 - 4 - k = 2$

and $\quad \lambda_1 - 4 + k = 6$

$\Rightarrow \quad \lambda_1 - 4 = 4$ and $k = 1$

$\lambda_1 = 8$

$\therefore \quad \alpha + \beta + \alpha\beta = 8 - 1 = 7.$

2. $16^5 5^{16} = (2^4)^5 \times 5^{16}$

$= 2^{20} \times 5^{16} = 2^4.2^{16}.5^{16}$

$= 16\ (2 \times 5)^{16}$

$= 16 \times (10)^{16}$

$\therefore \quad$ Total digits $= 2 + 16 = 18.$

3. $t^2 = at + b$; $ab \in I^+$

$t^3 = at^2 + bt$

$= a(at + b) + bt$

$= a^2t + bt + ab$

$\Rightarrow \quad t^3 = (a^2 + b)t + ab,$

check possibility for $a, b \in I^+$ from options

A. $a^2 + b = 4$, $ab = 3$ possible

B. $a^2 + b = 8$, $ab = 5$ not possible

C. $a^2 + b = 10$, $ab = 3$ possible

D. $a^2 + b = 6$, $ab = 5$ possible.

4. $(1 + a + b)^2 = 3(1 + a^2 + b^2)$

$(1 + a^2 + b^2) + 2a + 2ab + 2b = 3(1 + a^2 + b^2)$

$2(a + ab + b) = 2(1 + a^2 + b^2)$

$a + ab + b = 1 + a^2 + b^2$

This is possible when $1 = a = b$

$\therefore$ exactly one pair.

5. Note that for every real number a_i

$a_i.2^{ai} > a_i$ and $a_i.2^{-ai} < a_i$

Therefore, $\sum_{i=1}^{100} a_i.2^{ai} > \sum_{i=1}^{100} a_i$ and

$\sum_{i=1}^{100} a_i.2^{-ai} < \sum_{i=1}^{100} a_i$.

6. $\because \quad EB^2 = CB^2 + CE^2$

$\therefore \quad \angle BCE = 90°$

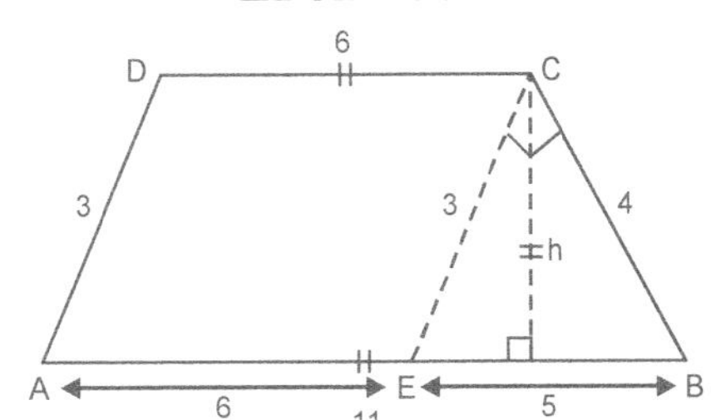

$\therefore \quad h = \frac{3\times4}{5} = \frac{12}{5} = 2.4.$

7.

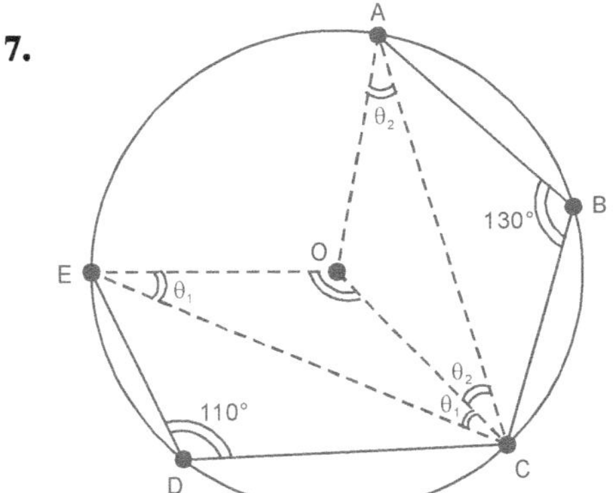

$\angle EOC = 2(180° - 110°) = 140°$

$\theta_1 = \frac{180-140}{2} = \frac{40°}{2} = 20°$

$\angle AOC = 2(180° - 130°) = 100$

$\theta_2 = \frac{180-100}{2} = \frac{80°}{2} = 40°$

$\therefore \quad \theta_1 + \theta_2 = 20 + 40 = 60°$ ($\angle ACE$).

8. $\because \quad O_1O_3^2 = O_1O_2^2 + O_2O_3^2$

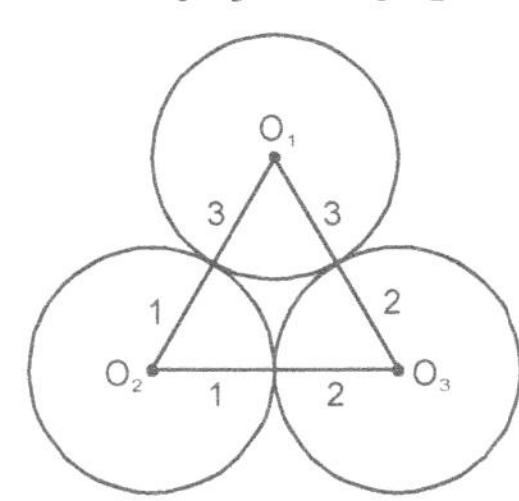

$\therefore \qquad \angle O_2O_1O_3 = 90°$

$$\text{Circumradius} = \frac{\text{Hypotenuse}}{2}$$

$$= \frac{5}{2} = 2.5 \text{ unit.}$$

9. $\therefore$ Distance between the circumcentres of triangle ABC and $P_1PP_2 = \dfrac{AC}{2}$

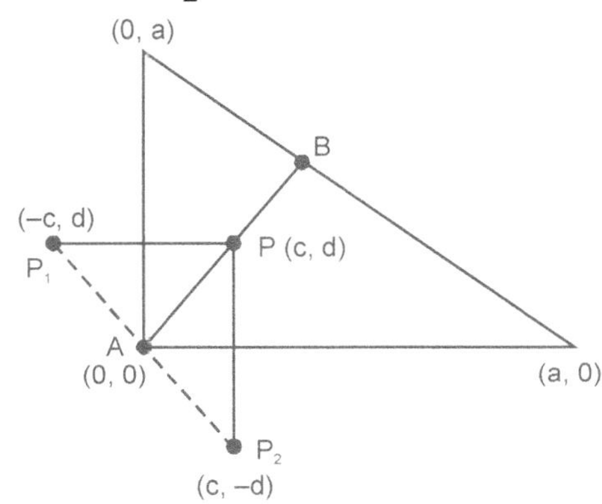

10. $$\frac{A_1}{A_2} = \frac{\pi(ab^3)^2}{\pi(b^2)^2} = \frac{a^2b^6}{b^4}$$

$$= a^2b^2$$

$\because \qquad a + 2b \le 1$

$\therefore$ $a + 2b$ maximum value = 1

$$\frac{a+2b}{2} \ge \sqrt[2]{(a)(2b)} \quad [\because \text{AM} \ge \text{GM}]$$

$$\frac{(a+2b)^2}{4} \ge 2ab$$

$$\frac{1}{4} \ge 2ab$$

$$\frac{1}{8} \ge ab$$

$$\frac{1}{64} \ge a^2b^2$$

$$\frac{1}{64} \ge \frac{A_1}{A_2}$$

Hence, the maximum value of $\dfrac{A_1}{A_2} = \dfrac{1}{64}$.

11.

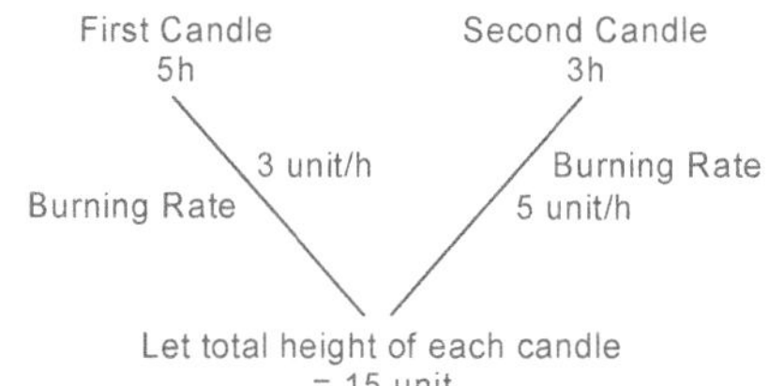

Let, after t hour their height ratio = 3 : 1

$$\frac{15-3t}{15-5t} = \frac{3}{1}$$

$$15 - 3t = 45 - 15t$$

$$12t = 30$$

$$t = \frac{30}{12} = \frac{5}{2} \text{ hour}$$

$$= 150 \text{ minutes.}$$

12. Let sides are a, a, h

So, $\qquad 4a + 4h + 4a = 2(a^2 + ab + ah)$

$\qquad 2a + 2b + 2a = a^2 + 2ah$

$\Rightarrow \qquad a^2 - 4a = 2h(1 - a)$

$\Rightarrow \qquad (a^2 - 1) + 1 - 4(a - 1) - 4 = 2h\,(1 - a)$

$\Rightarrow \qquad (a - 1)\,(a + 1) - 4(a - 1) - 3 = 2h\,(1 - a)$

$\Rightarrow \qquad 2h = \dfrac{3}{a-1} + 4 - (a+1)$

So, $a = 2$ and $h = 2$ are the only integral solution (a and h are positive integers).

$\therefore$ Sum of its edges $= 4a + 4h + 4a$

$= 4 \times 2 + 4 \times 2 + 4 \times 2$

$= 8 + 8 + 8 = 24.$

13. $|A_1| = 1$, $|A_2| = 2$, $|A_3| = 3$ ....$|A_m| = m$

[$\because$ $A_1, A_2, ..., A_m$ are disjoint]

$\therefore$ $1 + 2 + 3 + ... + m \le 100$

$$\frac{m(m+1)}{2} \le 100$$

$$m(m + 1) \le 200$$

Check the option,

Option (A) 13 satisfying the inequality

$\therefore$ maximum possible value of m is 13.

14. Let, $n = ab = 10a + b$

$\therefore \qquad 10a + b = a^2 + b^3$

$\qquad 10a - a^2 = b^3 - b$

$\qquad a(10 - a) = b(b^2 - 1)$

Check, $a = 1$, $b = 2$, $a \ne 6$ not possible

$a = 4$, $b = 3$, $\quad 4(10 - 4) = 3(3^2 - 1)$

$\qquad 24 = 24$ possible

$a = 6$, $b = 3$ $\quad 6(10 - 6) = 3(9 - 1)$

$\qquad 24 = 24$ possible

$\therefore$ only two possible numbers 43 and 63 only.

15. We have, $f(x, y) = f(x) + f(y)$

$$f(12) = 24 \quad [\because f(12) = f(4 \times 3)]$$
$$f(4) + f(3) = 24 \quad [\because f(4) = f(2 \times 2)]$$
$$f(2) + f(2) + f(3) = 24$$
$$2f(2) + f(3) = 24 \quad ...(i)$$
$$f(8) = 15$$
$$f(4) + f(2) = 15 \quad [\because f(8) = f(4 \times 2)]$$
$$f(2) + f(2) + f(2) = 15 \quad [\because f(4) = f(2 \times 2)]$$
$$3f(2) = 15$$
$$f(2) = 5$$

From equation (*i*), we get $f(3) = 14$

$$\therefore \quad f(48) = f(2^4 \times 3) = 4f(2) + f(3)$$
$$= 4 \times 5 + 14$$
$$= 20 + 14 = 34.$$

16.

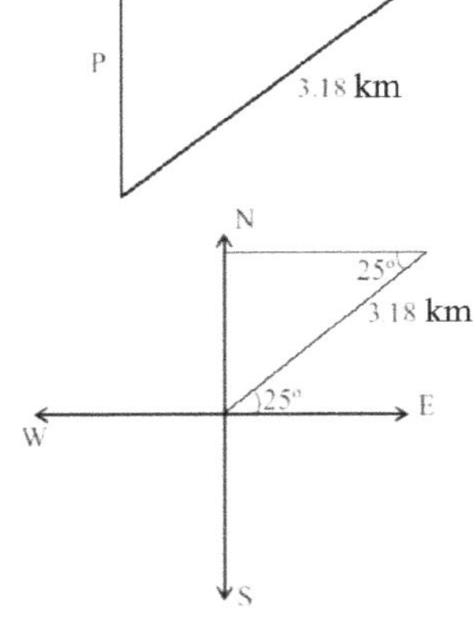

$$\therefore \quad \frac{P}{3.18} = \sin 25°$$
$$P = 3.18 \sin 25°$$
$$= 1.34 \text{ km along north}$$
$$B = 3.18 \cos 25°$$
$$= 2.88 \text{ km} \rightarrow \text{along east.}$$

17.

$$A = \ell B$$
$$dA = \ell\, dB + B\, d\ell$$
$$\frac{dA}{A} = \frac{\ell dB}{\ell B} + \frac{B d\ell}{\ell B}$$
$$\frac{dA}{A} = \frac{dB}{B} + \frac{d\ell}{\ell}$$
$$= \frac{0.05}{3.05} + \frac{0.05}{3.95}$$
$$= 0.016 + 0.012$$
$$= 0.028 \times 12.05$$
$$dA = 0.33$$
$$12.05 \pm 0.34.$$

18.

$$T = \frac{2\pi R}{V}$$
$$a_C = \frac{V^2}{R}$$
$$8\, a_C = \frac{V'^2}{2R}$$

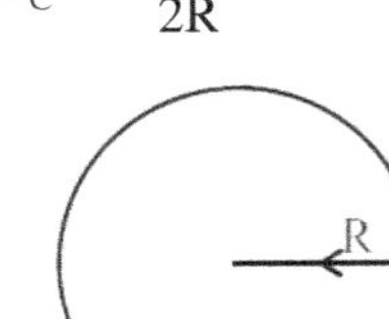

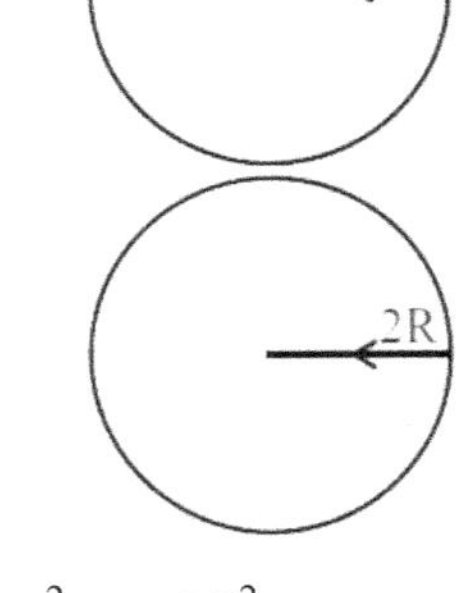

$$(8)\frac{V^2}{R} = \frac{V'^2}{2R}$$
$$V'^2 = 16V^2$$
$$V' = 4V$$
$$\therefore \text{ Time period } = \frac{(2\pi)R'}{V'}$$
$$= \frac{(2\pi)2R}{4V} = \frac{\pi R}{V} = (T/2)$$

19. Since the voltage production is based upon A.C supply and this voltage is D.C which is constant. Therefore, no flux will change in secondary and no voltage will be induced.

20. 500 m

$$P = \frac{mah}{time}$$
$$\eta = \frac{P_{out}}{P_{input}}$$
$$P_{in} = \frac{P_{out}}{\eta}$$
$$= \frac{10^9}{0.5}$$
$$P_{in} = 2 \times 10^9$$
$$\frac{mah}{time} = 2 \times 10^9$$
$$m/t = \frac{2 \times 10^9}{10 \times 500} = \frac{2}{5} \times 10^6$$
$$= 4 \times 10^5$$
$$= 400 \text{ m}^3.$$

22.

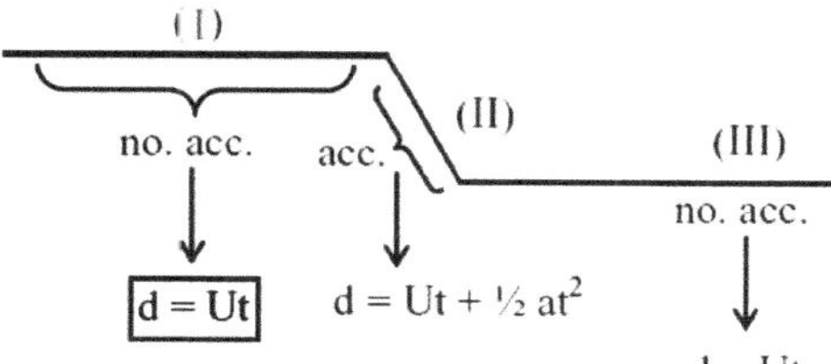

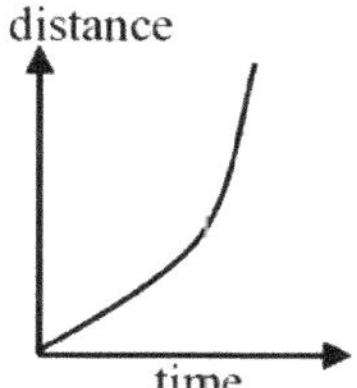

23. In setup B, A metal is placed, due to which metal may get magnetized and it may also exert force on current carrying wire but force between two wire remain same however net force on wire may get charge due to magnetic field produced by magnetized metal.

24.

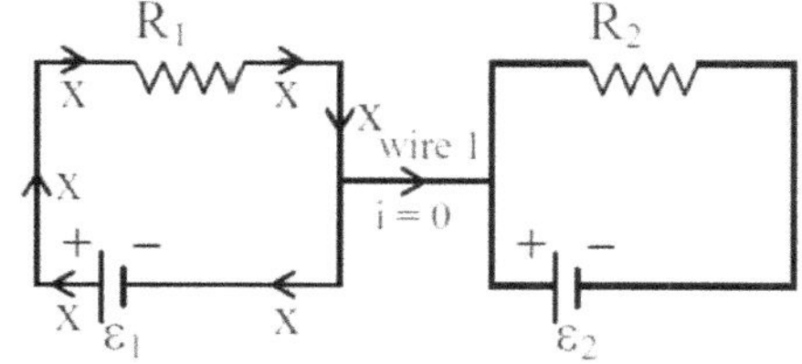

current through wire 1 = 0.

25.

$$r = r_0\, A^{1/3}$$

$$r_0 = 1.3 \times 10^{-15}$$

$$F = \frac{1}{4\pi \in_0} \times \frac{q_1 q_2}{r^2}$$

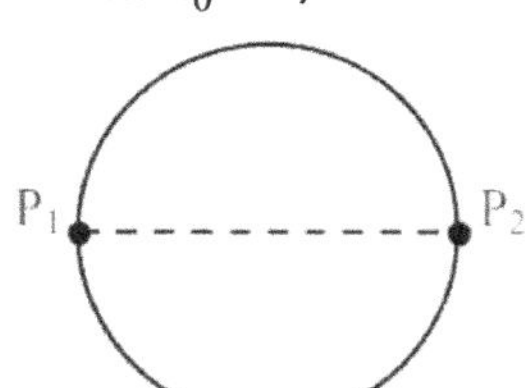

$$F = \frac{9\times10^9 \times 1.6\times10^{-19} \times 1.6\times10^{-19}}{r_0^2 A^{2/3}}$$

$$F = \frac{9\times10^9 \times 1.6\times10^{-19} \times 1.6\times10^{-19}}{(1.3)^2 \times 10^{-30} \times (206)^{2/3}}$$

$$= \frac{23.04\times10^{39} \times 10^{-38}}{(1.69)\times 34.81}$$

$$= \frac{23.04\times10}{1.69\times34.81}$$

= 3.91 Newton

= 0.039×10^2.

26.

$$\mu_{air} = 1$$

$$\mu_{water} = 1.33$$

$$\mu_{CS_2} = 1.6$$

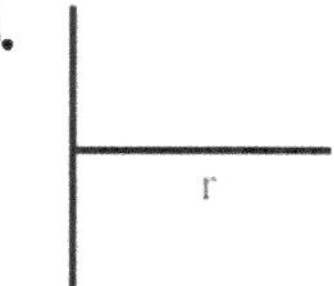

$$\frac{1}{f} = \left(\frac{n_2}{n_1} - 1\right)\left[-\frac{1}{R_1} - \frac{1}{R_2}\right]$$

$$\frac{1}{f} = -\left(\frac{n_2}{n_1} - 1\right)\left[\frac{1}{R_1} + \frac{1}{R_2}\right]$$

for diverging lens f must be –ve.

$\therefore$ for this $\frac{n_2}{n_1} > 1$

$n_2 > n_1$

$\therefore$ Lens should be filled with liquid which has more refractive index in comparison to liquid in which lens is immersed.

$\therefore$ Ans (D) is the correct option as $\mu_{cs_2} > \mu_{water}$.

28.

r

$$E = \frac{K}{r}$$

$\therefore$ $\boxed{F = qE}$

for first electron

$$(q)\frac{1}{r_1} = \frac{mv_1^2}{r_1}$$

$$\Rightarrow \quad q = mv_1^2$$

$$\boxed{v_1^2 = \frac{q}{M}}$$

$$v_1 = \sqrt{\frac{q}{M}}$$

$\therefore$ Similarly, $v_2 = \sqrt{\frac{q}{M}}$

$$v_1 = v_2$$

$$\frac{T_1}{T_2} = \frac{\frac{2\pi R_1}{v_1}}{\frac{2\pi R_2}{v_2}}$$

$$= \frac{2\pi R_1}{\nu_1} \times \frac{\nu_2}{2\pi R_2}$$

$$= \frac{R_1}{\nu_1} \times \frac{\nu_2}{R_2}$$

$$= \frac{1}{2}.$$

29. $V(r) = Kr^{-n}$

Gravitational field = $E = -\frac{dV}{dr}$

$$= (-K)\frac{d}{dr}(r^{-n})$$

$$= (-K)\ (-n)\ r^{-n-1}$$

$$= \frac{Kn}{r^{n+1}}$$

force on mass = E × M, where M = mass of body

$$\therefore \quad ME_1 = \frac{MV_1^2}{r_1}$$

$$ME_2 = \frac{MV_2^2}{r_2}$$

$$\therefore \quad \frac{V_1^2}{V_2^2} = \frac{r_1E_1}{r_2E_2}$$

$$\Rightarrow \quad \frac{V_1^2}{V_2^2} = \frac{r_1}{r_2}\frac{Kn}{r_1^{n+1}}\frac{r_2^{n+1}}{Kn}$$

$$\Rightarrow \quad \frac{V_1^2}{V_2^2} = \frac{r_2^n}{r_1^n}$$

$$\Rightarrow \quad V_1^2 r_1^n = V_2^2\ r_2^n.$$

30. High density is not the reason for its uses in clinical thermometers.

31. $2\,NaHCO_3 \xrightarrow{\Delta} Na_2CO_3 + H_2O + CO_2$

$$\%\ \text{of C} = \frac{12}{84} \times 100 = 14.28\%.$$

This Question can be done by checking % of carbon 14.2% comes only in $NaHCO_3$.

32. Formic Acid is Strongest Acid.

Acidic strength order

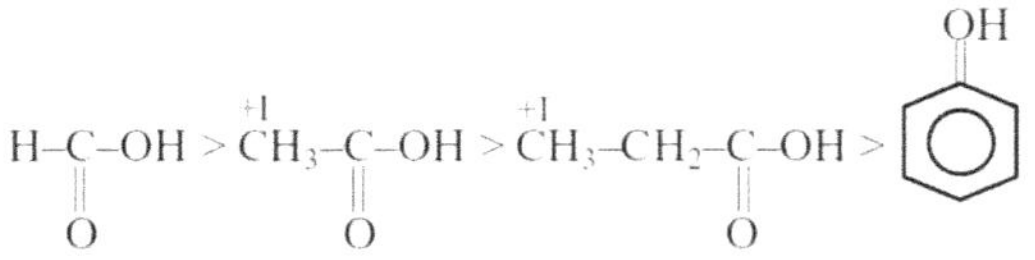

$$\underset{\underset{O}{\|}}{H-C-OH} > \underset{\underset{O}{\|}}{\overset{+I}{CH_3}-C-OH} > \underset{\underset{O}{\|}}{\overset{+I}{CH_3}-CH_2-C-OH} > \text{phenol (}C_6H_5OH\text{)}$$

→ +I decrease acidic strength

→ Carboxylic Acid are more acidic.

Then phenol

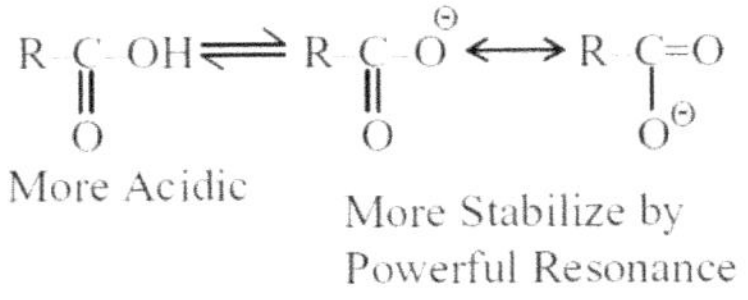

$$\underset{\text{More Acidic}}{R-\underset{\underset{O}{\|}}{C}-OH} \rightleftharpoons R-\underset{\underset{O}{\|}}{C}-\overset{\ominus}{O} \longleftrightarrow R-\underset{\underset{O^{\ominus}}{|}}{C}=O$$

More Stabilize by Powerful Resonance

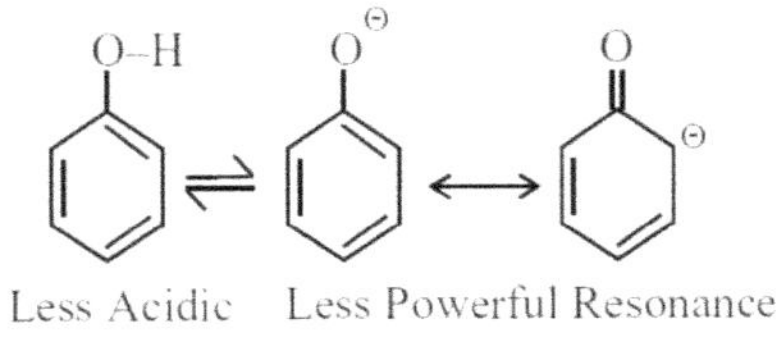

$$\underset{\text{Less Acidic}}{C_6H_5-OH} \rightleftharpoons C_6H_5-O^{\ominus} \longleftrightarrow O=C_6H_5^{\ominus}$$

Less Acidic — Less Powerful Resonance

33. $r \propto \frac{1}{\sqrt{M}}$ Rate of diffusion decrease with increase in molecular weight.

Rate of diffusion order $CO = N_2 > O_2 > CO_2$
(28) (28) (32) (44)

34. This is example of Reductive Ozonolysis

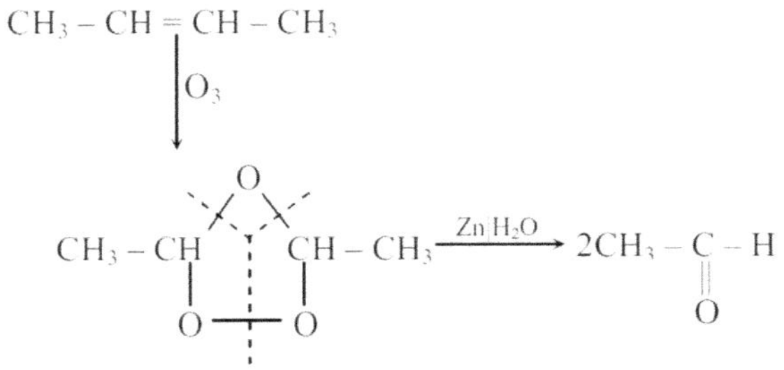

$$CH_3-CH=CH-CH_3 \xrightarrow{O_3} \text{ozonide } (CH_3-CH\overset{O}{\ }CH-CH_3 \text{ with } O-O) \xrightarrow{Zn/H_2O} 2CH_3-\underset{\underset{O}{\|}}{C}-H$$

35. ⑥ ⑤ ④ ③ ②

$$CH_3-CH_2-CH_2-CH_2-\underset{\underset{CH_2}{\|}}{C}-CH_2-CH_2-CH_3$$

① (CH_2)

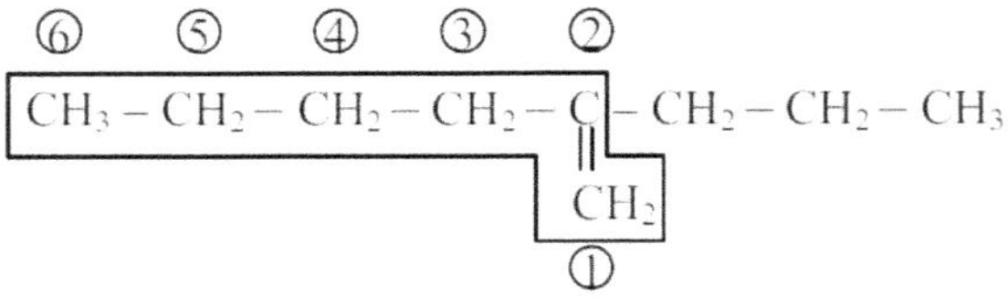

2 propyl hex-1-ene

36. $\underset{COOH}{\overset{COOH}{|}} + H_2SO_4 \xrightarrow{\Delta} H_2O + CO_{2(g)} + CO_{(g)} + H_2SO_4$

37. $2LiOH + CO_2 \rightarrow Li_2CO_3 + H_2O$

$$\frac{1}{24} \qquad \frac{1}{24 \times 2}$$

$$\text{No. of moles of } CO_2 = \frac{1}{48}$$

$$\text{Mass of } CO_2 = \frac{1}{48} \times 44$$

$$= 0.916\ \text{g}.$$

38. H_2S^{-2}
CS_2^{-2}
$Na_2\overset{+6}{S}O_4$
$Na_2\overset{+4}{S}O_3$ ·

39. Al_2O_3 is amphoteric so it dissolve in acid as well in alkalis.

40. $CH{\equiv}CH \xrightarrow{\text{Alkaline } KMnO_4}$ (H–O)(H–O)HC – CH(O–H)(O–H)

HO–C=O | H–C=O (Oxalic acid) $\xleftarrow{(O)}$ H–C=O | H–C=O

41. $P \propto T$ (V, $n \to$ const)

$$\frac{P_1}{P_2} = \frac{T_1}{T_2}$$

$$\frac{1}{P_2} = \frac{300}{600}$$

$P_2 = 2$ atm.

42. As we move left to right in a period atomic radius decrease due to increase in z_{eff}. So, greatest radius is of lithium.

43. Redox reaction is the reaction in which oxidation & reduction take place simultaneously.

So answer is (D)

$$2\overset{0}{Ca} + \overset{0}{O_2} \longrightarrow 2\overset{+2}{Ca}\overset{-2}{O}$$

Oxide (Ca → CaO); Red (O_2 → CaO)

44. C ⇒ $1s^2$ $2s^2$ $2p^2$

[⥮] [⥮] [↿ | ↿ |]
1s 2s 2p

→ Energy increases.

45. On increasing intensity of radiation, value of photo electric current increases because no. of photon incident increases.

46. The distance between 2 nucleotides / nitrogen bases is 3.4 Å and human DNA containing 6.6×10^9 bp multiplied by this distance gives a length of 2.2 meters.

47. Vaccine of *Diphtheria*, *Pertussis* and *Tetanus* (DPT) consist of:

(*i*) Toxoid of *Diphtherian* and *Tetanus*

(*ii*) Heat killed cells of *Pertussis.*

48. Lipase = Enzyme [Lipid digesting]

Amylase = Enzyme [Starch digesting]

Trypsin = Enzyme [Endopeptidase]

Bilirubin = Bile pigment.

49. pH of Blood of bird is maintained by HCO_3^-.

50. Podocyte are cells of squamous epithelium of Bowman capsule of nephron.

51. According to Chargaff's rule, the molar concentration of purines is equal to molar concentration of pyrimidines.

A + G = T + C

So, if Adenine is 20% then T is also 20% because A always pairs with T.

Hence, G is 30% and C is also 30%.

52. Pellagra can be cure by – Niacine
– Nicotinamide
– Tryptophan.

53. In all living organisms, there are 64 codons and 3 codons are stop or termination codons *i.e.* UAA, UAG and UGA which do not code for any amino acids.

54. Order of Silkworm ⇒ *Lepidoptera (Bombax mori).*

55. Relaxin hormone is secreted from ovary at the time of Parturition.

56. Connecting link between Reptile and Mammals is/are (1) Platypus (2) Echidina.

57. The genetic makeup of Turner's syndrome is 44 + XO, so these are a total of 45 chromosomes only.

58. Chipko movement was headed by social activist Sunder Lal Bahuguna in Uttarakhand to save trees from felling.

59. Lysine can not be converted in Glucose.

60. Causative agent of Syphilis is *Treponema pallidum.*

61. $a^5 - a^3 + a = 2;\ a \in R^+$

Let $f(a) = a^5 - a^3 + a - 2$;

{Note $f'(a) > 0\ a \in R$}

for, $a^6 = 3$

⇒ $a = 3^{\frac{1}{6}} = 1.2$

We get $f(1.2) < 0$ and at $a = 4^{\frac{1}{6}}$

⇒ $f(4^{1/6}) > 0$

So, one root in $a \in (3, 4)$.

62. $D = 49n - 4n^2 = n(49 - 4n)$

$D \neq 0$, for any $n \in I^+$.

So roots are distinct

For roots to be real $D \geq 0$

So, $$n \leq \frac{49}{4}$$

So, n can be {1, 2, 3, ..., 12}

Clearly product of the roots is 1.

63. 'E' is mid-point of AD

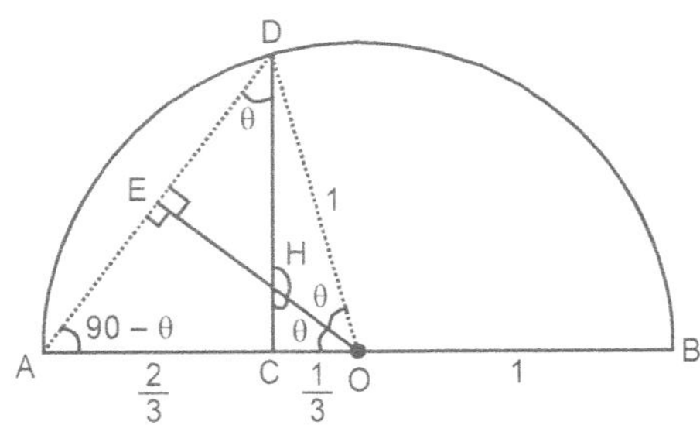

$$\cos 2\theta = \frac{1}{3}$$

$$\Rightarrow \quad 2\cos^2\theta - 1 = \frac{1}{3}$$

$$\Rightarrow \quad \cos^2\theta = \frac{2}{3}$$

$$\Rightarrow \quad \cos\theta = \frac{\sqrt{2}}{\sqrt{3}}$$

$$\Rightarrow \quad \sin\theta = \sqrt{1 - \frac{2}{3}}$$

$$= \frac{1}{\sqrt{3}}$$

$$\frac{ED}{1} = \frac{1}{\sqrt{3}}$$

$$ED = \frac{1}{\sqrt{3}}$$

$$\sec\theta = \frac{DH}{ED}$$

$$\frac{\sqrt{3}}{\sqrt{2}} = \frac{DH}{\left(\frac{1}{\sqrt{3}}\right)}$$

$$\therefore \quad DH = \frac{1}{\sqrt{2}}.$$

64. S_1 = Sum of Area of the square whose side are parallel to coordinate axes

$$S_1 = (a)^2 + \left(\frac{a}{2}\right)^2 + \left(\frac{a}{4}\right)^2 + \left(\frac{a}{8}\right)^2 + \ldots.\infty$$

$$S_1 = a^2\left[1 + \frac{1}{2^2} + \frac{1}{2^4} \ldots\infty\right]$$

$$= a^2\left[\frac{1}{1 - \frac{1}{4}}\right]$$

$$= \frac{4a^2}{3}$$

S_2 = Sum of Area of the square whose side are slanted

$$S_2 = \left(\frac{a}{\sqrt{2}}\right)^2 + \left(\frac{a}{2\sqrt{2}}\right)^2 + \left(\frac{a}{4\sqrt{2}}\right)^2 + \ldots.\ \infty$$

$$= a^2\left[\frac{1}{2} + \frac{1}{8} + \frac{1}{32} + \ldots\infty\right]$$

$$= \frac{a^2}{2}\left[1 + \frac{1}{4} + \frac{1}{16} + \ldots\infty\right]$$

$$= \frac{a^2}{2}\left[\frac{1}{1 - \frac{1}{4}}\right]$$

$$= \frac{a^2}{2} \times \frac{4}{3} = \frac{2a^2}{3}$$

$$\therefore \ S_1 : S_2 = \left(\frac{4a^2}{3}\right) : \left(\frac{2a^2}{3}\right)$$

$$= 2 : 1.$$

65. We need 3-digit number which is divisible by 4 and 5 both, *i.e.*, their last two digits are 00, 20, 40, 60 and 80

Now, ending with 00 are '9'

{100, 200, ..., 900}

If digit repeat other than '0' then they are

{220, 440, 660, 880}

But 220 numbers can be permuted according to the condition as {220, 202}. So, there are '8' other favourable cases.

If the number have no digit repeated like 320

320 can be permuted in 4 ways

{302, 230, 320, 203}

So, such numbers are 8 × 4 × 4 = 128

Total favourable = 9 + 8 + 128 = 145

So, required probability $= \frac{145}{900} = \frac{29}{180}$.

66.

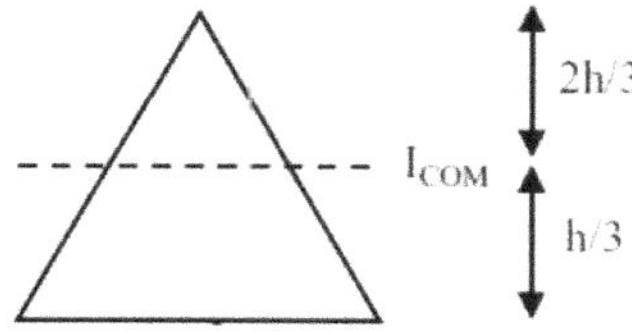

$I = I_{COM} + Mx^2$

First it will decrease because x is increasing and axis is coming closer to COM axis. After Passing COM axis, M & I will again increase

⇒ I is minimum about the axis passing through COM if we compare I about other parallel axis.

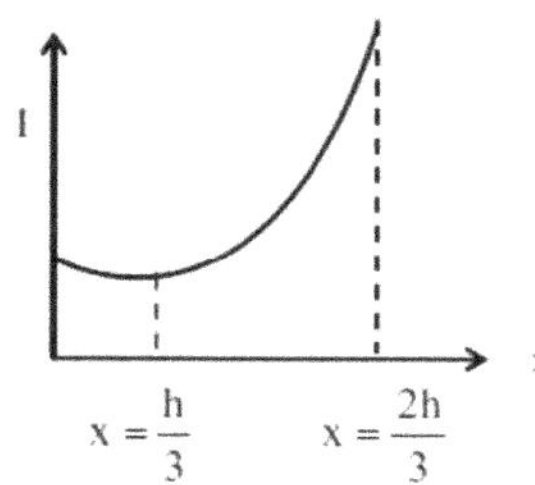

69.

$M_B = 20 \times 10^{-3}$ Kg
$C_B = 5000$ J / Kg-°C
$V = 2000$ M/s
$M_w = 1$ Kg
$C_w = 3000$ J/Kg-°C
$T_f = 25$°C
= 298 K

$$\frac{1}{2}MV^2 = M_wC_w\Delta T_w + M_BC_B\Delta T_B$$

$$\frac{1}{2}M_BV^2 = M_wC_w(\Delta T_w) + M_BC_B\Delta T_B$$

$$\Rightarrow \quad = \frac{1}{2} \times 20 \times 10^{-3} \times 4 \times 10^6$$

$$= (\Delta T)\{1 \times 3000 + 20 \times 10^{-3} \times 5000\}$$

$$\Rightarrow \quad 40 \times 10^3 = \Delta T\{3000 + 100\}$$

$$\Delta T = \frac{40 \times 10^3}{3100}$$

$\Delta T = 12.9$

$T_f - 25 = 12.9$

$T_f = 25 + 12.9$

= 37.9°C.

71. Benzene + CH_3Cl /Anhydrous $AlCl_3$ $\xrightarrow[\text{Craft reaction}]{\text{Friedel}}$ Toluene ($C_6H_5CH_3$)

$\xrightarrow{\text{Conc. } HNO_3 - \text{(Nitration Conc. } H_2SO_4)}$ CH_3–C_6H_4–NO_2

72. This is example of Dehydrohalogenation

$$CH_3-\underset{Br}{CH}-\underset{Br}{CH}-CH_3 \xrightarrow[\text{KOH} - \text{HBr}]{\text{Alcoholic}} CH_3-CH=\underset{Br}{C}-CH_3$$

$$\xrightarrow[-\text{HBr}]{NaNH_2} CH_3-C \equiv C-CH_3$$

$$CH_3-\underset{Br}{CH}-\underset{Br}{CH}-CH_3 \quad Br \longrightarrow CH_3-CH=C-CH_3$$

73. $NO + O_3 \longrightarrow NO_2 + O_2 \quad \Delta H = -198.9$ kJ/mole

$$O_3 \longrightarrow \frac{3}{2}O_2(g) \quad \Delta H = -142.3 \text{ kJ/mole}$$

$$O_2 \longrightarrow 2O_2(g) \quad \Delta H = +495.0 \text{ kJ/mole}$$

ΔH of $NO + O(g) \longrightarrow NO_2(g)$

For this $(i) - (ii) - \frac{(iii)}{2}$

$$= -198.9 - (-142.3) - \frac{495}{2}$$

$$= -304.1 \text{ kJ/mole.}$$

74. $3Pb^{2+} + 2AsO_4^{3-} \longrightarrow Pb_3(AsO_4)_2$

$n = M \times V \qquad n = \frac{2}{3} \times 2 \times 10^{-3}$

$$= 0.1 \times \frac{20}{1000}$$

= 0.00133

$= 2 \times 10^{-3}$

$\eta_{As} = \eta_{AsO_4^{3-}} = 0.00133$

$W_{As} = 0.00133 \times 74.9$

= 0.0996

$$\% \text{ of As} = \frac{0.0996}{1.85} \times 100 = 5.4\%.$$

75. $\underset{\text{conc.}}{MnO_2 + HCl} \longrightarrow Cl_2(g)(x)$

$Ca(OH)_2 + Cl_2 \longrightarrow CaOCl_2(y)$

$CaOCl_2 + dil.HCl \longrightarrow \underset{(X)}{Cl_2} + CaCl_2 + H_2O$

76. P_{CO_2} = 0.30 – 0.31 mm Hg in Air.

77. TTWW × ttww

↓

TtWw × TtWw (202 plants)

↓

2160 plants – (Total) in F_2

TW – 9
Tw – 3
tW – 3
tw – 1
} according to ratio of dihybrid cross

The total number of short and blue flowered plants is:

$$\frac{1}{16} \times 2130 = \frac{1080}{8} = 135.$$

78. – Neurogenic heart → King crab [Arthropod]

– Bronchial heart → Shark [Single circulation]

– Pulmonary heart → Human.

79. Being mostly proteinaceous enzymes are liable to temperature. Thermophiles are living at very high temperature while psychrophiles live in the range of –20°C to + 10°C. In either case rising temperature will first raise the rate of reaction but if temperature is still raised continuously enzyme get denatured hence reaction rate decreases.

80. (*i*) Hydrolase catalyses hydrolysis of ester, ether, peptide, glycosidic, C–C, C-halide or P–N bonds

(*ii*) Lyase catalyses removal of groups other than hydrolysis

(*iii*) Isomerase catalyses interconversion of optical, geometric or positional isomers.

(*iv*) Ligase catalyses linking together of two compounds.

Kishore Vaigyanik Protsahan Yojana (KVPY)

STREAM – SA

Part-I

Mathematics

1. Two distinct polynomial $f(x)$ and $g(x)$ are defined as follows:

$f(x) = x^2 + ax + 2$; $g(x) = x^2 + 2x + a$

If the equation $f(x) = 0$ and $g(x) = 0$ have a common root, then the sum of the roots of the equation $f(x) + g(x) = 0$ is:

A. $-\frac{1}{2}$ B. 0
C. $\frac{1}{2}$ D. 1

2. If n is the smallest natural number such that $n + 2n + 3n + ... + 99n$ is a perfect square, then the number of digits in n^2 is

A. 1 B. 2
C. 3 D. more than 3

3. Let x, y, z be positive reals. Which of the following implies $x = y = z$?

I. $x^3 + y^3 + z^3 = 3xyz$
II. $x^3 + y^2z + yz^2 = 3xyz$
III. $x^3 + y^2z + z^2x = 3xyz$
IV. $(x + y + z)^3 = 27xyz$

A. I, IV only B. I, II, IV only
C. I, II and III only D. All of them

4. In the figure given below, a rectangle of perimeter 76 units is divided into 7 congruent rectangles.

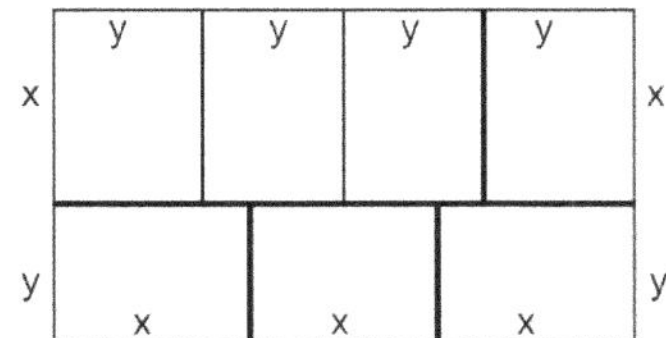

What is the perimeter of each of the smaller rectangles?

A. 38 B. 32
C. 28 D. 19

5. The largest non-negative integer k such that 24^k divides 13! is:

A. 2 B. 3
C. 4 D. 5

6. In a triangle ABC, points X and Y are on AB and AC, respectively, such that XY is parallel to BC. Which of the two following always hold? (Here [PQR] denotes the area of triangle PQR.)

I. [BCX] = [BCY].
II. [ACX] · [ABY] = [AXY] · [ABC]·

A. Neither I nor II B. I only
C. II only D. both I and II

7. Let P be an interior point of a triangle ABC. Let Q and R be the reflections of P in AB and AC, respectively. If Q, A, R are collinear then $\angle A$ equals:

A. 30° B. 60°
C. 90° D. 120°

8. Let ABCD be a square of side length l, and Γ a circle passing through B and C, and touching AD. The radius of Γ is:

A. $\frac{3}{8}$ B. $\frac{1}{2}$
C. $\frac{1}{\sqrt{2}}$ D. $\frac{5}{8}$

9. Let ABCD be a square of a side length l. Let P, Q, R, S be points in the interiors of the sides AD, BC, AB, CD, respectively, such that PQ and RS intersect at right angles. If $PQ = \frac{3\sqrt{3}}{4}$, then RS equals:

A. $\frac{2}{\sqrt{3}}$ B. $\frac{3\sqrt{3}}{4}$
C. $\frac{\sqrt{2}+1}{2}$ D. $4-2\sqrt{2}$

10. In the figure given below, if the areas of the two regions are equal, then which of the following is true?

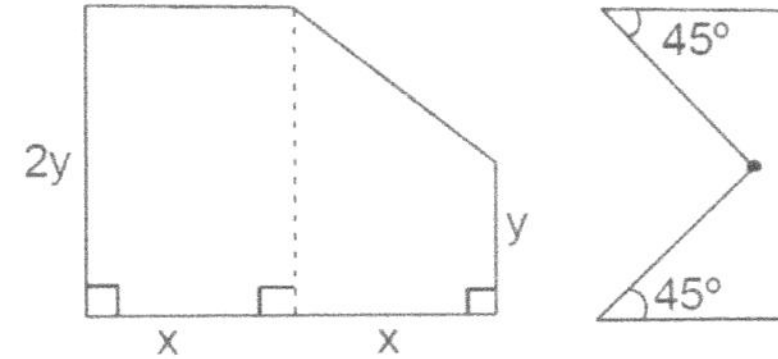

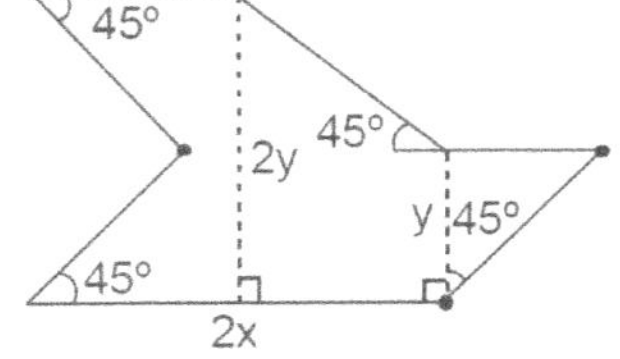

A. $x = y$ B. $x = 2y$
C. $2x = y$ D. $x = 3y$

11. A man standing on a railway platform noticed that a train took 21 seconds to cross the platform (this means the time elapsed from the moment the engine enters the platform till the last compartment leaves the platform) which is 88 meters long, and that it took 9 seconds to pass him. Assuming that the train was moving with uniform speed, what is the length of the train in metres?
A. 55 B. 60
C. 66 D. 72

12. The least positive integer n for which $\sqrt[3]{n+1} - \sqrt[3]{n} < \frac{1}{12}$ is:
A. 6 B. 7
C. 8 D. 9

13. Let $n > 1$ be an integer. Which of the following sets of numbers necessarily contains a multiple of 3?
A. $n^{19} - 1$, $n^{19} + 1$ B. n^{19}, $n^{38} - 1$
C. n^{38}, $n^{38} + 1$ D. n^{38}, $n^{19} - 1$

14. The number of distinct primes dividing 12! + 13! + 14! is:
A. 5 B. 6
C. 7 D. 8

15. How many ways are there to arrange the letters of the word **EDUCATION** so that all the following three conditions hold?
- the vowels occur in the same order **(EUAIO);**
- the consonants occur in the same order **(DCTN);**
- no two consonants are next to each other.
A. 15 B. 24
C. 72 D. 120

Physics

16. In an experiment, mass of an object is measured by applying a known force on it, and then measuring its acceleration. If, in the experiment, the measured values of applied force and the measured acceleration are F = 10.0 ± 0.2 N and a = 1.00 ± 0.01 m/s^2, respectively, the mass of the object is:
A. 10.0 kg B. 10.0 ± 0.1 kg
C. 10.0 ± 0.3 kg D. 10.0 ± 0.4 kg

17. A hollow tilted cylindrical vessel of negligible mass rests on a horizontal plane as known. The diameter of the base is a and the side of the cylinder makes an angle θ with the horizontal. Water is then slowly poured into the cylinder. The cylinder topples over when the water reaches a certain height h, given by:

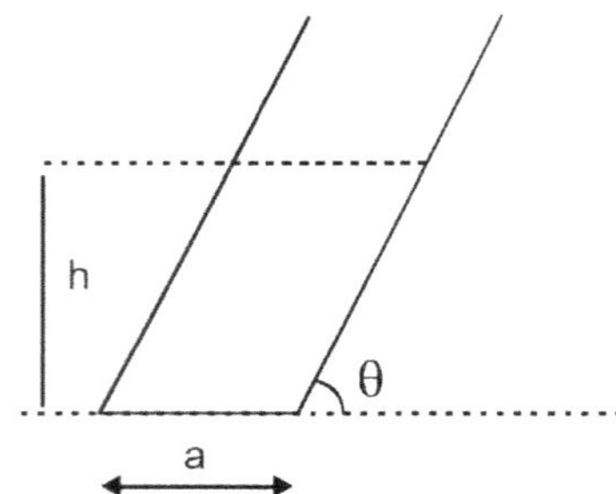

A. $h = 2a \tan \theta$ B. $h = a \tan^2 \theta$

C. $h = a \tan \theta$ D. $h = \frac{a}{2}\tan\theta$

18. An object at rest at the origin begins to move in the $+x$ direction with a uniform acceleration of 1 m/s^2 for 4s and then it continues moving with a uniform velocity of 4 m/s in the same direction. The $x - t$ graph for object's motion will be:

A. 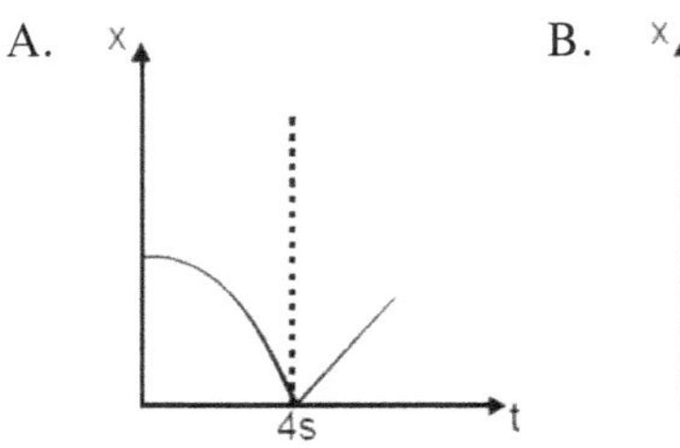

B. 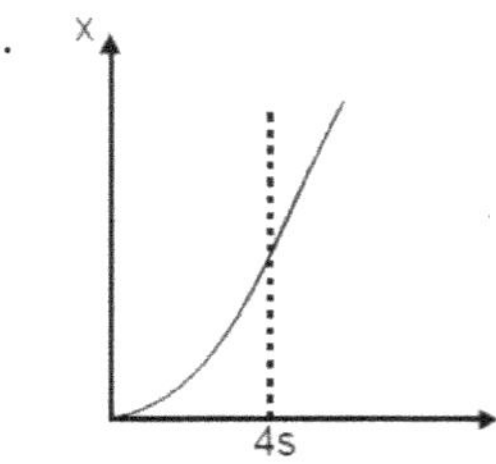

C. 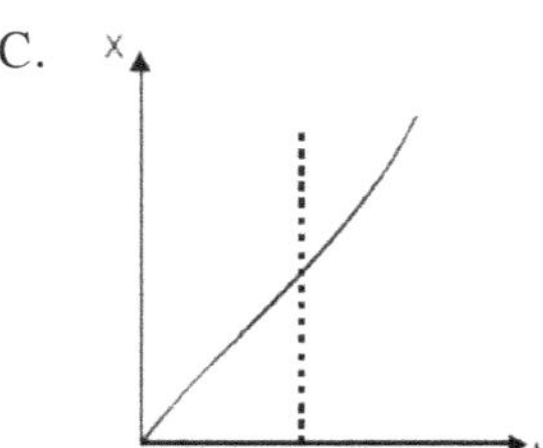

D. 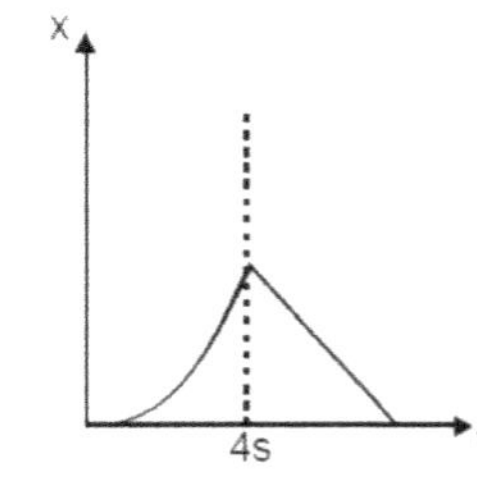

19. If the axis of rotation of the earth were extended into space, then it would pass close to:
A. the moon
B. the sun
C. the pole star
D. the centre of mass of all the planets in the solar system.

20. Methane is a greenhouse gas because:
A. it absorbs longer wavelengths of the electromagnetic spectrum while transmitting shorter wavelengths
B. it absorbs shorter wavelengths of the electromagnetic spectrum while transmitting longer wavelengths
C. it absorbs all wavelengths of the electromagnetic spectrum.
D. it transmits all wavelengths of the electromagnetic spectrum.

21. A parachutist with total weight 75 kg drops vertically onto a sandy ground with a speed of 2 ms^{-1} and comes to a halt over a distance of 0.25 m. The average force from the ground on her is close to:
A. 600 N B. 1200 N
C. 1350 N D. 1950 N

22. The beta particles of a radioactive metal originate from:
A. the free electrons in the metal
B. the orbiting electrons of the metal atoms
C. the photons released from the nucleus
D. the nucleus of the metal atoms

23. An optical device is constructed by fixing three identical convex lenses of focal lengths 10 cm each inside a hollow tube at equal spacing of 30 cm each. One end of the device is placed 10 cm away from a point source. How much does the image shift when the device is moved away from the source by another 10 cm?
A. 0 B. 5 cm
C. 15 cm D. 45 cm

24. An isosceles glass prism with angles 40° is clamped over a tray of water in a position such that the base is just dipped in water. A ray of light incident normally on the inclined face suffers total internal reflection at the base. If the refractive index of water is 1.33, then the condition imposed on the refractive index μ of the glass is:
A. $\mu < 2.07$ B. $\mu > 2.07$
C. $\mu < 1.74$ D. $\mu > 1.74$

25. A point source of light is moving at a rate of 2 $cm\text{-}s^{-1}$ towards a thin convex lens of focal length 10 cm along its optical axis. When the source is 15 cm away from the lens the image is moving at:
A. 4 $cm\text{-}s^{-1}$ towards the lens
B. 8 $cm\text{-}s^{-1}$ towards the lens
C. 4 $cm\text{-}s^{-1}$ away from the lens
D. 8 $cm\text{-}s^{-1}$ away from the lens

26. A light bulb of resistance R = 16 Ω is attached in series with an infinite resistor network with identical resistances *r* as shown below. A 10 V battery derives current in the circuit. What should be the value of *r* such that the bulb dissipated about 1 W of power?

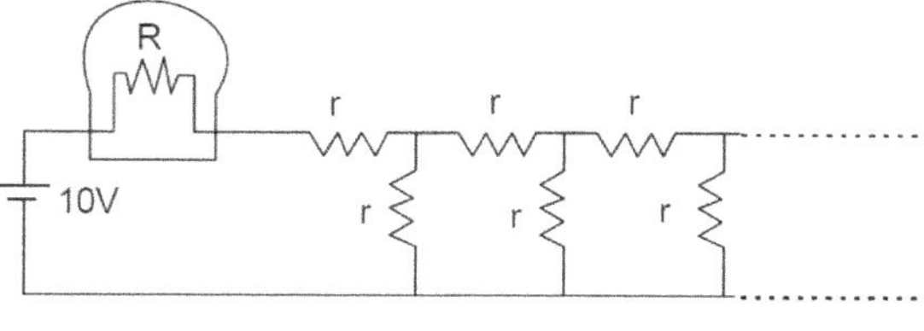

A. 14.8 Ω B. 29.6 Ω
C. 7.4 Ω D. 3.7 Ω

27. A ball is launched from the top of Mt. Everest which is at elevation of 9000 m. The ball moves in circular orbit around earth. Acceleration due to gravity near the earth's surface is *g*. The magnitude of the ball's acceleration while in orbit is:
A. close to *g*/2 B. zero
C. much greater than *g* D. nearly equal to *g*

28. A planet is orbiting the sun in an elliptical orbit. Let U denote the potential energy and K denote the kinetic energy of the planet at an arbitrary point on the orbit. Choose the correct statement.
A. $K < |U|$ always
B. $K > |U|$ always
C. $K = |U|$ always
D. $K = |U|$ for two positions of the planet in the orbit.

29. One mole of ideal gas undergoes a linear process as shown in figure below. Its temperature expressed as a function of volume V is:

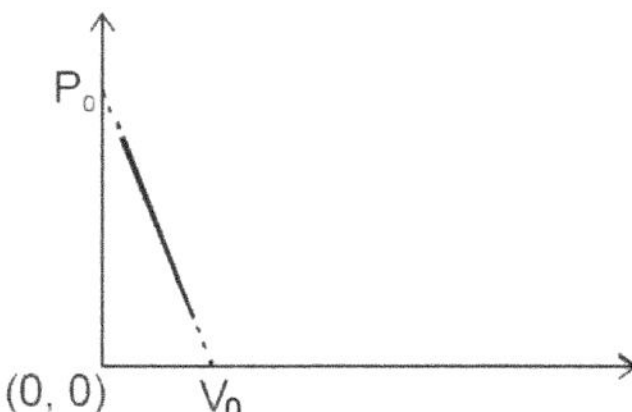

A. $\frac{P_0 V_0}{R}$ B. $\frac{P_0 V}{R}$

C. $\frac{P_0 V}{R}\left(1-\frac{V}{V_0}\right)$ D. $\frac{P_0 V}{R}\left(1-\left(\frac{V}{V_0}\right)^2\right)$

30. The international space station is maintained in a nearly circular orbit with a mean altitude of 330 km and a maximum of 410 km. An astronaut is floating in the space station's cabin. The acceleration of astronaut as measured from the earth is:
A. zero
B. nearly zero and directed towards the earth
C. nearly *g* and directed along the line of travel of the station
D. nearly *g* and directed towards the earth.

Chemistry

31. The percentage of nitrogen by mass in ammonium sulphate is closest to (atomic masses H = 1, N = 14, O = 16, S = 32)

A. 21% B. 24%
C. 36% D. 16%

32. Mendeleev's periodic law states that the properties of elements are a periodic function of their:

A. reactivity of elements B. atomic size
C. atomic mass D. electronic configuration

33. Maximum number of electrons that can be accommodated in the subshell with azimuthal quantum number l = 4, is:

A. 10 B. 8
C. 16 D. 18

34. The correct order of acidity of the following compounds is

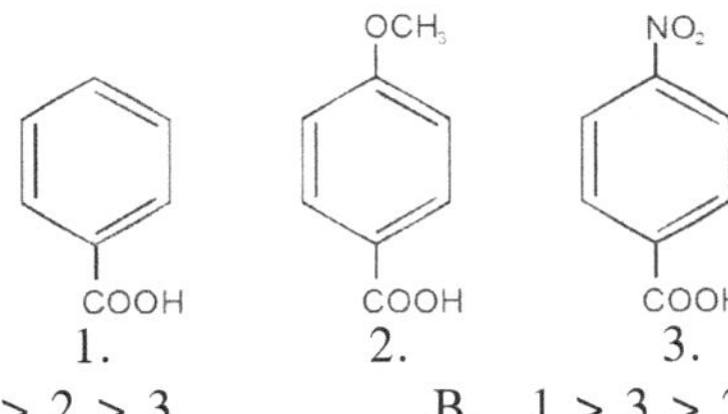

A. 1 > 2 > 3 B. 1 > 3 > 2
C. 3 > 1 > 2 D. 3 > 2 > 1

35. Reaction of 2-butane with acidic $KMnO_4$ gives:

A. CH_3CHO B. $HCOOH$
C. CH_3CH_2OH D. CH_3COOH

36. The gas released when baking soda is mixed with vinegar, is:

A. CO B. CO_2
C. CH_4 D. O_2

37. The element which readily forms an ionic bond has the electronic configuration?

A. $1s^2\ 2s^2\ 2p^3$ B. $1s^2\ 2s^2\ 2p^1$
C. $1s^2\ 2s^2\ 2p^2$ D. $1s^2\ 2s^2\ 2p^6\ 3s^1$

38. The major products of the following reaction

$ZnS(s) + O_2(g) \xrightarrow{\text{heat}}$ are:

A. ZnO and SO_2 B. $ZnSO_4$ and SO_3
C. $ZnSO_4$ and SO_2 D. Zn and SO_2

39. If Avogadro's number is A_0, the number of sulphur atoms present in 200 mL of 1 N H_2SO_4 is:

A. $A_0/5$ B. $A_0/2$
C. $A_0/10$ D. A_0

40. The functional group present in a molecule having the formula $C_{12}O_9$ is:

A. carboxylic acid B. anhydride
C. aldehyde D. alcohol

41. A sweet smelling compounds formed by reacting acetic acid with ethanol in the presence of hydrochloric acid is:

A. $CH_3COOC_2H_5$ B. C_2H_5COOH
C. $C_2H_5COOH_3$ D. CH_3OH

42. Among Mg, Cu, Fe, Zn, the metal that does not produce hydrogen gas in reaction with hydrochloric acid is:

A. Cu B. Zn
C. Mg D. Fe

43. The maximum number of isomeric ethers with the molecular formula $C_4H_{10}O$ is:

A. 2 B. 3
C. 4 D. 5

44. The number of electrons required to reduce chromium completely in $Cr_2O_7^{2-}$ to Cr^{3+} in acidic medium, is:

A. 5 B. 3
C. 6 D. 2

45. At constant pressure, the volume of a fixed mass of a gas varies as a function of temperature as shown in the graph.

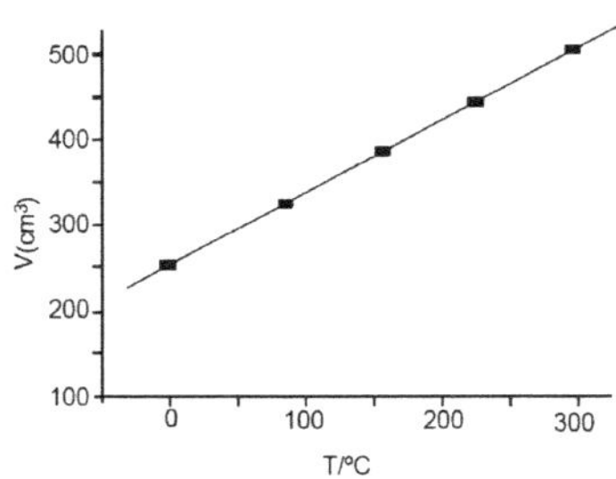

The volume of the gas at 300°C is larger than that at 0°C by a factor of:

A. 3 B. 4
C. 1 D. 2

Biology

46. Excess salt inhibits growth in pickles by:

A. endosmosis B. exosmosis
C. oxidation D. denaturation

47. Restriction endonucleases are enzymes that are used by biotechnologists to:

A. cut DNA at specific base sequences
B. join fragments of DNA
C. digest DNA from the 3′ end
D. digest DNA from the 5′ end

48. Enzyme X extracted from the digestive system hydrolyses peptide bonds. Which of the following are probable candidate to be enzyme X?

A. Amylase B. Lipase
C. Trypsin D. Maltase

49. A person with blood group AB has:
A. antigen A and B on RBCs and both anti-A and anti-B antibodies in plasma
B. antigen A and B on RBCs but neither anti-A and anti-B antibodies in plasma
C. no antigen on RBCs but both anti-A and anti-B antibodies present in plasma
D. antigen A on RBCs and antibodies in plasma

50. Glycolysis is the breakdown of glucose to pyruvic acid. How many molecules of pyruvic acid are formed from one molecule of glucose?
A. 1 B. 2
C. 3 D. 4

51. The process of transfer of electrons from glucose to molecular oxygen in bacteria and mitochondria is known as:
A. TCA cycle
B. Oxidative phosphorylation
C. Fermentation
D. Glycolysis

52. Which one of the following cell types is a part of innate immunity?
A. Skin epithelial cells B. B cells
C. T lymphocytes D. Liver cells

53. Deficiency of which of the following vitamins can cause impaired blood clotting?
A. Vitamin B B. Vitamin C
C. Vitamin D D. Vitamin K

54. Which one of the following is detrimental to soil fertility?
A. *Saprophytic bacteria* B. *Nitrosomes*
C. *Nitrobacter* D. *Pseudomonas*

55. In which one of the following phyla is the body segmented?
A. Porifera
B. Platyhelminthes
C. Annelida
D. Echinodermata

56. Widal test is prescribed to diagnose:
A. Typhoid B. Pneumonia
C. Malaria D. Filaria

57. Which, among grass, goat, tiger and vulture, in a food chain, will have the maximum concentration of harmful chemicals in its body due to contamination of pesticides in the soil?
A. Grass since it grows in the contaminated soil
B. Goat since it eats the grass
C. Tiger since it feed on the goat which feeds on the grass
D. Vulture since it eats the tiger, which in turns eats the goat, which eats the grass.

58. Considering the average molecular mass of a base to be 500 Da, what is the molecular mass of a double stranded DNA of 10 base pairs?
A. 500 Da B. 5 kDa
C. 10 kDa D. 1 kDa

59. Which of the following pairs are both polysaccharides?
A. Cellulose and glycogen
B. Starch and glucose
C. Cellulose and fructose
D. Ribose and sucrose

60. Which one of the following is a modified leaf?
A. Sweet potato B. Ginger
C. Onion D. Carrot

Part-II

Mathematics

61. A triangular corner is cut from a rectangular piece of paper and the resulting pentagon has sides 5, 6, 8, 9, 12 in some order. The ratio of the area of the rectangle is
A. $\frac{11}{18}$ B. $\frac{13}{18}$
C. $\frac{15}{18}$ D. $\frac{17}{18}$

62. For a real number x, let $[x]$ denote the largest integer less than or equal to x, and let $\{x\} = x - [x]$. The number of solutions x to be equation $[x]\ \{x\} = 5$ with $0 \le x \le 2015$ is:
A. 0 B. 3
C. 2008 D. 2009

63. Let ABCD be a trapezium with AD parallel to BC. Assume there is a point M is interior of the segment BC such that AB = AM and DC = DM. Then the ratio of the area of the trapezium to the area of triangle AMD is:
A. 2
B. 3
C. 4
D. not determinable from the data

64. Given are three cylindrical buckets X, Y, Z whose circular bases are of radii 1, 2, 3 units, respectively. Initially water is filled in these buckets upto the same height. Some water is then transferred from Z to X so that they both have the same volume of water. Some water is then transferred between X and Y so that they both have the same volume of water. If h_y, h_z denote the heights of water at this stage in the buckets Y, Z, respectively, then the ratio $\frac{h_y}{h_z}$ equals:

A. $\frac{4}{9}$ B. 1
C. $\frac{9}{4}$ D. $\frac{81}{40}$

65. The average incomes of the people in two villages are P and Q, respectively. Assume that $P \neq Q$. A person moves from the first village to the second village. The new average incomes are P′ and Q′, respectively. Which of the following is not possible?
A. $P' > P$ and $Q' > Q$
B. $P' > P$ and $Q' < Q$
C. $P' = P$ and $Q' = Q$
D. $P' < P$ and $Q' < Q$

Physics

66. A girl sees through a circular glass slab (refractive index 1.50 of thickness 20 mm and diameter 60 cm to the bottom of a swimming pool. Refractive index of water is 1.33. The bottom surface of the slab is in contact with the water surface.

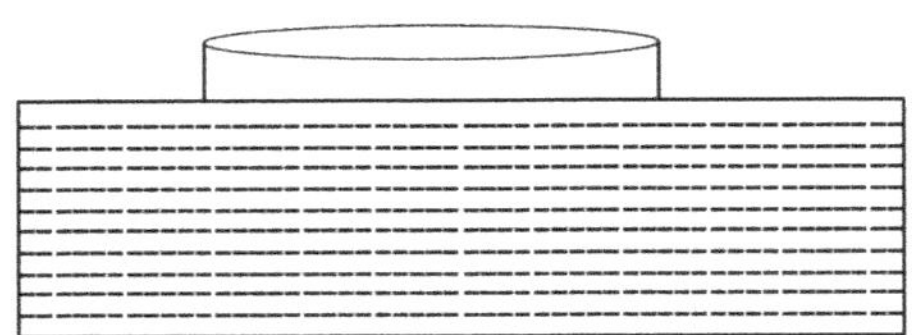

The depth of swimming pool is 6 m. The area of bottom of swimming pool that can be seen through the slab is approximately.
A. 100 m^2 B. 160 m^2
C. 190 m^2 D. 220 m^2

67. 1 kg of ice at –20°C is mixed with 2 kg of water at 90°C. Assuming that there is no loss of energy to the environment, what will be the final temperature of the mixture? (Assume latent heat of ice = 334.4 kJ/kg, specific heat of water and ice are 4.18 kJ/(kg.K) and 2.09 kJ/(kg.K), respectively.)
A. 30°C B. 0°C
C. 80°C D. 45°C

68. A rigid body in the shape of a "V" has two equal arms made of uniform rods. What must the angle between the two rods be so that when the body is suspended from one end, the other arm is horizontal?

A. $\cos^{-1}\left(\frac{1}{3}\right)$ B. $\cos^{-1}\left(\frac{1}{2}\right)$
C. $\cos^{-1}\left(\frac{1}{4}\right)$ D. $\cos^{-1}\left(\frac{1}{6}\right)$

69. A point object is placed 20 cm left of a convex lens of focal length $f = 5$ cm (see the figure). The lens is made to oscillate with small amplitude A along the horizontal axis. The image of the object will also oscillate along the axis with.

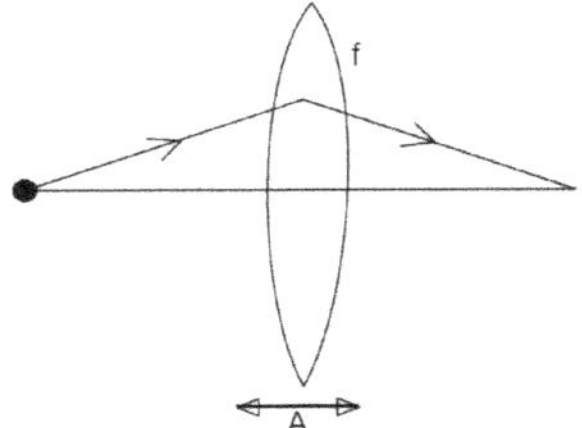

A. amplitude A/9, out of phase with the oscillations of the lens
B. amplitude A/3, out of phase with the oscillations of the lens
C. amplitude A/3, in phase with the oscillations of the lens
D. amplitude A/9, in phase with the oscillations of the lens

70. Stoke's law states that the viscous drag force F experience by a sphere of radius a, moving with a speed v through a fluid with coefficient of viscosity η, is given by $F = 6\pi\eta a v$.

If this fluid is flowing through a cylindrical pipe of radius r, length l and a pressure difference of P across its two ends, then the volume of water V which flows through the pipe in time t can be written as

$$\frac{v}{t} = k\left(\frac{p}{l}\right)^a \eta^b r^c$$

Where k is a dimensionless constant. Correct values of a, b and c are:
A. $a = 1, b = -1, c = 4$ B. $a = -1, b = 1, c = 4$
C. $a = 2, b = -1, c = 3$ D. $a = 1, b = -2, c = -4$

Chemistry

71. When 262 g of xenon (atomic mass = 131) reacted completely with 152 g of fluorine (atomic mass = 19), a mixture of XeF_2 and XeF_6 was produced. The molar ratio $XeF_2 : XeF_6$ is:
A. 1 : 2 B. 1 : 4
C. 1 : 1 D. 1 : 3

72. Reaction of ethanol with conc. sulphuric acid at 170°C produces a gas which is then treated with bromine in carbon tetrachloride. The major product obtained in this reaction is:
A. 1, 2-dibromoethane B. ethylene glycol
C. bromoethane D. ethyl sulphate

73. When 22.4 L of C_4H_8 at STP is burnt completely, 89.6 L of CO_2 gas at STP and 72 g of water are produced. The volume of the oxygen gas at STP consumed in the reaction is closest to:

A. 89.6 L B. 112 L
C. 134.4 L D. 22.4 L

74. The amount of Ag (atomic mass = 108) deposited at the cathode when a current of 0.5 amp is passed through a solution of $AgNO_3$ for 1 hour is closest to:

A. 2 g B. 5 g
C. 108 g D. 11 g

75. The major product of the reaction is:

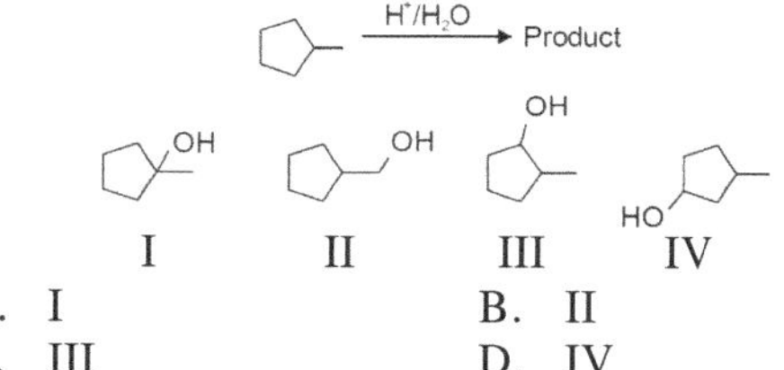

A. I B. II
C. III D. IV

Biology

76. Genomic DNA is digested with Alu I, a restriction enzyme which is a four base-pair cutter. What is the frequency with which it will cut the DNA assuming a random distribution of bases in the genome:

A. 1/4 B. 1/24
C. 1/256 D. 1/1296

77. If rice is cooked in a pressure cooker on the Siachen glacier, at sea beach, and on Deccan plain, which of the following is correct about the time taken for cooking rice:

A. Gets cooked faster on the Siachen glacier
B. Gets cooked faster at sea beach
C. Gets cooked faster on Deccan plain
D. Gets cooked at the same time at all the three places

78. A few rabbits are introduced in an un-inhabited island with plenty of food. If these rabbits breed in the absence of any disease, natural calamity and predation, which one of the following graphs best represents their population growth:

A.
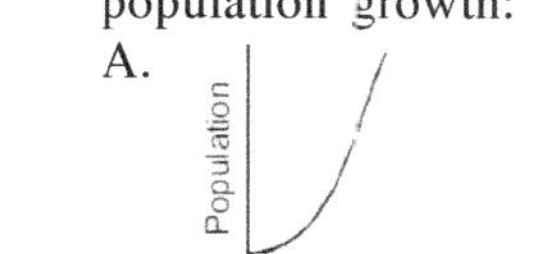

B.
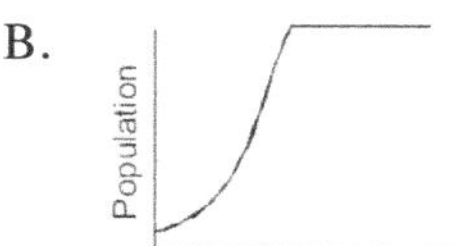

C.
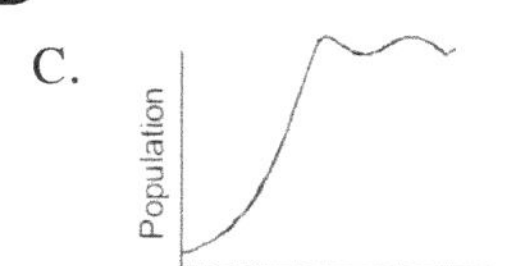

D.
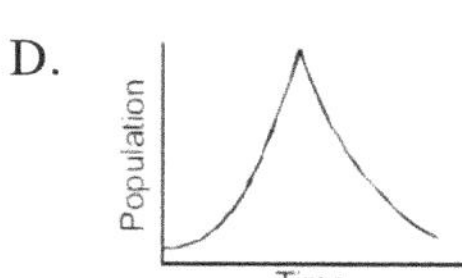

79. What is the advantage of storing glucose as glycogen in animals instead of as monomeric glucose:

A. Energy obtained from glycogen is more than that from the corresponding glucose monomers
B. Glucose present as monomers within the cell exerts more osmotic pressure than a single glycogen molecule, resulting in loss of water from the cells
C. Glucose present as monomers within the cell exerts more osmotic pressure than a single glycogen molecule, resulting in excess water within the cells
D. Glycogen gives more rigidity to the cells.

80. A line is drawn from the exterior of an animal cell to the centre of the nucleus, crossing through one mitochondrion. What is the minimum number of membrane bilayers that the line will cross:

A. 4 B. 3
C. 8 D. 6

ANSWERS

1	**2**	**3**	**4**	**5**	**6**	**7**	**8**	**9**	**10**
C	C	B	C	B	D	C	D	B	B
11	**12**	**13**	**14**	**15**	**16**	**17**	**18**	**19**	**20**
C	C	B	A	A	C	C	B	C	A
21	**22**	**23**	**24**	**25**	**26**	**27**	**28**	**29**	**30**
C	D	A	B	D	A	D	A	C	D
31	**32**	**33**	**34**	**35**	**36**	**37**	**38**	**39**	**40**
A	C	D	C	D	B	D	A	C	B
41	**42**	**43**	**44**	**45**	**46**	**47**	**48**	**49**	**50**
A	A	B	C	D	B	A	C	B	B
51	**52**	**53**	**54**	**55**	**56**	**57**	**58**	**59**	**60**
B	A	D	D	C	A	D	C	A	C
61	**62**	**63**	**64**	**65**	**66**	**67**	**68**	**69**	**70**
D	D	B	D	C	B	A	A	A	*
71	**72**	**73**	**74**	**75**	**76**	**77**	**78**	**79**	**80**
C	A	C	A	A	C	D	C	C	D

EXPLANATORY ANSWERS

1. $$f(x) = x^2 + ax + 2$$
$$g(x) = x^2 + 2x + a$$

Here a common Root then,

$$\begin{vmatrix} 1 & a \\ 1 & 2 \end{vmatrix}\begin{vmatrix} a & 2 \\ 2 & a \end{vmatrix} = \begin{vmatrix} 2 & 1 \\ a & 1 \end{vmatrix}^2$$

$$a = 2, -3$$

$$f(x) + g(x) = 2x^2 + (a+2)x + a + 2$$

$$\text{Sum of roots} = \frac{-(a+2)}{2}$$

if $a = -3$, then sum $= \frac{1}{2}$.

2. $n + 2n + 3n + ... + 99n$

$n(1 + 2 + 3 + ... + 99)$

$$n\frac{(99)(100)}{2} = 9 \times 25 \times 22 \times n$$

is a perfect square when $n = 22 \because n^2 = 484$

$\therefore$ Number of digits in $n^2 = 3$.

3. For option (C) if $x = z = 1$ and $y = 2$, then option (C) is right. So, by option (C) we can't say $x = y = z$. Remaining options implies $x = y = z$.

4. Let sides of Rectangle are x & y

Then, $5x + 6y = 76$

$4y = 3x$

After solving we get, $y = 6$, $x = 8$

Perimeter $= 2(x + y) = 28$.

5. $24^k \rightarrow (2^3 \times 3)^k$

Exponent of 2 in 13!

$$\left[\frac{13}{2}\right]+\left[\frac{13}{2^2}\right]+\left[\frac{13}{2^3}\right] = 10$$

Exponent of 3 in 13!

$$\left[\frac{13}{3}\right]+\left[\frac{13}{3^2}\right] = 5$$

So, $(2^3 \times 3)^3$. So, K = 3.

6.

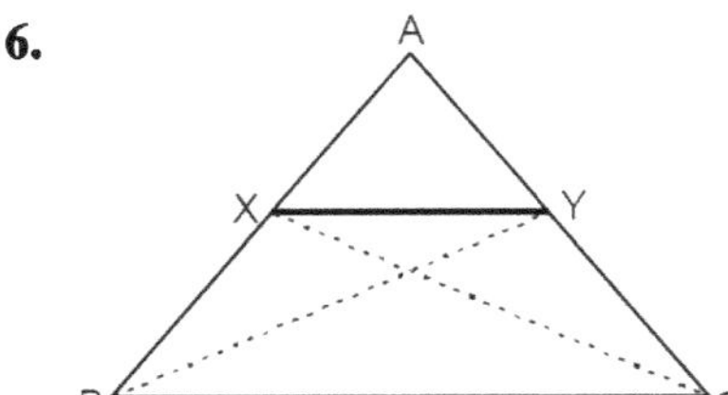

$\Delta BCX = \Delta BCY$ (Obvious)

Same base and same height

Now, Let $A(\vec{O})$, $\overrightarrow{AB} = \vec{b}$, $\overrightarrow{AC} = \vec{c}$

So, $\overrightarrow{AX} = \lambda\vec{b}$, $\overrightarrow{AY} = \lambda\vec{c}$

$$\Delta ACX = \frac{1}{2}\lambda\,|\vec{b}\times\vec{c}|$$

$$\Delta ABY = \frac{1}{2}\lambda\,|\vec{b}\times\vec{c}|$$

$$\Delta AXY = \frac{1}{2}\lambda^2\,|\vec{b}\times\vec{c}|$$

$$\Delta ABC = \frac{1}{2}|\vec{b}\times\vec{c}|.$$

7.

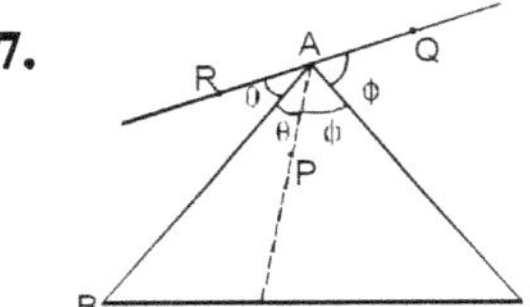

So, from Diagram

$$\theta + \theta + \phi + \phi = 180°$$

$$\angle A = \theta + \phi = 90°.$$

8.

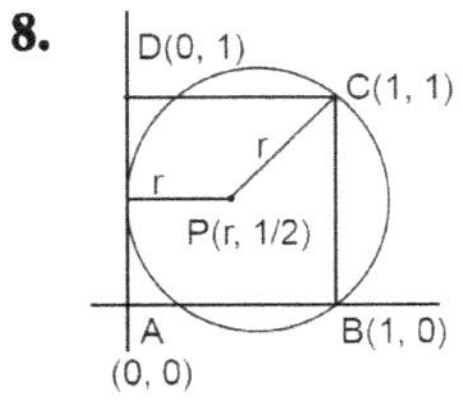

$$PC = r$$

$$PC^2 = r^2$$

$$(r-1)^2 + \left(\frac{1}{2}-1\right)^2 = r^2$$

$$1 - 2r + \frac{1}{4} = 0$$

$$r = \frac{5}{8}.$$

9.

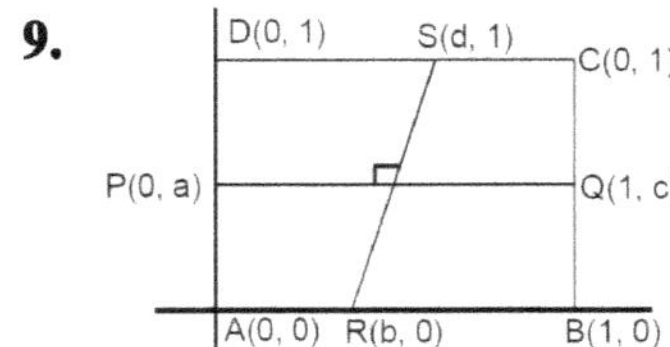

$PQ \perp RS \Rightarrow$

$\boxed{c - a = b - d}$ ...(i)

$$PQ = \frac{3\sqrt{3}}{4}$$

$$PQ^2 = \frac{27}{16}$$

$$1 + (a-c)^2 = \frac{27}{16} \quad ...(ii)$$

$$RS = \sqrt{(b-d)^2 + 1} \quad ...(iii)$$

By equations (*i*), (*ii*) and (*iii*)

$$RS = \frac{3\sqrt{3}}{4}.$$

10. 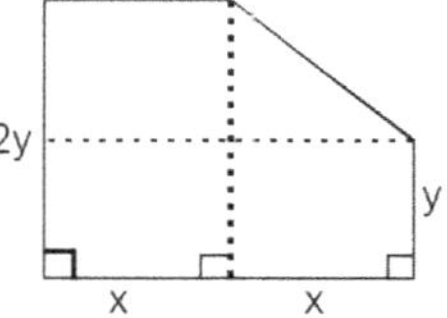

$$A_1 = x \times 2y + \frac{1}{2}(y+2y).x = \frac{7}{2}xy$$

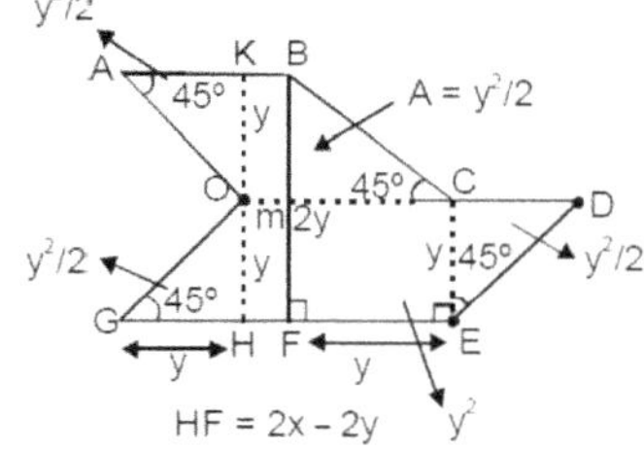

$$A_2 = 4\left(\frac{y^2}{2}\right) + (2x-2y).2y + y^2$$

$A_1 = A_2$

$x = 2y.$

11. 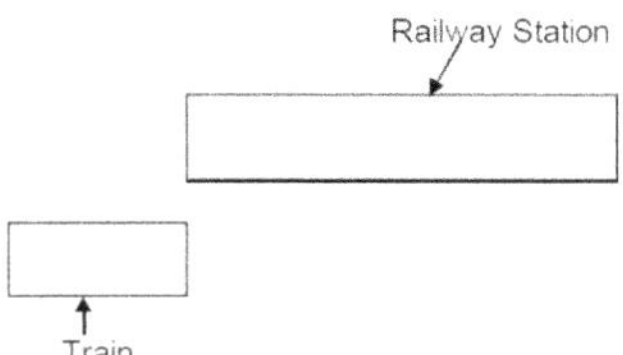

$$9V + 88 = 21V$$

$$12V = 88$$

$$V = \frac{88}{12}$$

$$\text{Required} = 9V = 9 \times \frac{88}{12} = 66.$$

12. $(n+1)^{1/3} - (n)^{1/3} < \frac{1}{12}$

$$(n+1)^{1/3} < (n)^{1/3} + \frac{1}{12}$$

Cube Both sides are get

$$(n)^{1/3}\left(n^{1/3} - \frac{1}{12}\right) > \frac{1727}{432}$$

So, $n = 8$ only possible least positive integer.

13. If $n = 3m$ then n^{19} is multiple of 3

If $n = 3m + 1$ or $3m + 2$

then $n^{38} - 1$ is multiple of 3 by binomial expansion.

14. 12! + 13! + 14!

12! (1 + 13 + 14 × 13)

12! × 196

Which is only divided by possible distinct primes 2, 3, 5, 7, 11.

15. First arrange EUAIO → 1

For consonant $\left.\begin{matrix} |\bar{E}|\bar{U}|\bar{A}|\bar{I}|\bar{O}| \\ {}^6C_4 \times (1) \end{matrix}\right\} \Rightarrow {}^6C_4 = 15.$

16. F = Ma

$$M = \frac{F}{a}$$

$$\frac{\Delta M \times 100}{M} = \frac{\Delta F}{F} \times 100 + \frac{\Delta a}{a} \times 100$$

$$= \frac{0.2}{10} + \frac{0.01}{1}$$

$$\Delta M = 0.03 \times 10$$

$\therefore$ $M = 10 \pm 0.3$ kg.

17. 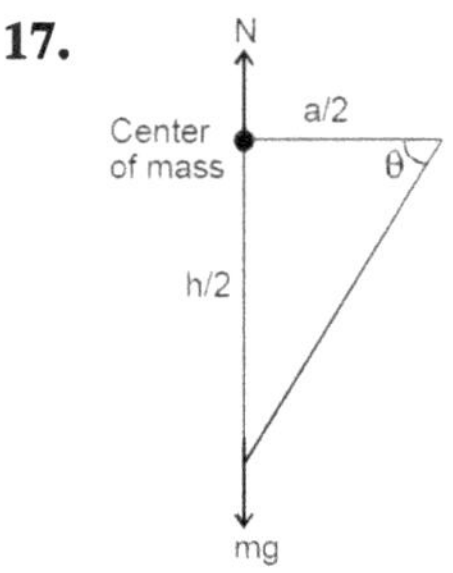

$$\tan\theta = \frac{\frac{h}{2}}{a/2}$$

$$h = a \tan\theta.$$

18. $v = 0 + 1 \times t$

$$\frac{dx}{dt} = t$$

$$dx = t\,dt$$

$x \propto t^2$ ... Parabolic (*i*)

$$\frac{dx}{dt} = 4$$

$$dx = 4dt$$

$x \propto t$ .... Linear (*ii*)

21. $0^2 = 2^2 - 2a\frac{1}{4}$

$a = 8$ m/s²

$a_T = 10 + 8 = 18$ m/s²

$f = ma = 75 \times 18 = 1350$ N.

23. 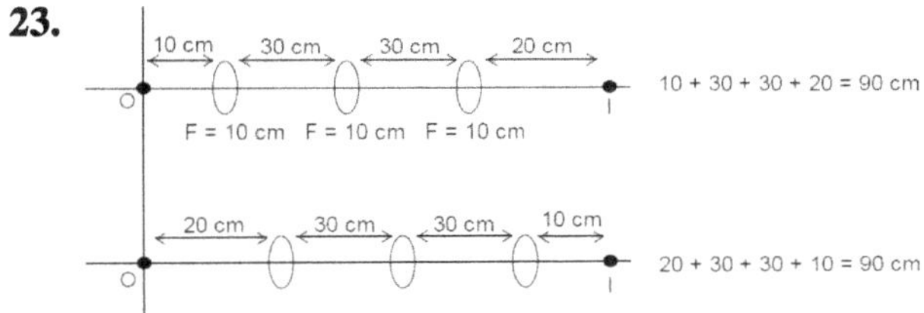

24.

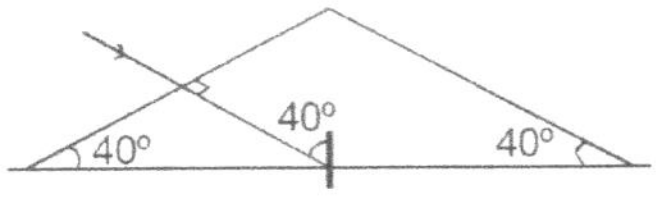

$1.33 \times \sin 90° = \mu . \sin 40°$

$= \frac{1.33 \times 1}{\sin 40°} = \mu$

$= \frac{1.33}{3/5} \approx \mu$

$= \frac{1.33 \times 5}{3} \approx \mu$

$= \mu \approx 2.07$

$= \mu > 2.07$ (For TIR).

25. $\frac{dv}{dt} = \frac{-v^2}{u^2}\frac{du}{dt}$

and $\frac{1}{v} = \frac{1}{F} + \frac{1}{u}$

$\frac{1}{v} = \frac{1}{10} + \frac{1}{-15}$

$\frac{1}{v} = \frac{3-2}{30}$

$v = 30$ cm

$\frac{dv}{dt} = \left(\frac{30}{15}\right)^2 .2$

= 8 cm/s away from lens.

26. $P_{bulb} = \frac{V^2}{R} = i^2R$

$1 = \frac{V^2}{16}$

$V_B = 4$ V

$1 = i^2 \times 16$

$I_B = \frac{1}{4}$ Amp.

$6 = \frac{1}{4} \times r_{eq.}$ (equivalent of groups of r)

Where, $r_{eq} = r + \frac{r_{eq}.r}{r_{eq}+r}$.

27. $\frac{mv^2}{r} = mg'$ (where g' is nearly equal to g).

28. Total energy must be less than zero and as potential energy is negative so answer is A.

29. $P = \frac{-P_0}{V_0}V + P_0$ ...(*i*)

and $PV = nRT$ ...(*ii*)

$\therefore$ $T = \frac{P_0V}{R}\left[1 - \frac{V}{V_0}\right]$.

31. Ammonium sulphate $(NH_4)_2 SO_4$ =

% of nitrogen = $\frac{28 \times 100}{36+96} = \frac{28 \times 100}{132} \cong 21.21\%$.

33. Total number of electrons = $2(2l + 1) = 18$.

34.

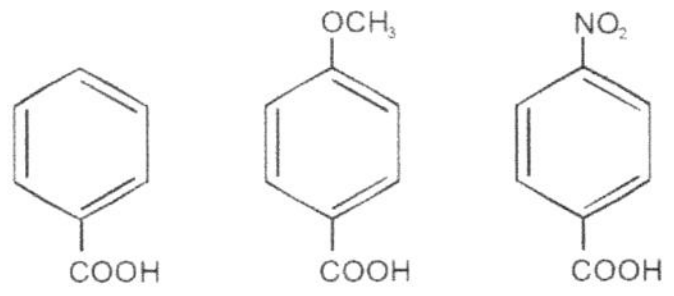

(Structures: 1 — benzoic acid (COOH); 2 — p-methoxybenzoic acid (OCH_3, COOH); 3 — p-nitrobenzoic acid (NO_2, COOH))

B. OCH_3 exerts + M effect destabilizes the conjugate base of the acid.

C. NO_2 exerts – M effect and stabilizes the conjugate base of the acid

35. $CH_3 - CH = CH - CH_3 \xrightarrow{KMnO_4/H^+} 2CH_3COOH$

37. Metals form ionic bond as they have low ionization energies.

$1s^2\ 2s^2\ 2p^6\ 3s^1$: Sodium metal.

38. $2ZnS_{(s)} + 3O_{2(g)} \xrightarrow{heat} 2ZnO_{(s)} + 2SO_{2(g)}$.

39. Avogadro's number = A_0

Normality = $n_f \times$ Molarity

$1 = 2 \times M$

$M = \frac{1}{2}$ mol L^{-1}

Moles of H_2SO_4 = $\frac{1}{2} \times 0.2$ = 0.1 moles

Normality = 1; Volume = 200 ml (0.2 litre)

Moles of hydrogen = 0.2 moles

Moles of sulphur = 0.1 moles

Atoms = 0.1 A_0.

40.

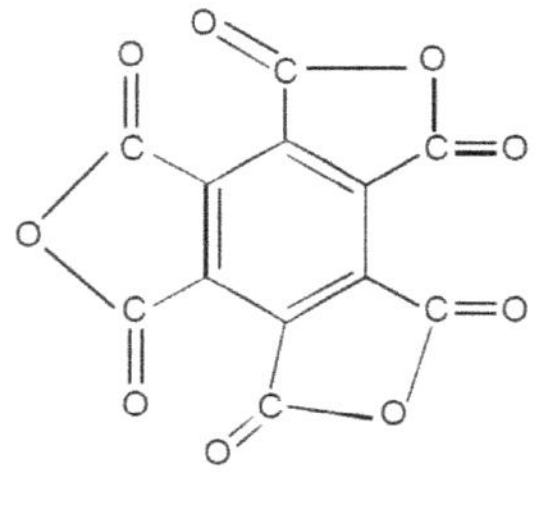

(Structure: benzene ring fused with three anhydride rings, C=O and O)

41. $CH_3 - \underset{\underset{O}{\|}}{C} - OH + HOC_2H_5 \xrightarrow{H^+} CH_3 - \underset{\underset{O}{\|}}{O} - OC_2H_5$

Ethyl acetate

42. Metals having more standard reduction potential than $H^+/H_{2(g)}$ can't produce $H_{2(g)}$ in acidic medium.

43. $C_4H_{10}O \Rightarrow$ $CH_3 - CH_2 - CH_2 - O - CH_3$

$CH_3 - CH(CH_3) - O - CH_3$

$CH_3 - CH_2 - O - CH_2 - CH_3$

44. $Cr_2O_7^{2-} + 14H^+ + 6e^- \rightarrow 2Cr^{3+} + 7H_2O$.

45. From graph,

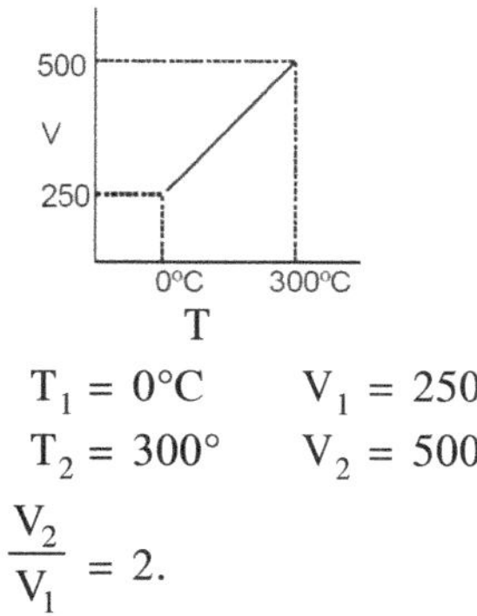

$T_1 = 0°C \quad V_1 = 250$

$T_2 = 300° \quad V_2 = 500$

$\frac{V_2}{V_1} = 2.$

46. Due to hypertonic solution outside the bacterial cell, bacteria will die by plasmolysis.

47. Restriction endonucleases cut ds DNA from specific base sequence (Palindromic sequence).

48. Trypsin is proteolytic enzyme.

49. Person with blood group AB having both A and B antigens in membrane of his RBC but lacks antibodies (*a*, *b*) in his plasma.

50. In glycolysis one mol. Glucose ($C_6H_{12}O_6$) forms two mol. of pyruvic acid ($CH_3COCOOH$).

51. ETS or electron transport system is also known as oxidative phosphorylation.

52. Skin, mucus membranes and phagocytes are part of innate immunity.

53. Vit. K is useful in synthesis of prothrombin and fibrinogen in liver which are necessary for blood clotting.

54. Pseudomonas is denitrifying bacterium.

55. Annelids show metameric segmentation.

56. Typhoid is caused by *Salmonella typhi* which is diagnosed by widal test.

57. It is due to biomagnifications.

58. 1 Base = 500 Da, ds DNA having 10 BP or 20 bases, thus 20 × 500 = 10 kDa.

59. Cellulose is polymer of β, D-glucose and glycogen of α, D-glucose. Glucose, fructose and ribose are monosaccharides.

60. Onion is bulb forms by fleshy scaly leaves sweet potato and carrot (root), Ginger – rhizome (stem).

61.

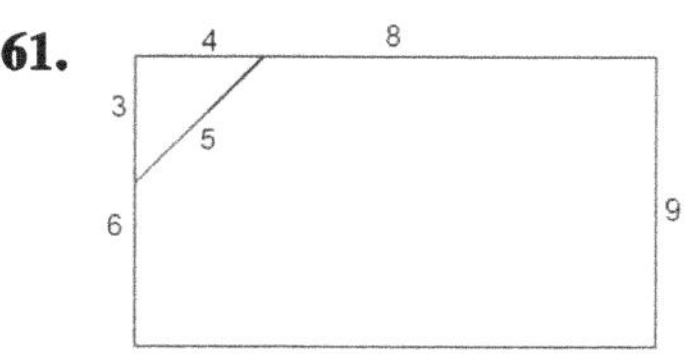

Angle of Rectangle = 12 × 9

$$\text{Area of Pentagon} = 12\times9-\frac{1}{2}\times3\times4 = 12 \times 9 - 6$$

$$\text{Required Ratio} = \frac{12\times9-6}{12\times9} = \frac{17}{18}.$$

62.

$\{x\} = x - [x]$

$[x]\{x\} = 5 \qquad f \neq 0$

$I\,f = 5$

$0 < f < 1$

Possible solutions

$$\left(6+\frac{5}{6}\right),\left(7+\frac{5}{7}\right),.....,\left(2014+\frac{5}{2014}\right) = 2009.$$

63.

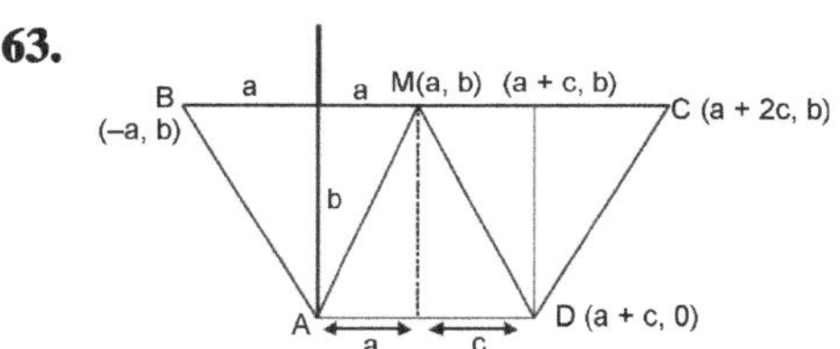

$$\text{Required} = \frac{\frac{1}{2}[(a+c)+2(a+c)]b}{\frac{1}{2}(a+c)b} = 3.$$

64.

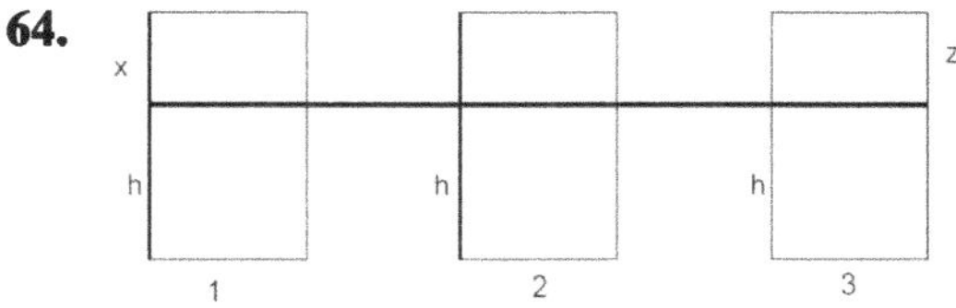

V = πh	$\pi 4h$	$\pi 9h$	...stage (*i*)
$5\pi h$	$4\pi h$	$5\pi h$	...stage (*ii*)
$4.5\pi h$	$4.5\pi h$	$5\pi h$	...stage (*iii*)

$$4\pi.h_y = \frac{9\pi h}{2} \qquad \pi 9h_z = 5\pi h$$

$$h_y = \frac{9h}{8} \qquad h_z = \frac{5}{9}h$$

$$\frac{h_y}{h_z} = \frac{9h}{8}/\frac{5h}{9} = \frac{81}{40}.$$

65.

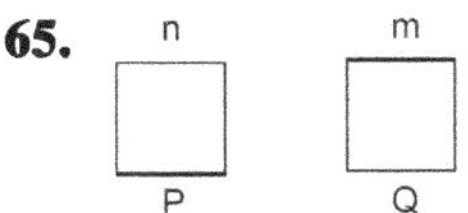

Let number of peoples in two villages are *n* and *m* respectively

So, $nP - P'(n-1) = (m+1)Q' - mQ$

$n(P - P') + P' = m(Q' - Q) + Q'.$

66. For maximum possible area
I should be 90°

$$1 \times \sin 90° = \frac{4}{3}\sin r'$$

$$\sin r' = \frac{3}{4}$$

$$\tan r' = \frac{3}{\sqrt{7}}$$

Total base area $\pi\left(6\times\frac{3}{\sqrt{7}}+0.3\right)^2 \approx 160 \text{ m}^2.$

67. $m_i s_i (\Delta T) + m_i L + m_i s_w (T - 0) = m_w s_w (90 - T)$

$1 \times 2.09(20) + 1 \times 334.4 + 1 \times 4.18 \times T$

$= 2 \times 4.18 \times (90 - T)$

$T = 60 - 30 = 30°C.$

68.
$$m_1 r_1 + m_2 r_2 = 0$$
$$mr_1 = mr_2$$
$$r_1 = r_2$$
$$\frac{l}{2}\cos\theta = \frac{l}{2} - l\cos\theta$$
$$\frac{3l}{2}\cos\theta = \frac{l}{2}$$
$$\cos\theta = \frac{1}{3}.$$

69.
$$\frac{1}{v}+\frac{1}{20} = \frac{1}{5}$$
$$v = \frac{20}{3}\text{cm}$$
$$\Delta x_i = \frac{+v^2}{u^2}\Delta x_0$$
$$\Delta x_i = \frac{A}{9} \text{ out of phase with lens.}$$

Hence, (A) is correct.

71. Xe + F_2 → XeF_2 + XeF_6

$\frac{262}{131}$ $\frac{152}{38}$ a mole b mole

= 2 mole 4 mole

Let a mole XeF_2 form and b mole XeF_6 form

Apply POAC

$a \times 1 + b \times 1 = 2$ ...(*i*)

$2a + 6b = 8$ ...(*ii*)

After solving equations (*i*) & (*ii*)

a = 1 mole & b = 1 mole.

72. $CH_3-CH_2-OH \xrightarrow[170°]{\text{Conc. } H_2SO_4} CH_2$ Ethane

$= CH_2 \xrightarrow[CCl_4]{Br_2} \underset{Br}{CH_2} - \underset{Br}{CH_2}$

1, 2–Dibromoethane

73.

C_4H_8	+	$6O_2$	→	$4CO_2$	+	$4H_2O$
22.4 lit				89.6 lit.		72 g
At S.T.P.				at S.T.P.		
1 mole				4 mole		$\frac{72}{18}$ = 4 mole

For complete combustion of 1 mole C_4H_8
6 mole O_2 required

$$n_{O_2} = 6 \text{ mole}$$
$$V_{O_2} = 6 \times 22.4$$
$$V_{O_2} = 134.4 \text{ lit.}$$

74. $W = \frac{E}{96500} \times I \times t$

$$W = \frac{108}{96500}\times 0.5\times 3600 = 2 \text{ gm.}$$

75. 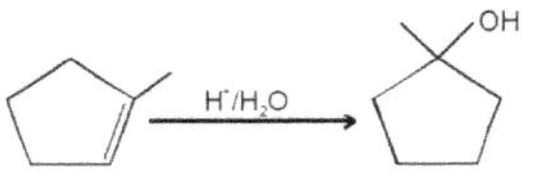 1-methylcyclopentene $\xrightarrow{H^+/H_2O}$ 1-methylcyclopentanol (OH)

Mechanism electrophilic addition reaction of alkenes.

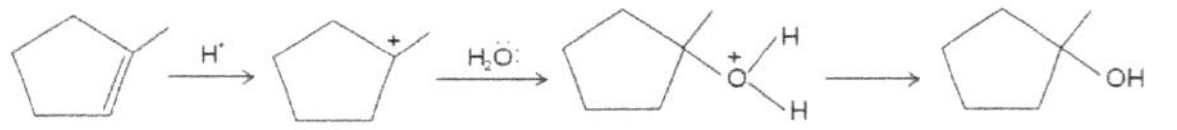

1-methylcyclopentene $\xrightarrow{H^+}$ carbocation $\xrightarrow{H_2\ddot{O}}$ $-\overset{+}{O}H_2$ ⟶ 1-methylcyclopentanol (OH)

76. Alu, I is a restriction endonuclease which is a four base pair cutter its frequency is 1/256 BP, while frequency of 6 cutter Bam HI, ECORI is 1/4096.

79. Glucose maintaining high osmotic pressure inside cell.

Kishore Vaigyanik Protsahan Yojana (KVPY)

STREAM – SA

Part-I

Mathematics

1. Let r be a root of the equation $x^2 + 2x + 6 = 0$. The value of $(r + 2)(r + 3)(r + 4)(r + 5)$ is equal to:

A. 51 B. –51

C. –126 D. 126

2. Let R be the set of all real numbers and let f be a function R to R such that $f(x) + \left(x + \frac{1}{2}\right) f(1 - x) = 1$, for all $x \in$ R. Then $2f(0) + 3f(1)$ is equal to:

A. 2 B. 0

C. –2 D. –4

3. The sum of all positive integers n for which $\dfrac{1^3 + 2^3 + ... - (2n)^3}{1^2 + 2^2 + ... + n^2}$ is also an integer is:

A. 8 B. 9

C. 15 D. Infinite

4. Let x and y be two 2-digit numbers such that y is obtained by reversing the digits of x. Suppose they also satisfy $x^2 - y^2 = m^2$ for some positive integer m. The value of $x + y + m$ is:

A. 88 B. 112

C. 144 D. 154

5. Let $p(x) = x^2 - 5x + a$ and $q(x) = x^2 - 3x + b$, where a and b are positive integers. Suppose hof$(p(x), q(x)) = x - 1$ and $k(x) = 1$ cm $(p(x), q(x))$. If the coefficient of the highest degree term of $k(x)$ is 1, the sum of the roots of $(x - 1) + k(x)$ is:

A. 4 B. 5

C. 6 D. 7

6. In a quadrilateral ABCD, which is not a trapezium, it is known that $\angle DAB = \angle ABC = 60°$. Moreover, $\angle CAB = \angle CBD$. Then,

A. AB = BC + CD B. AB = AD + CD

C. AB = BC + AD D. AB = AC + AD

7. A semi-circle of diameter 1 unit sits at the top of a semi-circle of diameter 2 units. The shaded region inside the smaller semi-circle but outside the larger semi-circle is called a *lune*. The area of the lune is:

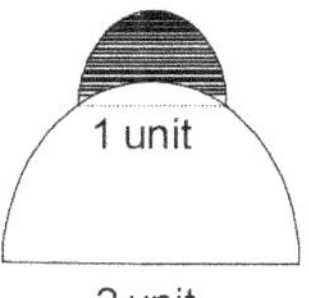

A. $\frac{\pi}{6} - \frac{\sqrt{3}}{4}$ B. $\frac{\sqrt{3}}{4} - \frac{\pi}{24}$

C. $\frac{\sqrt{3}}{4} - \frac{\pi}{12}$ D. $\frac{\sqrt{3}}{4} - \frac{\pi}{8}$

8. The angle bisectors BD and CE of a triangle ABC are divided by the incentre I in the ratios 3 : 2 and 2 : 1 respectively. Then the ratio in which I divides the angle bisector through A is:

A. 3 : 1 B. 11 : 4

C. 6 : 5 D. 7 : 4

9. Suppose S_1 and S_2 are two unequal circles; AB and CD are the direct common tangents to these circles. A transverse common tangent PQ cuts AB in R and CD in S. If AB = 10, then RS is:

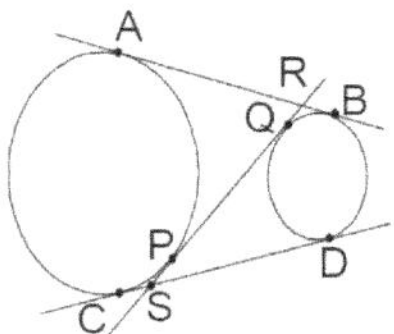

A. 8 B. 9

C. 10 D. 11

10. On the circle with center O, points A, B are such that OA = AB. A point C is located on the tangent at B to the circle such that A and C are on the opposite sides of the line OB and AB = BC. The line segment

AC intersects the circle again at F. Then the ratio ∠BOF : ∠BOC is equal to:

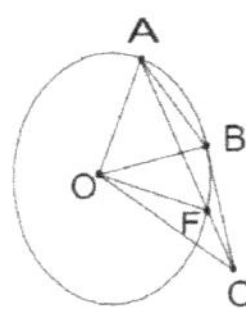

A. 1 : 2   B. 2 : 3
C. 3 : 4   D. 4 : 5

11. In a cinema hall, the charge per person is ₹ 200. On the first day, only 60% of the seats were filled. The owner decided to reduce the price by 20% and there was in increase of 50% in the number of spectators on the next day. The percentage increase in the revenue on the second day was:

A. 50   B. 40
C. 30   D. 20

12. The population of cattle in a farm increases so that the difference between the population in year $n + 2$. If the populations in year 2010, 2011 were 39, 60 and 123, respectively, then the population in 2012 was:

A. 81   B. 84
C. 87   D. 90

13. The number of 6-digit numbers of the form ababab (in base 10) each of which is a product of exactly 6 distinct primes is

A. 8   B. 10
C. 13   D. 15

14. The houses on one side of a road are numbered using consecutive even numbers. The sum of the numbers of all the houses in that row is 170. If there are at least 6 houses in that row and a is the number of the sixth house, then

A. $2 \le a \le 6$ B. $8 \le a \le 12$
C. $14 \le a \le 20$ D. $22 \le a \le 30$

15. Suppose $a_2, a_3, a_4, a_5, a_6, a_7$ are integers such that $\frac{5}{7} = \frac{a_2}{2!} + \frac{a_3}{3!} + \frac{a_4}{4!} + \frac{a_5}{5!} + \frac{a_6}{6!} + \frac{a_7}{7!}$ where $0 \le a < j$ for $j = 2, 4, 5, 6, 7$. The sum $a_2 + a_3 + a_4 + a_5 + a_6 + a_7$ is:

A. 8   B. 9
C. 10   D. 11

Physics

16. In the following displacement (x) vs time (t) graph, at which among the points P, Q and R is the object's speed increasing?

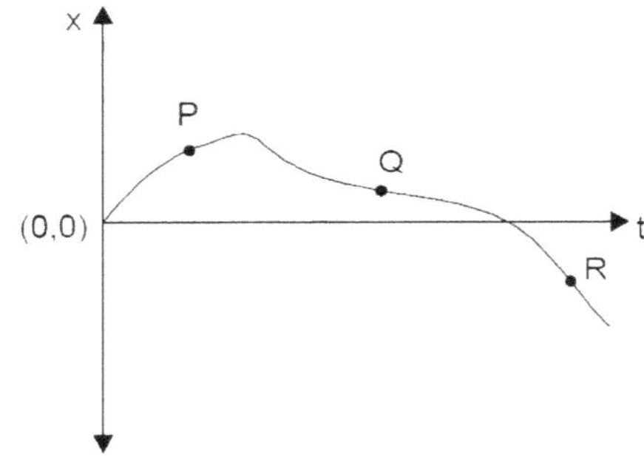

A. R only   B. P only
C. Q and R only   D. P, Q, R

17. A box, when hung from a spring balance shows a reading of 50 kg. If the same box is hung from the same spring balance inside an evacuated chamber, the reading on the scale will be

A. 50 kg because the mass of the box remains unchanged
B. 50 kg because the effect of the absence of the atmosphere will be indentical on the box and the spring balance
C. Less than 50 kg because the weight of the column of air on the box will be absent
D. More than 50 kg because the atmospheric buoyancy force will be absent

18. Two positively charged spheres of masses m_1, and m_2, are suspended from a common point at the ceiling by identical insulating massless strings of length l. Charges on the two spheres are q_1 and q_2, respectively. At equilibrium both strings make the same angle θ with the vertical. Then

A. $q_1 m_1 = q_2 m_2$ B. $m_1 = m_2$
C. $m_1 = m_2 \sin \theta$ D. $q_2 m_1 = q_1 m_2$

19. A box when dropped from a certain height reaches the ground with a speed v. When it skides from rest from the same height down a rough inclined plane inclined at in angle 45° to the horizontal, it reaches the ground with a speed $v/3$. The coefficient of sliding friction between the box and the plane is (acceleration due to gravity is 10 ms^{-2}):

A. $\frac{8}{9}$ B. $\frac{1}{9}$
C. $\frac{2}{3}$ D. $\frac{1}{3}$

20. A thin paper cup filled with water does not catch fire when placed over a flame. This is because:

A. The water cuts off oxygen supply to the paper cup
B. Water is an excellent conductor of heat
C. The paper cup does not become appreciably hotter than the water it contain
D. Paper is a poor conductor of heat

21. Ice is used in a cooler in order to cool its contents. Which of the following will speed up the cooling process?
A. Wrap the ice in a metal foil
B. Drain the water from the cooler periodically
C. Put the ice as a single block
D. Crush the ice

22. The angle of a prism is 60°. When light is incident at an angle of 60° on the prism, the angle of emergence is 40°. The angle of incidence i for which the light ray will deviate the least is such that
A. $i < 40°$ B. $40° < i < 50°$
C. $50° < i < 60°$ D. $i > 60°$

23. A concave lens made of material of refractive index 1.6 is immersed in a medium of refractive index 2.0. The two surfaces of the concave lens have the same radius of curvature 0.2 m. The lens will behave as a
A. Divergent lens of focal length 0.4 m
B. Divergent lens of focal length 0.5 m
C. Convergent lens of focal length 0.4 m
D. Convergent lens of focal length 0.5 m

24. A charged particle, initially at rest at O. When released follows a trajectory as shown. Such a trajectory is possible in the presence of

A. Electric field of constant magnitude and varying direction
B. Magnetic field of constant magnitude and varying direction
C. Electric field of constant magnitude and constant direction
D. Electric and magnetic fields of constant magnitudes and constant directions which are parallel to each other

25. Two equal charges of magnitude Q each are placed at a distance d apart. Their electrostatic energy is E. A third charge –Q/2 is brought midway between these two charges.The electrostatic energy of the system is now:
A. –2E   B. –E
C. 0   D. E

26. A bar magnet falls with its north pole pointing down through the axis of a copper ring. When viewed from above, the current in the ring will be
A. Clockwise while the magnet is above the plane of the ring and counter clockwise while below the plane of the ring
B. Counter clockwise throughout
C. Counter clockwise while the magnet is above the plane of the ring, and clockwise while below the plane of the ring
D. Clockwise throughout

27. Two identical bar magnets are held perpendicular to each other with a certain separation, as shown below. The area around the magnets is divided into four zones

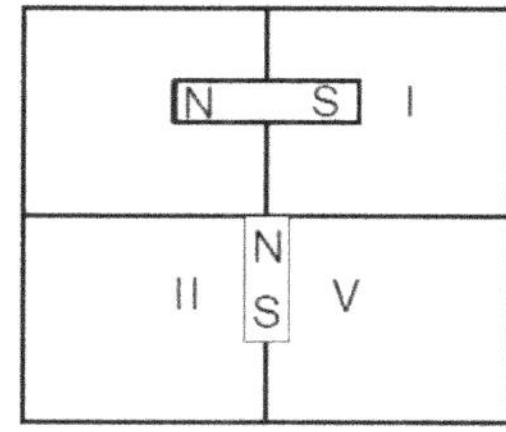

Given that there is a neutral point it is located in:
A. Zone I   B. Zone II
C. Zone III   D. Zone IV

28. A large number of random snap shots using a camera are taken of a particle in simple harmonic motion between $x = -x_0$ and $x = +x_0$ with origin $x = 0$ as the mean position. A histogram of the total number of times the particle is recorded about a given position (Event no.) would most closely resemble:

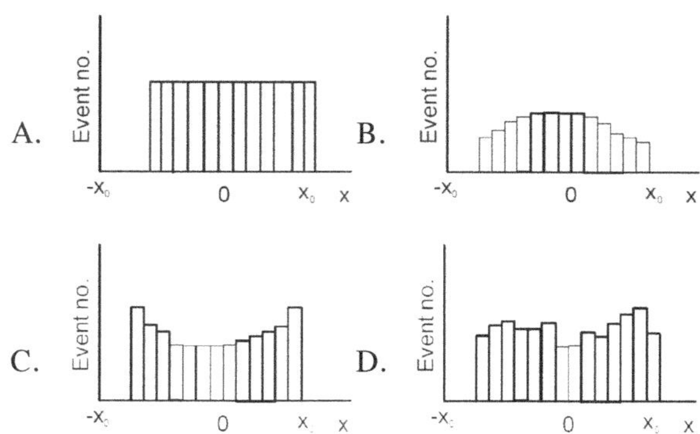

29. In 1911, the physicist Ernest Rutherford discovered that atoms have a tiny, dense nucleus by shooting positively charged particles at a very thin gold foil. A key physical property which led Rutherford to use gold that it was
A. Electrically conducting
B. Highly malleable
C. Shiny
D. None-reactive

30. Consider the following statements
(i) All isotopes of an element have the same number of neutrons
(ii) Only one isotope of an element can be stable and non-radioactive
(iii) All elements have isotopes
(iv) All isotopes of Carbon can form chemical compounds with Oxygen-16

The correct option regarding an isotope is:
A. (iii) and (iv) only
B. (ii), (iii) and (iv) only
C. (i), (ii) and (iii) only
D. (i), (iii) and (iv) only

Chemistry

31. The isoelectronic pair is:
A. CO, N_2 B. O_2, NO
C. C_2, HF D. F_2, HCl

32. The numbers of lone pairs and bond pairs in hydrazine are, respectively
A. 2 and 4 B. 2 and 6
C. 2 and 5 D. 1 and 5

33. The volume of oxygen at STP required to burn 2.4 g of carbon completely is
A. 1.12 L B. 8.96 L
C. 2.24 L D. 4.48 L

34. The species that exhibits the highest R_f value in a thin layer chromatogram using a nonpolar solvant on a silica gel olate is:

A. 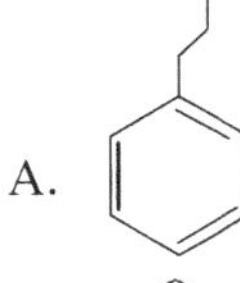 B. 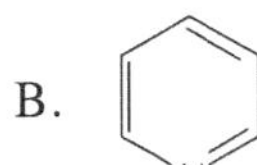

C. 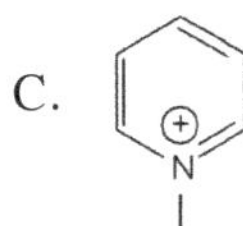

D.

35. The number of C-C sigma bonds in the compound:

A. 16 B. 17
C. 18 D. 11

36. If the radius of the hydrogen atom is 53 pm, the radius of the He^+ ion is closest to:
A. 108 pm B. 81 pm
C. 27 pm D. 13 pm

37. The diamagnetic species is:
A. NO B. NO_2
C. O_2 D. CO_2

38. The pH of 0.1 M aqueous solutions of NaCl, CH_3COONa and NH_4Cl will follow the order
A. NaCl < CH_3COONa < NH_4Cl
B. NH_4Cl < NaCl < CH_3COONa
C. NH_4Cl < CH_3COONa < NaCl
D. NaCl < NH_4Cl < CH_3COONa

39. At room temperature the average seed of Helium is higher than that of Oxygen by a factor of:
A. $2\sqrt{2}$ B. $6\sqrt{2}$
C. 8 D. 6

40. Ammonia is NOT produced in the reaction of:
A. NH_4Cl with KOH B. AlN with water
C. NH_4Cl with $NaNO_2$ D. NH_4Cl with $Ca(OH)_2$

41. The number of isomers which are ethers and having the molecular formula $C_4H_{10}O$, is:
A. 2 B. 3
C. 4 D. 5

42. The major product of the reaction of 2-butene with alkaline $KMnO_4$ solution is:

A. 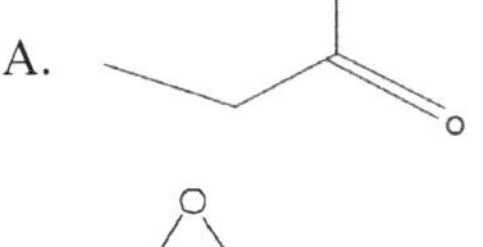

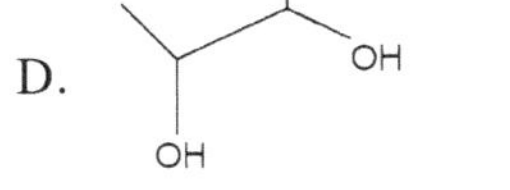

B. 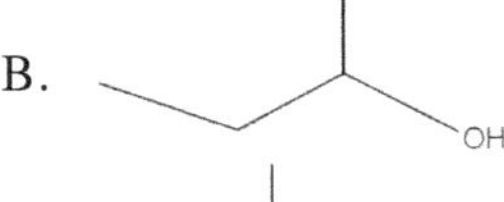

C. D.

43. Among the compounds I-IV, the compound having the lowest boiling point is

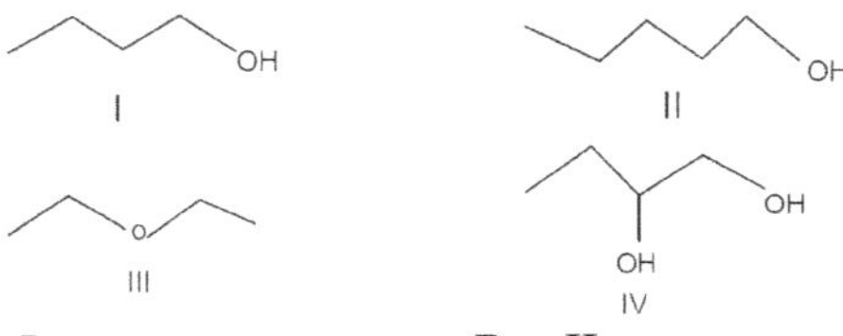

A. I B. II
C. III D. IV

44. Of the following reactions
(*i*) A $\rightleftharpoons$ B $\Delta G^\circ = 250$ kJ mol^{-1}
(*ii*) D $\rightleftharpoons$ E $\Delta G^\circ = -100$ kJ mol^{-1}
(*iii*) F $\rightleftharpoons$ G $\Delta G^\circ = -150$ kJ mol^{-1}
(*iv*) M $\rightleftharpoons$ N $\Delta G^\circ = 150$ kJ mol^{-1}
the reaction with the largest equilibrium constant is:
A. (*i*) B. (*ii*)
C. (*iii*) D. (*iv*)

45. The first ionization enthalpies for three elements are 1314, 1680 and 2080 kJ mol^{-1}, respectively. The correct sequence of the elements is:
A. O, F and Ne B. F, O and Ne
C. Ne, F and O D. F, Ne and O

Biology

46. Individuals of one kind occupying a particular geographic area at a given time are called:
A. Community B. Population
C. Species D. Biome

47. What fraction of the assimilated energy is used in respiration by the herbivores?
A. 10 per cent B. 60 per cent
C. 30 per cent D. 80 per cent

48. Athletes are often trained at high altitude because:
A. Training at high altitude increase muscle mass
B. Training at high altitude increases the number of red blood cells
C. There is less change of an injury at high altitude
D. Athletes sweat less at high altitude

49. In human brain two hemispheres are connected by bundle of fibers which is known as:
A. Medulla oblongata B. Cerebrum
C. Cerebellum D. Corpus callosum

50. Which one of the following hormones is produced by the pancreas?
A. Prolactin B. Glucagon
C. Leutinizing hormone D. Epinephrine

51. The stalk of a leaf is derived from which one of the following types of plant tissue?
A. Sclerenchyma B. Paranchyma
C. Chlorenchyma D. Collenchyma

52. Which of the following muscle types CANNOT be used voluntarily?
A. Both striated and smooth
B. Both cardiac and striated
C. Both smooth and cardiac
D. Cardiac, striated and smooth

53. The pulmonary artery carries:
A. Deoxygenated blood to the lungs
B. Oxygenated blood to the brain
C. Oxygenated blood to the lungs
D. Deoxygenated blood to the kidney

54. Both gout and kidney stone formation is caused by:
A. Calcium oxalate B. Uric acid
C. Creatinine D. Potassium chloride

55. The auditory nerve gets its input from which of the following?
A. The sense cells of the cochlea
B. Vibration of the last ossicle
C. Eustachian tube
D. Vibration of the tympanic membrane

56. Which of the following organelles contain circular DNA?
A. Peroxisomes and Mitochondria
B. Mitochondria and Golgi complex
C. Chloroplasts and Lysosomes
D. Mitochondria and Chloroplast

57. A reflex action does NOT involve:
A. Neurons B. Brain
C. Spinal cord D. Muscle fiber

58. Which one of the following options is true in photosynthesis?
A. CO_2 is oxidized and H_2O is reduced
B. H_2O is oxidized and CO_2 is reduced
C. Both CO_2 and H_2O are reduced
D. Both CO_2 and H_2O are oxidized

59. Human mature red blood cells (RBCs) do NOT contain:
A. Iron B. Cytoplasm
C. Mitochondria D. Haemoglobin

60. A person was saved from poisonous snake bite by antivenom injection. Which of the following immunity explains this form of protection?
A. Naturally acquired active immunity
B. Artificially acquired active immunity
C. Naturally acquired passive immunity
D. Artificially acquired passive immunity

Part-II

Mathematics

61. Let a, b, c be non-zero real numbers such that $a + b + c = 0$; let $q = a^2 + b^2 + c^2$ and $r = a^4 + b^4 + c^4$. Then:
A. $q^2 < 2r$ always
B. $q^2 = 2r$ always
C. $q^2 > 2r$ always
D. $q^2 - 2r$ can take both positive and negative value

62. The value of $\sum_{n=0}^{1947} \frac{1}{2^n + \sqrt{2^{1947}}}$ is equal to:
A. $\frac{847}{\sqrt{2^{1945}}}$ B. $\frac{1946}{\sqrt{2^{1947}}}$
C. $\frac{1947}{\sqrt{2^{1947}}}$ D. $\frac{1948}{\sqrt{2^{1947}}}$

63. The number of integers a in the interval [1, 2014] for which the system of equations

$$x + y = a\frac{x^2}{x-1} + \frac{y^2}{y-1} = 4$$

has finitely many solutions is:
A. 0 B. 1007
C. 2013 D. 2014

64. In a triangle ABC with $\angle A = 90°$, P is a point on BC such that PA : PB = 3 : 4. If AB = $\sqrt{7}$ and AC = $\sqrt{5}$, then BP : PC is:
A. 2 : 1 B. 4 : 3
C. 4 : 5 D. 8 : 7

65. The number of all 3-digit numbers abc (in base 10) for which $(a \times b \times c) + (a \times b)\ 6 + (c \times a) + a + b + c = 29$ is:
A. 6 B. 10
C. 14 D. 18

Physics

66. A uniform square wooden sheet of side a has its center of mass located at point O as shown in the figure on the left. A square portion of side b of this sheet is cut out to produce and L-shaped sheet as shown in the figure on the right.

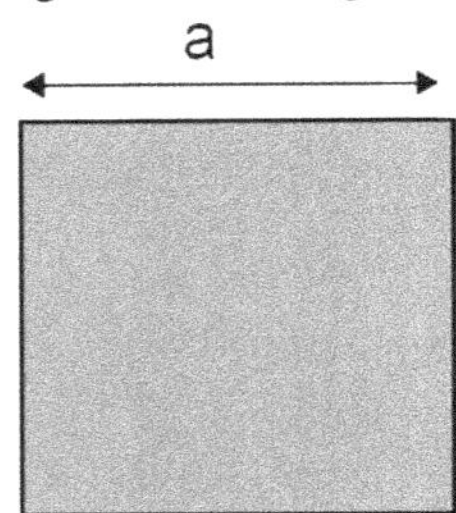

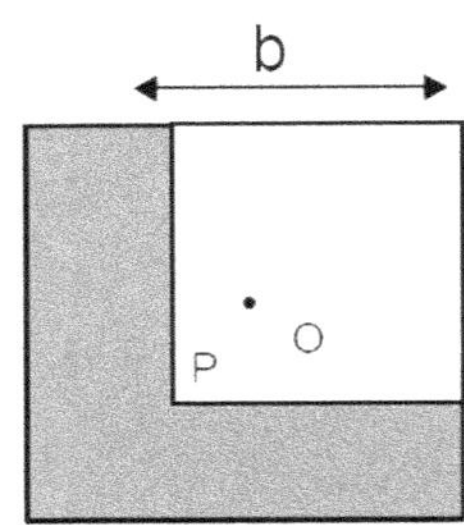

The center of mass of the L-shaped sheet lies at the point P (in the diagram) when:

A. $\frac{a}{b} = \frac{(\sqrt{5}-1)}{2}$ B. $\frac{a}{b} = \frac{(\sqrt{5}+1)}{2}$

C. $\frac{a}{b} = \frac{(\sqrt{3}-1)}{2}$ D. $\frac{a}{b} = \frac{(\sqrt{3}+1)}{2}$

67. A machine is blowing spherical soap bubbles of different radii filled with helium gas. It is found that if the bubbles have a radius smaller than 1 cm, then they sink to the floor in still air. Larger bubbles float in the air. Assume that the thickness of the soap film in all bubbles is uniform and equal. Assume that the density of soap solution is same as that of water (= 1000 kgm^{-3}). The density of helium inside the bubbles and air are 0.18 kgm^{-3} and 1.23 kgm^{-3}, respectively. Then the thickness of the soap film of the bubbles is (note 1 μm = 10^{-6} m)

A. 0.50 μm B. 1.50 μm
C. 7.00 μm D. 3.50 μm

68. An aluminum piece of mass 50 g initially at 300°C is dipped quickly and taken out of 1 kg of water, initially at 30 °C. If the temperature of the aluminum piece be 160 °C, what is the temperature of the water then (Specific heat capacities of aluminum and water are 900 $Jkg^{-1}\,K^{-1}$ and 4200 $Jkg^{-1}\,K^{-1}$, respectively):

A. 165 °C B. 45 °C
C. 31.5 °C D. 28.5 °C

69. A ray of light incident paralled to the base PQ of an isosceles right-angled triangular prism PQR suffers two successive total internal reflections at the faces PQ and QR before emerging reversed in direction as shown

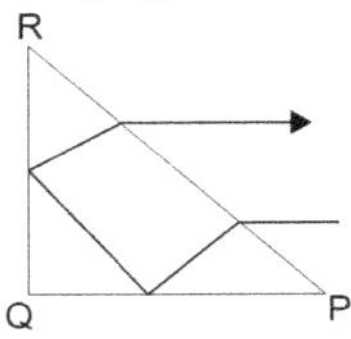

If the refractive index of the material of the prism is μ, then

A. $\mu > \sqrt{5}$ B. $\sqrt{3} < \mu < \sqrt{5}$

C. $\sqrt{2} < \mu < \sqrt{5}$ D. $\mu < \sqrt{2}$

70. Consider the circuit shown below where all resistors are of 1 kΩ

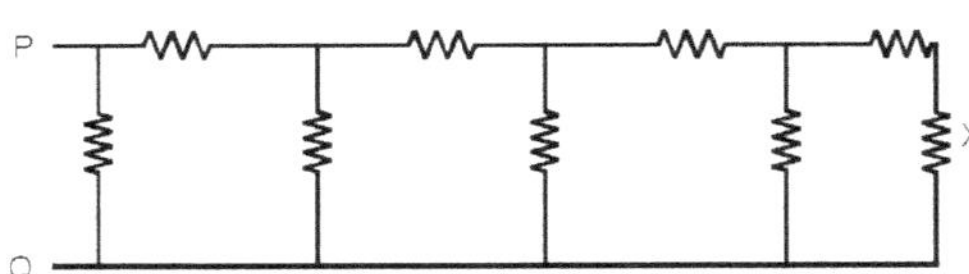

If a current of magnitude 1 mA flows through the resistor marked X, what is the potential difference measured between point P and Q?

A. 21 V B. 68 V
C. 55 V D. 34 V

Chemistry

71. 10 moles of a mixture of glycogen and oxygen gases at a pressure of 1 atm at constant volume and temperature, react to form 3.6 g of liquid water. The pressure of the resulting mixture will be closest to:

A. 1.07 atm B. 0.97 atm
C. 1.02 atm D. 0.92 atm

72. The ammonia evolved from 2 g of a compound in Kjeldahl's estimation of nitrogen neutralizes 10 mL of 2 M H_2SO_4 solution. The weight percentage of nitrogen in the compound is:

A. 28 B. 14
C. 56 D. 7

73. Complete reaction of 2.0 g of calcium (at. wt. = 40) with excess HCl produces 1.125 L of H_2 gas. Complete reaction of the same quantity of another metal "M" with excess HCl produces 1.85 L of H_2 gas under indentical conditions. The equivalent weight of "M" is closest to:

A. 23 B. 9
C. 7 D. 12

74. A compound X formed after heating coke with lime react with water to give Y which on passing over red-hot iron at 873 produces Z. The compound Z is:

A. 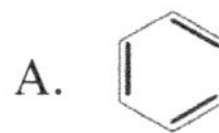 B.

C.  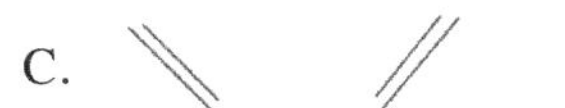 D.

75. In the following reaction sequence

Br, Br, Ph — 1. Alcoholic KOH, 2. NaNH$_2$ → X — 3. $HgSO_4$/dil H_2SO_4, heat, 4. Con HNO_3/H_2SO_4 → Y

X and Y are, respectively

A. Ph—≡ and (O, NO_2)

B. (OH, Ph, NO_2) and (O, NH_2, NO_2)

C. (NH_2, Ph, OH) and (H_2N, O, NO_2)

D. (OH, Ph, NH_2) and (O, NO_2)

Biology

76. In which of the following cellular compartment(s) do respiratory reactions occur?

A. Cytoplasm and endoplasmic reticulum
B. Mitochondria and golgi complex
C. Mitochondria and cytoplasm
D. Mitochondria only

77. A women heterozygous for color blindness marries a colour blind man. What is the ratios of carrier daughters, colour blind daughters, normal sons and colour blind sons in F1 generation?

A. 1 : 2 : 2 : 1 B. 2 : 1 : 1 : 2
C. 1 : 1 : 1 : 1 D. 1 : 1 : 2 : 2

78. Two semi-permeable bags containing 2% sucrose placed in two beakers, 'P' containing water and 'Q' containing 10% sucrose. Which one of the following outcomes is true?

A. Bag in 'P' becomes flaccid due to exosmosis
B. Bag in 'P' becomes turgid due to endosmosis
C. Bag in 'Q' becomes turgid due to endosmosis
D. Concentration of sucrose remain unchanged both

79. Children suffering from phenylketonuria are given food low in phenylalanine and supplemented with tyrosine. This is because they.

A. Are unable to utilize phenylalanine
B. Do not require phenylalanine
C. Have increased tyrosine anabolism
D. Have increased tyrosine catabolism

80. Two bottles were half filled with water from Ganga ('P') and Kaveri ('Q') and kept under indentical airtight conditions for 5 days. The oxygen was determined to be 2% in bottle ('P') and 10% in bottle ('Q'). What could be the cause of this difference?

A. Ganga is more polluted than Kaveri
B. Both the rivers are equally polluted
C. Kaveri is more polluted than Ganga
D. Kaveri has more minerals than Ganga

ANSWERS

1	**2**	**3**	**4**	**5**	**6**	**7**	**8**	**9**	**10**
C	C	A	D	D	C	B	B	C	B
11	**12**	**13**	**14**	**15**	**16**	**17**	**18**	**19**	**20**
D	B	C	C	B	A	D	B	A	C
21	**22**	**23**	**24**	**25**	**26**	**27**	**28**	**29**	**30**
D	B	D	A	B	C	A	C	B	A
31	**32**	**33**	**34**	**35**	**36**	**37**	**38**	**39**	**40**
A	C	D	A	B	C	D	B	A	C
41	**42**	**43**	**44**	**45**	**46**	**47**	**48**	**49**	**50**
B	D	C	C	A	B	C	B	D	B
51	**52**	**53**	**54**	**55**	**56**	**57**	**58**	**59**	**60**
D	C	A	B	A	D	B	B	C	D
61	**62**	**63**	**64**	**65**	**66**	**67**	**68**	**69**	**70**
B	A	C	A	C	B	D	C	A	D
71	**72**	**73**	**74**	**75**	**76**	**77**	**78**	**79**	**80**
B	A	D	A	A	C	C	B	A	A

EXPLANATORY ANSWERS

1. r be a root $\Rightarrow r^2 + 2r + 6 = 0$ ...(*i*)

Now $(r + 2)(r + 3)(r + 4)(r + 5)$

$= (r^2 + 5r + 6)(r^2 + 9r + 20)$

$= (3r)(7r + 14)$ using (*i*)

$= 21(r^2 + 2r)$

$= -126$ using (*i*).

2. Given $f(x)+\left(x+\frac{1}{2}\right)f(1-x) = 1$ ...(*i*)

but $x = 0$

$$f(0)+\frac{1}{2}f(1) = 1$$

$\Rightarrow \quad 2f(0) + f(1) = 2$ ...(*ii*)

put $x = 1$ in (*i*)

$\Rightarrow \quad f(1)+\frac{3}{2}f(0) = 1$

$\Rightarrow \quad 2f(1) + 3f(0) = 2$ ...(*iii*)

Solving (*ii*) & (*iii*) we have

F(0) = 2 & $f(1) = -2$

$\therefore \quad 2f(0) + f(1) = 4 - 6 = -2.$

3. $$\frac{1^3+2^3+\ldots+(2n)^3}{1^2+2^2+\ldots+n^2} = \left(\frac{2n(2n+1)}{2}\right)^2 \cdot \frac{6}{n(n+1)(2n+1)}$$

$$= \frac{6n(2n+1)}{n+1} = \frac{12n^2+6n}{n+1}$$

$$= \frac{12(n^2-1)+6(n+1)+6}{n+1}$$

$$= l+\frac{6}{n+1}$$

If the given terms is an integer, then $\frac{6}{n+1}$ must be an integer

$\Rightarrow \quad n = 1, 2, 5$

Sum = 8.

4. $x \rightarrow \quad ab$ or $x = 10a + b$

$y \rightarrow \quad ba$ or $y = 10b + a$

Now $\quad x^2 - y^2 = (10a + b)^2 - (10b + a)^2$

$= 99(a^2 - b^2)$

$= 3^2 \times 11(a + b)(a - b)$ ...(*i*)

According of question

$(a + b)(a - b) = 11$ and $a - b = 1$

$\Rightarrow \quad a + b = 11$ and $a - b = 1$

$\Rightarrow \quad a = 6, b = 5$

Hence, $x = 65$, $y = 56$ and $m = 33$

$\Rightarrow \quad x + y + m = 154.$

5. $\therefore \quad$ HCF $= x - 1$

$\Rightarrow \quad p(x) = x^2 - 5x + a$

$= x^2 - 5x + 4$

$= (x - 1)(x - 4)$ ...(*i*)

and $q(x)\ x^2 - 3x + b = x^2 - 3x + 2$

$= (x - 1)(x - 2)$ ...(*ii*)

$\Rightarrow \quad k(x) = (x - 1)(x - 2)(x - 4)$

Hence

$(x - 1) + R(x) = (x - 1) + (x - 1)(x - 2)(x - 2)(x - 4)$

$= (x - 1)(x - 3)^2$

Hence sum of roots = 7.

7.

Area of sector OACB $= \frac{r^2}{2}\theta = \frac{1}{2}.\frac{\pi}{3} = \frac{\pi}{6}$

Area of shaded region $= \frac{\pi}{6}$ – area of ΔOAB

$$= \frac{\pi}{6} - \frac{\sqrt{3}}{4}$$

Hence, area of line = Area of semi-circle – Area of shaded region

$$= \frac{1}{2}\pi\left(\frac{1}{2}\right)^2 - \left(\frac{\pi}{6}-\frac{\sqrt{3}}{4}\right)$$

$$= \frac{\sqrt{3}}{4}+\frac{\pi}{8}-\frac{\pi}{6} = \frac{\sqrt{3}}{4}-\frac{\pi}{24}.$$

8. $\because \quad \frac{AI}{IF} = \frac{b+c}{a}$ ...(*i*)

$\because \quad \frac{BI}{ID} = \frac{a+c}{b} = \frac{3}{2}$ ...(*ii*)

$\because \quad \frac{CI}{IE} = \frac{a+c}{c} = \frac{2}{1}$

$\Rightarrow \quad a + b = 2c$ ...(*iii*)

(*ii*) $\quad 2a + 2c = 3b \quad$ using to

$\Rightarrow \quad 2a + a + b = 3b \quad$ using (*iii*)

$\Rightarrow \quad 3a = 2b$

$\Rightarrow \quad b = \frac{3}{2}a$ ...(*iv*)

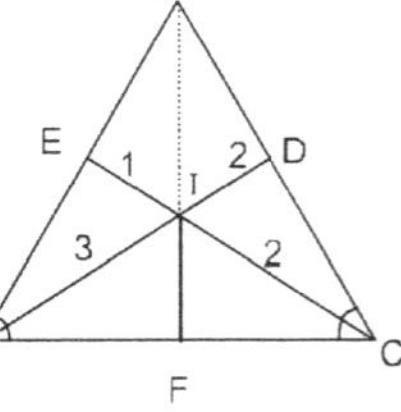

Now again (*iii*) $\Rightarrow 2c = a + b$

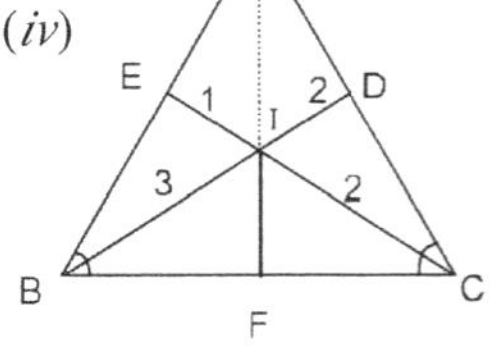

$$= a+\frac{3}{2}a$$

$\Rightarrow \quad c+\dfrac{5}{4}a$

Hence $\quad \dfrac{AI}{IF} = \dfrac{b+c}{a} = \dfrac{\frac{1}{2}a+\frac{5}{4}a}{a} = \dfrac{11}{4}$.

9.

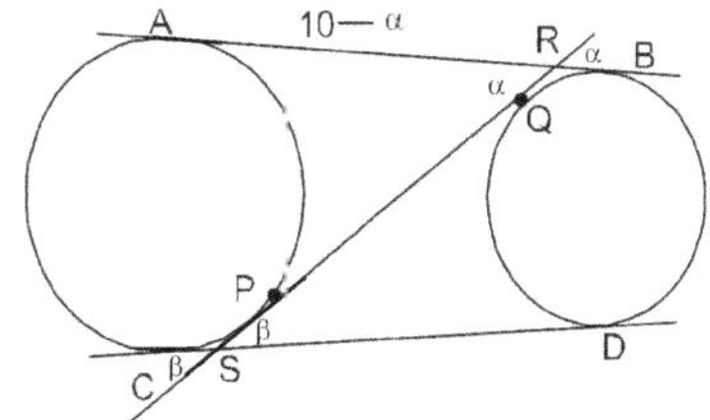

$\therefore \qquad RP = RA = 10 - \alpha$

$\Rightarrow \qquad RS = 10 - \alpha + \beta \qquad ...(i)$

Also $\qquad SQ = SD = 10 - \beta$

$\Rightarrow \qquad RS = 10 - \beta + \alpha \qquad ...(ii)$

(*i*) and (*ii*) $\Rightarrow \alpha = \beta$. Hence RS = 10.

10.

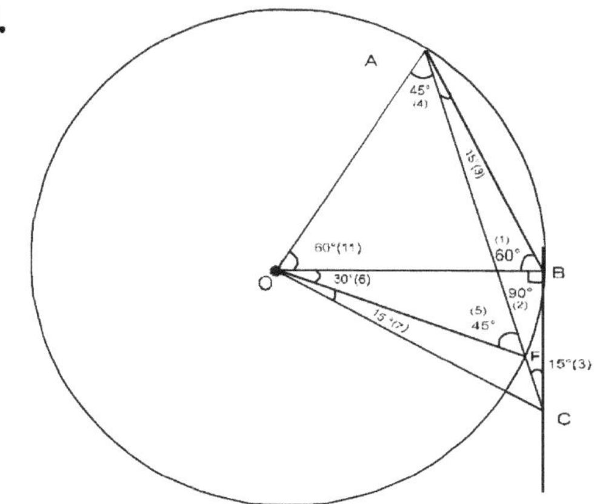

1. ΔAOB is equilateral ($\angle AOB = \angle OAB = \angle OBA = 60°$)
2. ΔOBC is right angled isosceles ($\angle OBC = 90°$)
3. ΔABC is isosceles ($\angle BAC = \angle BCA = 15°$)
4. $\angle OAC = 60° - \angle CAB = 45°$
5. ΔAOF is right angled isosceles ($\angle AOF = 90°$, $\angle OFA = 45°$)
6. $\angle BOF = 90° - \angle AOB = 30°$
7. ΔOBC is right angled isosceles ($\angle BOC = 45°$)

$\therefore \quad \dfrac{\angle BOF}{\angle BOC} = \dfrac{30°}{45°} = \dfrac{2}{3}$.

11. Let total seats = 100

On first day,

Ticket price = 200

Seats full = 60% $= \dfrac{60}{100} \times 100 = 60$

$\therefore \quad$ Revenue = 60 × 200

$R_1 = 12000$

On second day

Ticket price = 200 – 20% of 200

$= 200 - \dfrac{20}{100} \times 200$

$= 200 - 40 = 160$

Seats full 60 + 50% of 60

$= 60 + \dfrac{50}{100} \times 60$

$= 60 + 30 = 90$

Revenue = 160 × 90

$R_2 = 14400$

% Increase in Revenue $= \dfrac{R_2 - R_1}{R_1} \times 100$

$= \dfrac{14400 - 12000}{12000} \times 100$

$= \dfrac{2400}{12000} \times 100 = 20\%$.

12. Year – Population

2010 – 39

2011 – 60

2012 – x

2013 – 123

According to question,

$x - 39 = k(60)$ & $63 = kr$

$\Rightarrow \quad x - 39 = \dfrac{63}{x}.63$

$\Rightarrow \quad x^2 - 39x = -(60)(63) = 0$

$x = 84$ & -40.

13. $N = ab\ ab\ ab$

$1 < a \le 9 \qquad 0 < b \le 9 \qquad a, b \in I$

$N = 10^5a + 10^4b + 10^3a + 10^2b + 10a + b$

$= (10^4 + 10^2 + 1)(10a + b)$

$= (10^2 + 10 + 1)(10^2 - 10 + 1)(10a + b)$

$= 3 \times 37 \times 13 \times 7(10a + b) \quad ...(i)$

then $\quad 10a + b = P_1 \times P_2 \qquad p_1, p_2 \in$ prime and $10 \le 10a + b \le 99$

a	b	$10a + b$
1	0	10 = 2 × 5
2	2	22 = 2 × 11
3	4	34 = 2 × 17
3	8	38 = 2 × 19
4	6	46 = 2 × 23
5	5	55 = 5 × 11
5	8	58 = 2 × 29
6	2	62 = 2 × 31
7	4	74 = 2 × 37
8	2	82 = 2 × 41
8	5	85 = 5 × 17
9	4	94 = 2 × 47
9	5	95 = 5 × 19

14. Let house no. are α, α + 2, α + 4, α + 6, α + 8, α + 10, ...

$$\alpha + 10 = a \Rightarrow \alpha = a - 10 \quad ...(i)$$

House no. will be (+)

$\Rightarrow \quad \alpha = a - 10 > 0$

$\Rightarrow \quad \alpha > 10$

$\Rightarrow \quad \alpha \geq 12$ as a is each too ...(*ii*)

Now, $\quad S_n = \frac{n}{2}[2\alpha + (n-1)(d)]$

$$170 = \frac{n}{2}[2\alpha + (n-1)(2)]$$

$$= n(\alpha + (n-1))$$

$$= n(a - 10 + n - 1)$$

$$= n(a - 11 + n)$$

$\Rightarrow n^2 + n(a - 11) - 170 = 0$

$\Rightarrow \quad n = \frac{(11-a) \pm \sqrt{(a-11)^2 + 680}}{2}$ ...(*iii*)

$\because \quad n \geq 6$

$\Rightarrow \quad \frac{(11-a) \pm \sqrt{(a-11)^2 + 680}}{2} \geq 6$

$\Rightarrow \quad a \leq \frac{800}{24}$ ...(*iv*)

From (*ii*) and (*iv*) $\Rightarrow 12 \leq a \leq 32$

Now checking through (*iii*) for a = 12, 14, ...;

We have $a = 18$, $n = 10$ and $S_n = 170$.

15. $\frac{5}{7} = \frac{2520a_2 + 840a_3 + 210a_4 + 42a_5 + 7a_6 + a_7}{\lfloor 7}$

$2520a_2 + 840a_3 + 210a_4 + 42a_5 + 7a_6 + a_7 = 3600$

Let $a_2 = a_3 = a_4 = 1$, $a_5 = 0$, $a_6 = 4$, $a_7 = 2$.

16. |slope| is increasing at point R.

17. No Buoyancy force in vacuum.

18.

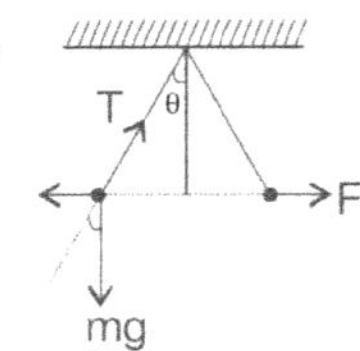

$$\tan\theta = \frac{F}{mg} \quad (F \rightarrow \text{same})$$

$$\tan\theta \ \alpha \ \frac{1}{m}$$

$\therefore \quad m_1 = m_2$.

19. Case-1, $\quad v = \sqrt{2gh}$

Case-2, $\quad \Delta U + \Delta kE = w_f$

$$-mgh + \frac{1}{2}m\left(\frac{2gh}{9}\right) = -\mu mgh$$

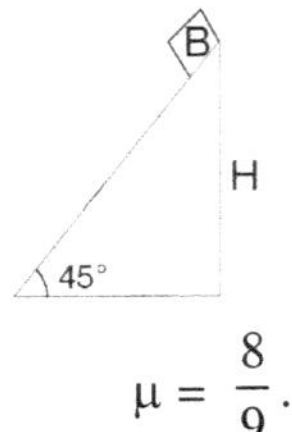

$$\mu = \frac{8}{9}.$$

22. For minimum deviation

$i = e$

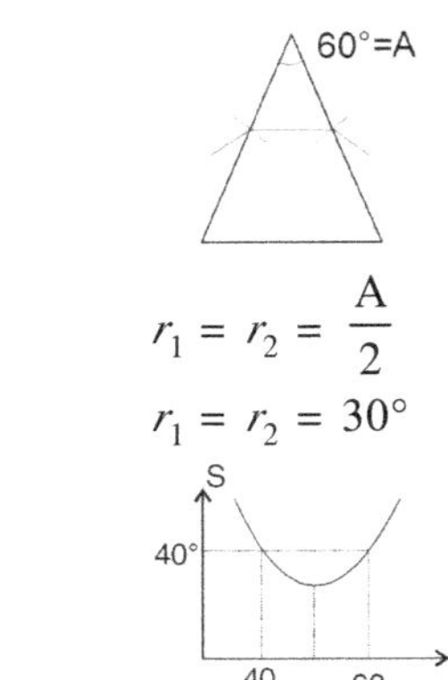

$$r_1 = r_2 = \frac{A}{2}$$

$\therefore \quad r_1 = r_2 = 30°$

For minimum deviation i should lie between 40 to 50°.

23.

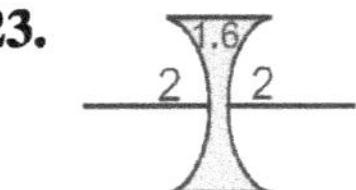

$$\frac{1}{F} = \left(\frac{1.6}{2} - 1\right)\left(\frac{1}{-0.2} - \frac{1}{0.2}\right)$$

$$= \frac{0.4}{2} \times \frac{1}{0.1}$$

F = 0.5 converging lens.

24. In option B it will not move, in option C & D path will be straight line.

25. $\quad \mu_i = \frac{kQ^2}{d} = E$

−Q/2

Q° ° °

Q

$$\mu_f = \frac{kQ^2}{d} + \frac{k(-Q)^2}{d} + \frac{k - Q^2}{d}$$

$$= -\frac{kQ^2}{d} = -E.$$

26. Using Lenz's law upper face first become North pole then South pole

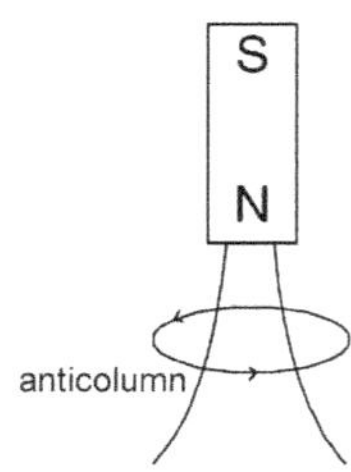

28. In SHM particle comes 2 times at every position in 1 oscillation, so actual histogram may be option (A) but since at it random snap shots so it should be option (C).

31. CO & N_2 are isoelectronic.

32. HYDRAZINE N_2H_4

H H
N — N
H H

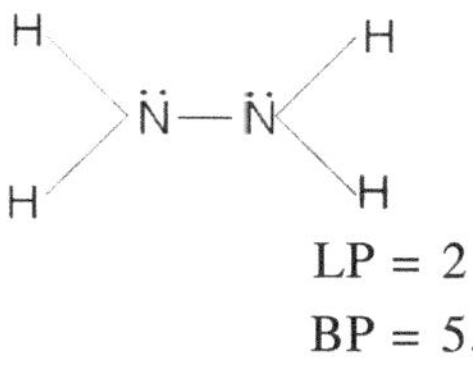

LP = 2

BP = 5.

33. $C(s) + O_2(g) \rightarrow CO_2(g)$

moles = 1 mole 1 mole 1 mole

weight = 12 gm 32 gm 44 gm

12 gm of C require → 1 mole of O_2

$\therefore$ 2.4 gm of C will require → $\frac{1}{12} \times 2.4$ mole of O_2

volume of 2.4/12 mole O_2 at STP

$$= \frac{22.4 \times 2.4}{12} \text{ litre.}$$

$$= 4.48 \text{ litre.}$$

34. Nonpolar substance will have high R_f value as solvent is nonpolar therefore option (A) will have high R_f value as it have low dipole moment.

36.
$$r_n = \frac{R_H n^2}{Z}$$

$$r_{H_e} = \frac{53n^2}{Z}$$

$$= \frac{53 \times 1^2}{2} = 27 \text{ approx.}$$

38. NH_4Cl → Acidic salt (pH < 7)

NaCl → Neutral salt (pH = 7)

CH_3COONa → Basic salt (pH > 7).

39. Average speed $\alpha \frac{1}{\sqrt{M}}$

$$\frac{V_{He}}{V_{O_2}} = \sqrt{\frac{32}{4}} = \sqrt{\frac{M_{O_2}}{M_{H_e}}}$$

$$= \sqrt{8} = 2\sqrt{2}.$$

40. $NH_4Cl + NaNO_2 \rightarrow NaCl + N_2 + 2H_2O$.

41. $CH_3 - O - CH_2 - CH_2 - CH_3$

$CH_3 - CH_2 - O - CH_2 - CH_3$

CH_3
|
$CH_3 - O - CH - CH_3$

42. Alkaline $KMnO_4$ (Syn) Oxidation → OH, OH

43. I, II & IV compound form H–bond III do not form H–bond.

44. $\boxed{\Delta G^\circ = -RT \ln K_{eq}}$.

45. As we move from left to right in period ionisation energy increases.

61. $a + b + c = 0$, $a, b, c \in R \neq 0$

$a^2 + b^2 + c^2 + 2(ab + bc + ca) = 0$

$q = a^2 + b^2 + c^2$, $r = a^4 + b^4 + c^4$

$r = q^2 - 2(a^2b^2 + b^2c^2 + c^2a^2)$

$r = q^2 - 2[(ab + bc + ca)^2 - 2abc(a + b + c)]$

$r = q^2 - 2(q^2 / 4)$

$r = q^2 / 2$.

62.
$$\frac{1}{1+\sqrt{2^{1947}}} + \frac{1}{2^{1947} + 2^{\frac{1947}{2}}} = \frac{1}{2^{\frac{1947}{2}}}$$

Similarly,

$$\sum_{n=0}^{1947} \frac{1}{2^4 + \sqrt{2^{1947}}} = \frac{974}{\sqrt{2^{1947}}} = \frac{487}{\sqrt{2^{1945}}}.$$

63.
$$\frac{x^2-1+1}{x-1} + \frac{y^2-1+1}{y-1} = 4$$

$$x+1+\frac{1}{x-1} + y+1+\frac{1}{y-1} = 4$$

$$a+2+\frac{1}{x-1} + \frac{1}{(a-1)-x} = 4$$

$$\frac{(a-1)-x+x-1}{(x-1)[(a-1)-x]} = 2 - a$$

$\because$ $a \neq 2$ [for $a = 2$ equation have infinitely many solution]

$\therefore$ $(x - 1)[(a - 1) - x] = -1$

$(x - 1)[x - (a - 1)] = 1$

$x^2 - ax + (a - 2) = 0$

$D > 0$

$\therefore$ equation have 2 real roots. So a can be 1, 3, 4....... 2014.

64.

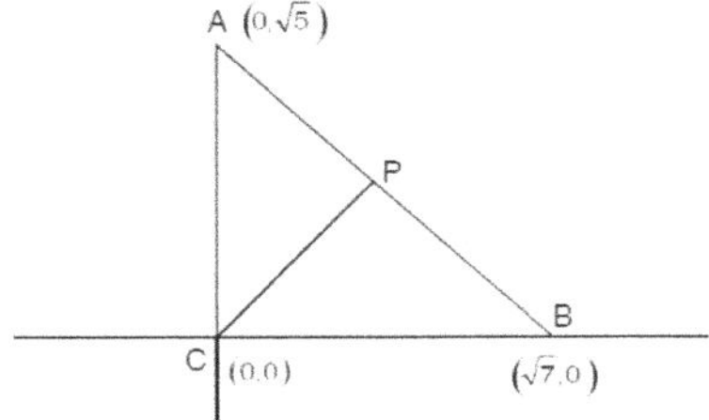

Equation of line AB is

$$\frac{x}{\sqrt{7}} + \frac{y}{\sqrt{5}} = 1$$

Let $P\left[\alpha, \sqrt{5}\left(1-\frac{\alpha}{\sqrt{7}}\right)\right]$

On solving 16(PA)2 = 9(PB)2

$P\left[\frac{\sqrt{7}}{3}, \frac{2\sqrt{5}}{3}\right]$

Let BP : PC = λ : 1

then $\lambda = 2$

BP : PC = 2 : 1.

65. $(a \times b \times c) + (a \times b) + (c \times a) + (a + b + c) = 29$

$(1 + a)(1 + b)(1 + c) = 30$

$= 2 \times 3 \times 5 \rightarrow (a, b, c) \Rightarrow (1, 2, 3) \Rightarrow 6$

$= 1 \times 6 \times 5 \rightarrow (a, b, c) \Rightarrow (0, 5, 4) \Rightarrow 4$

$= 1 \times 3 \times 10 \rightarrow (a, b, 1) \Rightarrow (0, 2, 9) \Rightarrow 4$

14

66. Finally come at p

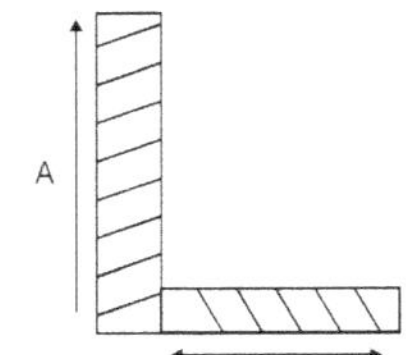

$$X_{am} = \frac{A_1X_1 + A_2X_2}{A_1 + A_2}$$

$$(a - b) = \frac{a(a-b)\frac{(a-b)}{2} + b(a-b)(a-b+b/2)}{a(a-b)+(a-b)b}$$

$$\therefore \quad \left(\frac{a}{b}\right)^2 - \left(\frac{a}{b}\right) - 1 = 0$$

$$\frac{a}{b} = \frac{1+\sqrt{5}}{2}.$$

67. Weight = F_0

$4\pi r^2 t\, \rho_w g + 4/3\pi r^3\, \rho_{Ne} g = 4/3\, \pi r^3\, \rho_{air} g$

$\therefore t = 3.5$ um.

68. Heat lost = heat gain

$0.05 \times 900 \times (300 - 160) = 1 \times 4200 \times (T - 30)$

T = 31.5 °.

69.

$45 + r > C$

also $45 - r > C$

$90 > 2C \qquad 45 > C$

$\because \qquad \mu > \sqrt{2}.$

70.

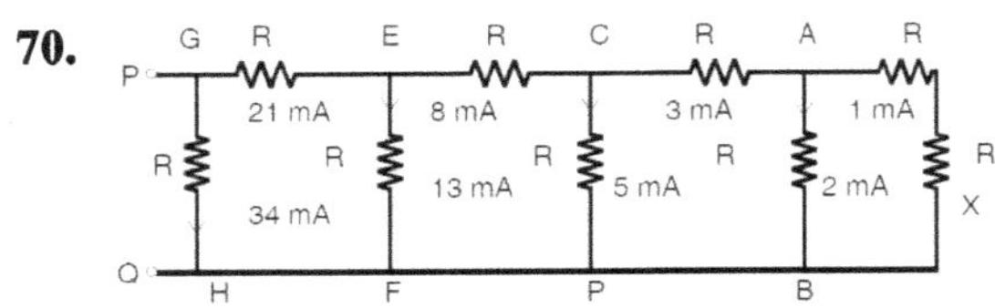

Using KCL

At point A Current is 3 mA

At point C Current is 8 mA

At point E Current is 21 mA

At point G Current through GH is 34 mA

$\therefore \qquad V_{PQ} = V_{GH} = i\,R_{GH}$

$= 34$ V.

71. $2H_2(g) \ + \ O_2(g) \ \rightarrow \ 2H_2O(l)$

0.2 mole 0.1 mole 0.2 mole

moles of gas remaining = 9.7

at constant (T) & (V)

$$\frac{n_1}{n_2} = \frac{p_1}{p_2}$$

$$\frac{10}{9.7} = \frac{1}{p_2} \ \& \ p_2 = 0.97.$$

72. $2NH_3 + H_2SO_4 \rightarrow (NH_4)_2SO_4$

10ml

2M

$$\text{millimole of } H_2SO_4 = \frac{\text{mmol of } NH_3}{2} = 20$$

$$\text{mmol of } NH_3 = \text{mmol of N} = 40$$

$$W_N = \frac{40 \times 14}{1000} = \frac{560}{1000} = 0.56 \text{ g}$$

$$\% \text{ of N} = \frac{0.56}{2} \times 100 = 28.$$

73. 1.125 L of H_2 produced by 0.1 equivalent of metal

1.85 L of H_2 will be produced by = $\frac{0.1 \times 1.85}{1.125}$ equivalents

$\therefore$ No of gram equivalent of metal

$$= \frac{2}{\text{Equivalent weight}} = \frac{2}{x}$$

$$\therefore \quad \frac{0.1}{1.125} \times 1.85 = \frac{2}{x}$$

$x = 12.16.$

74. $CaO + C \rightarrow CaC_2 + CO_2$

$CaC_2 + H_2O \rightarrow HC \equiv CH + Ca(OH)_2$

$3HC \equiv CH \xrightarrow[\text{Fe}]{\text{Red-hot}}$ (benzene).

Kishore Vaigyanik Protsahan Yojana (KVPY)

STREAM – SA

Part-I

Mathematics

1. Let x, y, z be three non-negative integers such that $x + y + z = 10$. The maximum possible value of $xyz + xy + yz + zx$ is:

A. 52 B. 64
C. 69 D. 73

2. If a, b are natural numbers such that $2013 + a^2 = b^2$, then the minimum possible value of ab is:

A. 671 B. 668
C. 658 D. 645

3. The number of values of b for which there is an isosceles triangle with sides of length $b + 5$, $3b - 2$ and $6 - b$ is:

A. 0 B. 1
C. 2 D. 3

4. Let a, b be non-zero real numbers. Which of the following statements about the quadratic equation $ax^2 + (a + b)x + b = 0$ is necessarily true?

(I) It has at least one negative root
(II) It has at least one positive root.
(III) Both its roots are real.

A. (I) and (II) only B. (I) and (III) only
C. (II) and (III) only D. All of them

5. Let x, y, z be non-zero real numbers such that $\frac{x}{y}+\frac{y}{z}+\frac{z}{x}=7$ and $\frac{y}{x}+\frac{z}{y}+\frac{x}{z}=9$, then $\frac{x^3}{y^3}+\frac{y^3}{z^3}+\frac{z^3}{x^3}-3$ is equal to:

A. 152 B. 153
D. 154 D. 155

6. In a triangle ABC with $\angle A < \angle B < \angle C$, points D, E, F are on the interior of segments BC, CA, AB, respectively. Which of the following triangles CANNOT be similar to ABC?

A. Triangle ABD B. Triangle BCE
C. Triangle CAF D. Triangle DEF

7. Tangents to a circle at points P and Q on the circle intersect at a point R. If PQ = 6 and PR = 5, then the radius of the circle is:

A. $\frac{13}{3}$ B. 4
C. $\frac{15}{4}$ D. $\frac{16}{5}$

8. In an acute-angled triangle ABC, the altitudes from A, B, C when extended intersect the circumcircle again at points A_1, B_1, C_1, respectively. If $\angle ABC = 45°$ then $\angle A_1B_1C_1$ equals:

A. 45° B. 60°
C. 90° D. 135°

9. In a rectangle ABCD, points X and Y are the midpoints of AD and DC, respectively. Lines BX and CD when extended intersect at E, lines BY and AD when extended intersect at F. If the area of ABCD is 60 then the area of BEF is:

A. 60 B. 80
C. 90 D. 120

10. In the figure given below, ABCDEF is a regular hexagon of side length 1, AFPS and ABQR are squares. Then the ratio Area (APQ)/ Area (SRP) equals:

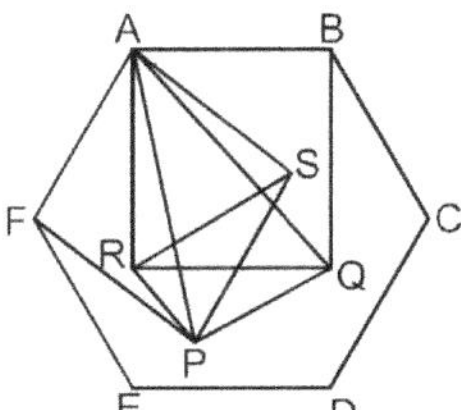

A. $\frac{\sqrt{2}+1}{2}$ B. $\sqrt{2}$
C. $\frac{3\sqrt{3}}{4}$ D. 2

11. A person X is running around a circular track completing one round every 40 seconds. Another person Y running in the opposite direction meets X every 15 second. The time, expressed in seconds, taken by Y to complete one round is:

A. 12.5 B. 24
C. 25 D. 55

12. The least positive integer n for which $\sqrt{n+1}-\sqrt{n-1}<0.2$ is:

A. 24 B. 25
C. 26 D. 27

13. How many natural numbers n are there such that $n! + 10$ is a perfect square?

A. 1
B. 2
C. 4
D. infinitely many

14. Ten points lie in a plane so that no three of them are collinear. The number of lines passing through exactly two of these points and dividing the plane into two regions each containing four of the remaining points is

A. 1
B. 5
C. 10
D. dependent on the configuration of points

15. In a city, the total income of all people with salary below ₹ 10000 per annum is less than the total income of all people with salary above ₹ 10000 per annum. If the salaries of people in the first group increases by 5% and the salaries of people in the second group decreases by 5% then the average income of all people

A. increases
B. decreases
C. remains the same
D. cannot be determined from the data

Physics

16. A man inside a freely falling box throws a heavy ball towards a side wall. The ball keeps on bouncing between the opposite walls of the box. We neglect air resistance and friction. Which of the following figures depicts the motion of the centre of mass of the entire system (man, the ball and the box)?

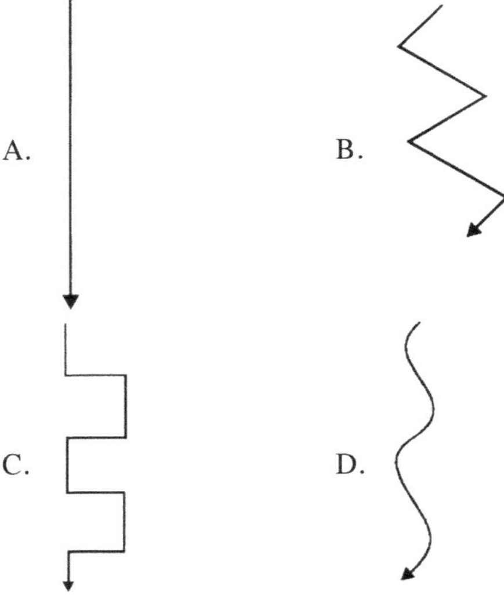

17. A ball is thrown horizontally from a height with a certain initial velocity at time $t = 0$. The ball bounces repeatedly from the ground with the coefficient of restitution less than 1 as shown.

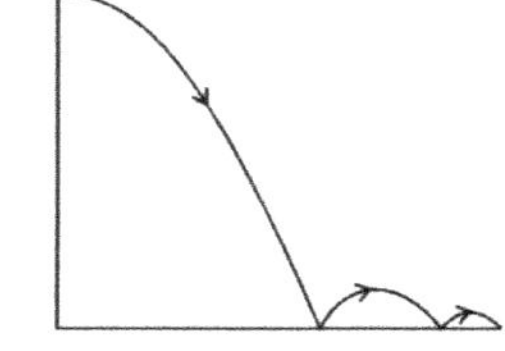

Neglect air resistance and taking the upward direction as positive, which figure qualitatively depicts the vertical component of the ball's velocity (V_y) as a function of time (t)?

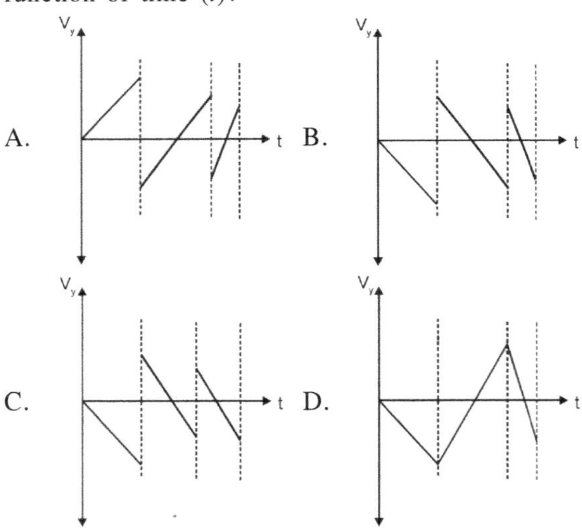

18. A tall tank filled with water has an irregular shape as shown. The wall CD makes an angle of 45° with the horizontal; the wall AB is normal to the base BC. The lengths AB and CD are much smaller than the height h of water (figure not to scale).

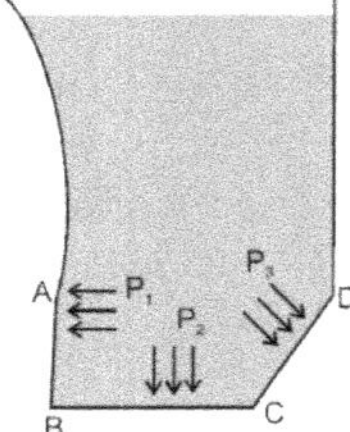

Let P_1, P_2 and P_3 be the pressures exerted by the water on the wall AB, base BC and the wall CD respectively. Density of water is ρ and g is acceleration due to gravity. Then, approximately:

A. $P_1 = P_2 = P_3$ B. $P_1 = 0, P_3 = \frac{1}{\sqrt{2}} P_2$

C. $P_1 = P_3 = \frac{1}{\sqrt{2}} P_2$ D. $P_1 = P_3 = 0, P_2 = h\rho g$

19. The accompanying graph of position x versus time t represents the motion of a particle. If p and q are both positive constants, the expression that best describes the acceleration α of the particle is:

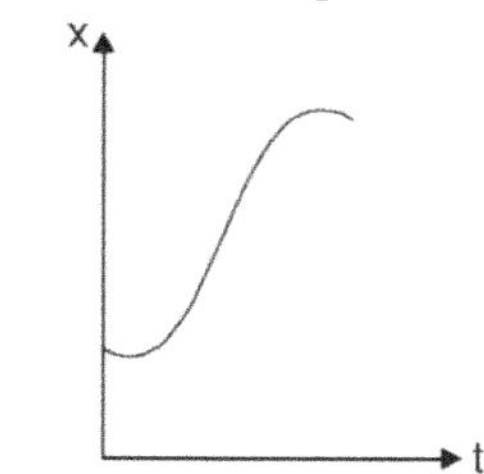

A. $a = -p - qt$ B. $a = -p + qt$

C. $a = p + qt$ D. $a = p - qt$

20. Two stones of mass m_1 and m_2 (such that $m_1 > m_2$) are dropped Δt time apart from the same height towards the ground. At a later time t the difference in their speed is ΔV and their mutual separation is ΔS. While both stones are in flight

A. ΔV decreases with time and ΔS increases with time

B. Both ΔV and ΔS increase with time

C. ΔV remains constant with time and ΔS decreases with time

D. ΔV remains constant with time and ΔS increases with time

21. The refractive index of a prism measured using three lines of a mercury vapour lamp. If μ_1, μ_2 and μ_3 are the measured refractive indices for these green, blue and yellow lines respectively, then

A. $\mu_2 > \mu_3 > \mu_1$ B. $\mu_2 > \mu_1 > \mu_3$

C. $\mu_3 > \mu_2 > \mu_1$ D. $\mu_1 > \mu_2 > \mu_3$

22. A horizontal parallel beam of light passes through a vertical convex lens of focal length 20 cm and is then reflected by a tilted plane mirror so that it converges to a point I. The distance PI is 10 cm.

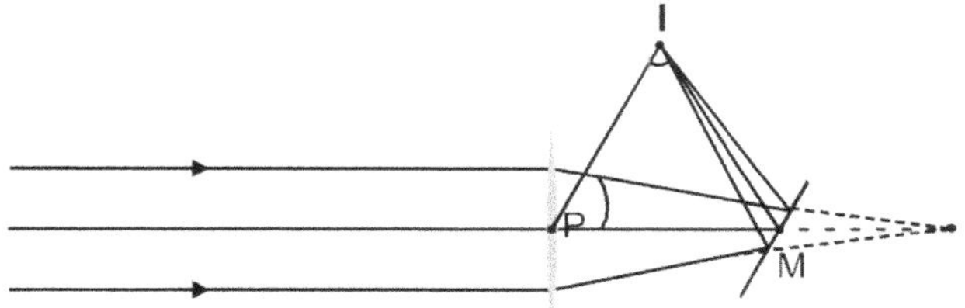

M is a point at which the axis of the lens intersects the mirror. The distance PM is 10 cm. The angle which the mirror makes with the horizontal is

A. 15° B. 30°

C. 45° D. 60°

23. In a car a rear view mirror having a radius of curvature 1.50 m forms a virtual image of a bus located 10.0 m from the mirror. The factor by which the mirror magnifies the size of the bus is close to:

A. 0.06 B. 0.07

C. 0.08 D. 0.09

24. Consider the circuit shown in the figure below:

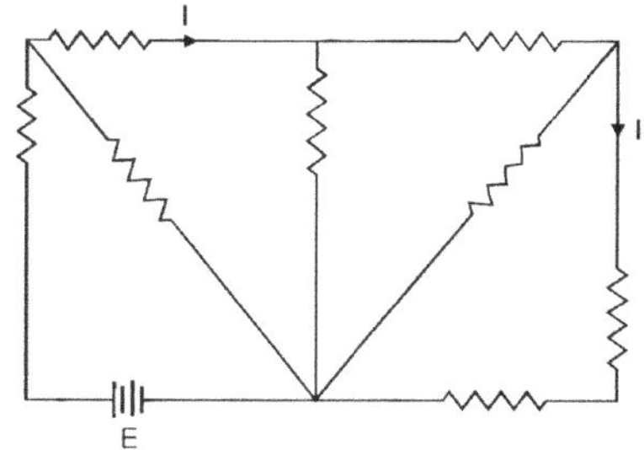

All the resistors are identical. The ratio I/I′ is:

A. 8 B. 6

C. 5 D. 4

25. The figure shows a bar magnet and a metallic coil. Consider four situations.

(I) Moving the magnet away from the coil.

(II) Moving the coil towards the magnet.

(III) Rotating the coil about the vertical diameter.

(IV) Rotating the coil about its axis.

An emf in the coil will be generated for the following situations.

A. (I) and (II) only B. (I), (II) and (IV) only

C. (I), (II) and (III) only D. (I), (II), (III) and (IV)

26. A current of 0.1 A flows through a 25 Ω resistor represented by the circuit diagram. The current in the 80 Ω resistor is:

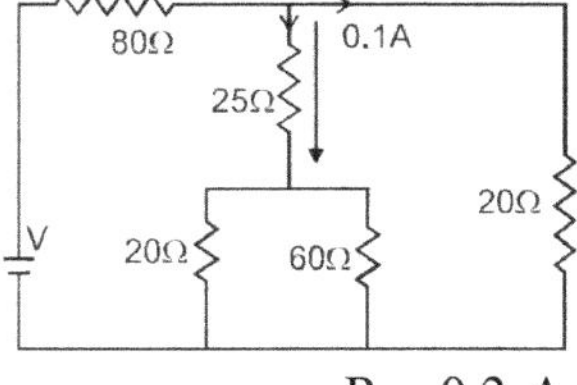

A. 0.1 A B. 0.2 A

C. 0.3 A D. 0.4 A

27. Solar energy is incident normally on the earth's surface at the rate of about 1.4 kW m^{-2}. The distance between the earth and the sun is 1.5×10^{11} m. Energy (E) and mass (m) are related by Einstein equation $E = mc^2$ where c (3×10^8 ms^{-1}) is the speed of light in free space. The decrease in the mass of the sun is:

A. 10^9 kg s^{-1} B. 10^{30} kg s^{-1}

C. 10^{26} kg s^{-1} D. 10^{11} kg s^{-1}

28. If the current through a resistor in a circuit increases by 3%, the power dissipated by the resistor
A. increases approximately by 3%
B. increases approximately by 6%
C. increases approximately by 9%
D. decreases approximately by 3%

29. An ideal gas filled in a cylinder occupies volume V. The gas is compressed isothermally to the volume V/3. Now the cylinder valve is opened and the gas is allowed to leak keeping temperature same. What percentage of the number of molecules escape to bring the pressure in the cylinder back to its original value.
A. 66% B. 33%
C. 0.33% D. 0.66%

30. An electron enters a chamber in which a uniform magnetic field is present as shown

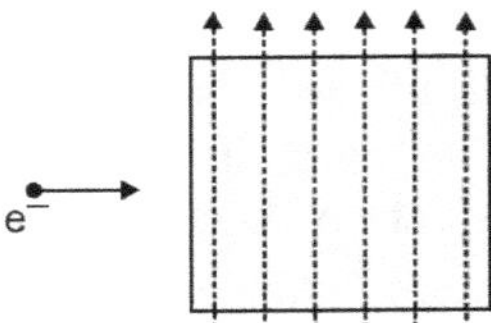

An electric field of appropriate magnitude is also applied so that the electron travels undeviated without any change in its speed through the chamber. We are ignoring gravity. Then, the direction of the electric field is
A. opposite to the direction of the magnetic field
B. opposite to the direction of the electron's motion
C. normal to the plane of the paper and coming out of the plane of the paper
D. normal to the plane of the paper and into the plane of the paper

Chemistry

31. The molecule having a formyl group is:
A. acetone
B. acetaldehyde
C. acetic acid
D. acetic anhydride

32. The structure of cis-3-hexene is:

A. 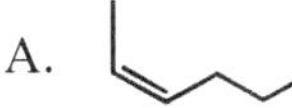 B. 

C.  D. 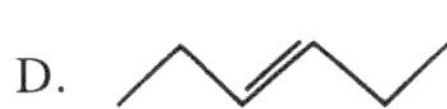

33. The number of sp^2 hybridized carbon atoms in

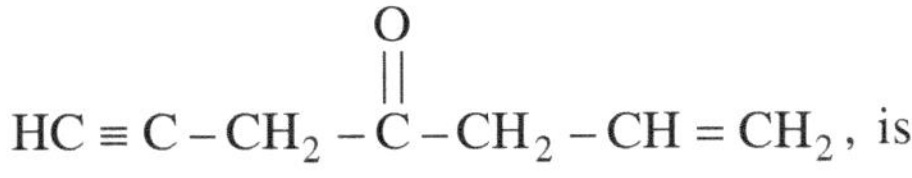

$$HC \equiv C-CH_2-\overset{\overset{\displaystyle O}{\|}}{C}-CH_2-CH=CH_2$$, is:

A. 3 B. 5
C. 4 D. 6

34. The number of valence electrons in an atom with electronic configuration $1s^2\ 2s^2\ 2p^6\ 3s^2\ 3p^3$ is:
A. 2 B. 3
C. 5 D. 11

35. The pair of atoms having the same number of neutrons is:
A. ${}^{12}_{6}C$, ${}^{24}_{12}Mg$ B. ${}^{23}_{11}Na$, ${}^{19}_{9}F$
C. ${}^{23}_{11}Na$, ${}^{24}_{12}Mg$ D. ${}^{23}_{11}Na$, ${}^{39}_{19}K$

36. Which of the following molecules has no dipole moment?
A. CH_3Cl B. $CHCl_3$
C. CH_2Cl_2 D. CCl_4

37. The decay profiles of three radioactive species A, B and C are given below:

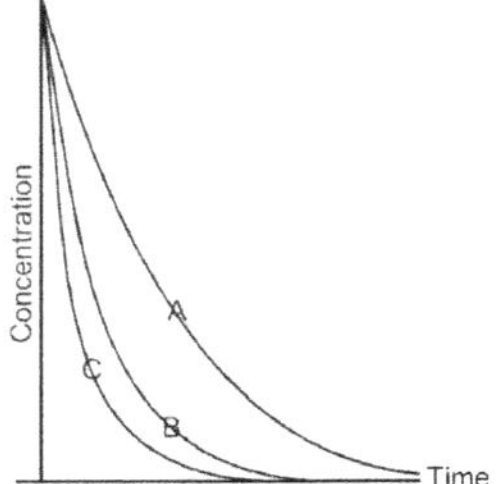

These profiles imply that the decay constants k_A, k_B and k_C follow the order:
A. $k_A > k_B > k_C$ B. $k_A > k_C > k_B$
C. $k_B > k_A > k_C$ D. $k_C > k_B > k_A$

38. A specific volume of H_2 requires 24 s to diffuse out of a container. The time required by an equal volume of O_2 to diffuse out under identical conditions, is:
A. 24 s B. 96 s
C. 384 s D. 192 s

39. Acetic acid reacts with sodium metal at room temperature to produce:
A. CO_2 B. H_2
C. H_2O D. CO

40. The equilibrium constant, K_C for $3C_2H_2(g) \rightleftharpoons C_6H_6(g)$ is 4 $L^2\ mol^{-2}$. If the equilibrium concentration of benzene is 0.5 mol L^{-1}, that of acetylene in mol L^{-1} must be:
A. 0.025 B. 0.25
C. 0.05 D. 0.5

41. The weight percent of sucrose (formula weight = 342 g mol^{-1}) in an aqueous solution is 3.42. The density of the solution is 1 g mL^{-1}, the concentration of sucrose in the solution in mol L^{-1} is:
A. 0.01 B. 0.1
C. 1.0 D. 10

42. The order of reactivity of K, Mg, Au and Zn with water is:
A. K > Zn > Mg > Au B. K > Mg > Zn > Au
C. K > Au > Mg > Zn D. Au > Zn > K > Mg

43. Which of the following is an anhydride?

A. O O H_3C C CH_3 B. O H_3C O O CH_3

C. O H_3C O CH_3 O D. O H_3C O CH_3

44. Which of the following metals will precipitate copper from copper sulphate solution?
A. Hg B. Sn
C. Au D. Pt

45. The radii of the first Bohr orbit of H (r_H), He^+ (r_{He^+}) and Li^{2+} ($r_{Li^{2+}}$) are in the order:
A. $r_{He^+} > r_H > r_{Li^{2+}}$
B. $r_H < r_{He^+} < r_{Li^{2+}}$
C. $r_H > r_{He^+} > r_{Li^{2+}}$
D. $r_{He^+} < r_H < r_{Li^{2+}}$

Biology

46. The Bowman's capsule, a part of the kidney is the site of:
A. filtration of blood constituents
B. re-absorption of water and glucose
C. formation of ammonia
D. formation of urea

47. In human brain the sensation of touch, pain and temperature is controlled by the
A. parietal lobe of cerebrum
B. limbic lobe of cerebrum
C. temporal lobe of cerebrum
D. frontal lobe of cerebrum

48. A pathogen which can not be cultured in an artificial medium is:
A. protozoan B. virus
C. becterium D. fungus

49. Meiosis I and Meiosis II are characterised by the separation of:
A. homologous chromosomes; sister chromatids
B. sister chromatids; homologous chromosomes
C. centromere; telomere
D. telomere; centromere

50. People suffering from albinism cannot synthesize:
A. suberin B. melanin
C. keratin D. collagen

51. Short sightedness in humans can be corrected by using:
A. concave lens B. convex lens
C. cylindrical lens D. plain glass

52. A person with blood group "A" can (a) donate blood to, and (b) receive blood from:
A. (a) persons with blood group "AB", and (b) persons with any blood group
B. (a) person with blood group "A" or "AB", and (b) "A" or "O" blood groups
C. (a) person with blood group "B" or "AB", and (b) "B" or "O" blood groups
D. (a) person with any blood group, and (b) "O" blood group only

53. Animal cells after removal of nuclei still contained DNA. The source of this DNA is:
A. nucleosomes B. mitochondria
C. peroxisomes D. lysosome

54. Which one of the following combinations is found in DNA?
A. Guanine and guanidine B. Guanidine and cytosine
C. Guanine and cytosine D. Adenine and guanidine

55. Which one of the following is NOT a mode of asexual reproduction?
A. Binary fission B. Multiple fission
C. Budding D. Conjugation

56. Which one of the following class of animals constitutes the largest biomass on earth?
A. Insects B. Fish
C. Mammals D. Reptilians

57. In the digestive system, the pH of the stomach and the intestine, respectively are:
A. alkaline; acidic B. acidic; alkaline
C. acidic; neutral D. acidic; acidic

58. The major nitrogenous excretory product in mammals is:
A. amino acids B. ammonia
C. urea D. uric acid

59. Which of the following plant traits (characters) is NOT an adaptation to dry (Xeric) habitats?
A. Sunken stomata on leaves
B. Highly developed root system
C. Thin epidermis without a cuticle on stem and leaves
D. Small leaves and photosynthetic stem

60. Biological diversity increases with the productivity of an ecosystem. In which of the following habitats do we see the greatest diversity of species?
A. Tropical dry grasslands
B. Temperate deciduous forests
C. Alpine grasslands
D. Tropical evergreen forests

Part-II

Mathematics

61. Let a, b, c, d, e be natural numbers in an arithmetic progression such that $a + b + c + d + e$ is the cube of an integer and $b + c + d$ is square of an integer. The least possible value of the number of digits of c is:

A. 2 B. 3
C. 4 D. 5

62. On each face of a cuboid, the sum of its perimeter and its area is written. Among the six numbers so written, there are three distinct numbers and they are 16, 24 and 31. The volume of the cuboid lies between:

A. 7 and 14 B. 14 and 21
C. 21 and 28 D. 28 and 35

63. Let ABCD be a square and let P be point on segment CD such that DP : PC = 1 : 2. Let Q be a point on segment AP such that $\angle BQP = 90°$. Then the ratio of the area of quadrilateral PQBC to the area of the square ABCD is:

A. $\frac{31}{60}$ B. $\frac{37}{60}$
C. $\frac{39}{60}$ D. $\frac{41}{60}$

64. Suppose the height of a pyramid with a square base is decreased by $p\%$ and the lengths of the sides of its square base are increased by $p\%$ (where $p > 0$). If the volume remains the same, then:

A. $50 < p < 55$ B. $55 < p < 60$
C. $60 < p < 65$ D. $65 < p < 70$

65. There are three kinds of liquids X, Y, Z. Three jars J_1, J_2, J_3 contain 100 ml of liquids X, Y, Z, respectively. By an operation we mean three steps in the following order:

– stir the liquid in J_1 and transfer 10 ml from J_1 into J_2;
– stir the liquid in J_2 and transfer 10 ml from J_2 into J_3;
– stir the liquid in J_3 and transfer 10 ml from J_3 into J_1;

After performing the operation four times, let x, y, z be the amounts of X, Y, Z, respectively, in J_1. Then

A. $x > y > z$ B. $x > z > y$
C. $y > x > z$ D. $z > x > y$

Physics

66. Two identical uniform rectangular blocks (with longest side L) and a solid sphere of radius R are to be balanced at the edge of a heavy table such that the centre of the sphere remains at the maximum possible horizontal distance from the vertical edge of the table without toppling as indicated in the figure.

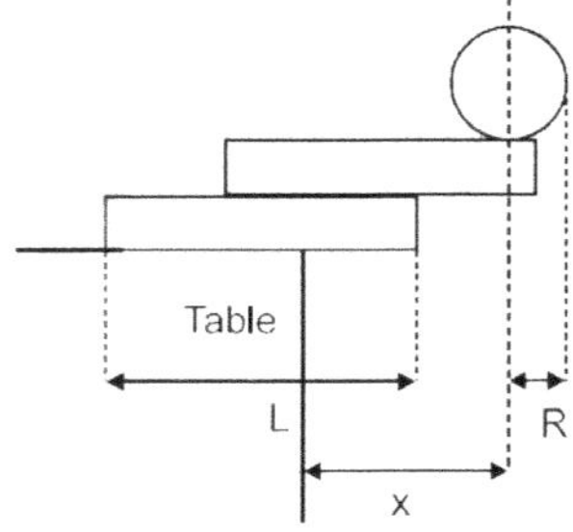

If the mass of each block is M and of the sphere is M/2, then the maximum distance x that can be achieved is:

A. 8L/15 B. 5L/6
C. (3L/4 + R) D. (7L/15 + R)

67. Two skaters P and Q are skating towards each other. Skater P throws a ball towards W every 5 s such that it always leaves her hand with speed 2 ms^{-1} with respect to the ground. Consider two cases:

(I) P runs with speed 1 ms^{-1} towards Q while Q remains stationary.

(II) Q runs with speed 1 ms^{-1} towards P while P remains stationary.

Note that irrespective of speed of P, ball always leaves P's hand with speed 2 ms^{-1} with respect to the ground. Ignore gravity. Balls will be received by Q.

A. one every 2.5 s in case (I) and one every 3.3 s in case (II)
B. one every 2 s in case (I) and one every 4 s in case (II)
C. one every 3.3 s in case (I) and one every 2.5 s in case (II)
D. one every 2.5 s in case (I) and one every 2.5 s in case (II)

68. A 10.0 W electrical heater is used to heat a container filled with 0.5 kg of water. It is found that the temperature of the water and the container rise by 3 K in 15 minutes. The container is then emptied, dried, and filled with 2 kg of an oil. It is now observed that the same heater raises the temperature of the container-oil system by 2 K in 20 minutes. Assuming no other heat losses in any of the processes, the specific heat capacity of the oil is:

A. 2.5×10^3 JK^{-1} kg^{-1} B. 5.1×10^3 JK^{-1} kg^{-1}
C. 3.0×10^3 JK^{-1} kg^{-1} D. 1.5×10^3 JK^{-1} kg^{-1}

69. A ray of light incident on a transparent sphere at an angle $\pi/4$ and refracted at an angle r, emerges from the sphere after suffering one internal reflection. The total angle of deviation of the ray is:

A. $\frac{3\pi}{2} - 4r$ B. $\frac{\pi}{2} - 4r$

C. $\frac{\pi}{4} - r$ D. $\frac{5\pi}{2} - 4r$

70. An electron with an initial speed of 4.0×10^6 ms^{-1} is brought to rest by an electric field. The mass and charge of an electron are 9×10^{-31} kg and 1.6×10^{-19} C, respectively. Identify the correct statement

A. The electron moves from a region of lower potential to higher potential through a potential difference of 11.4 μV.

B. The electron moves from a region of higher potential to lower potential through a potential difference of 11.4 μV.

C. The electron moves from a region of lower potential to higher potential through a potential difference of 45 V.

D. The electron moves from a region of higher potential to lower potential through a potential difference of 45 V.

Chemistry

71. The degree of dissociation of acetic acid (0.1 mol L^{-1}) in water (K_a of acetic acid is 10^{-5}) is:

A. 0.01 B. 0.5

C. 0.1 D. 1.0

72. Compound 'X' on heating with Zn dust gives compound 'Y' which on treatment with O_3 followed by reaction with Zn dust gives propionaldehyde. The structure of 'X' is:

A. 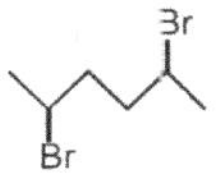 B.

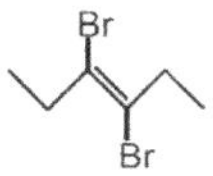

C. 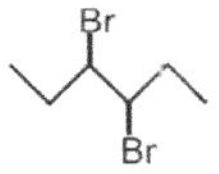 D.

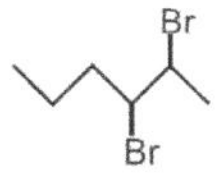

73. The amount of metallic Zn (Atomic weight = 65.4) required to react with aqueous sodium hydroxide to produce 1 g of H_2, is:

A. 32.7 g B. 98.1 g

C. 65.4 g D. 16.3 g

74. Natural abundances of ^{12}C and ^{13}C isotopes of carbon are 99% and 1%, respectively. Assuming they only contributes to the mol. wt. of C_2F_4, the percentage of C_2F_4 having a molecular mass of 101 is:

A. 1.98 B. 98

C. 0.198 D. 99

75. 2, 3-Dimethylbut-2-ene when reacted with bromine forms a compound which upon heating with alcoholic KOH produce the following major product:

A. 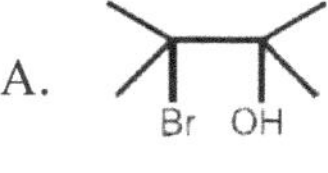

B.

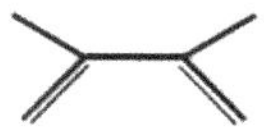

C.

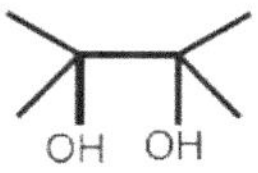

D. 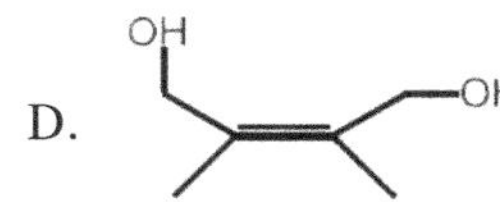

Biology

76. Sister chromatids of a chromosome have:

A. different genes at the same locus

B. different alleles of the same gene at the same locus

C. same alleles of the same gene at the same locus

D. same alleles at different loci

77. A diabetic individual becomes unconscious after self-administering insulin. What should be done immediately to revive the individual?

A. Provide him sugar

B. Give him high dose of insulin

C. Provide him salt solution

D. Provide him lots of water

78. A regular check on the unborn baby of a lady towards the end of her pregnancy showed a heart rate of 80 beats per minute. What would the doctor infer about the baby's heart condition from this?

A. Normal heart rate

B. Faster heart rate

C. Slower heart rate

D. Defective brain function

79. Three uniformly watered plants (*i*), (*ii*) and (*iii*) were kept in 45% relative humidity, 45% relative humidity with blowing wind and 95% relative humidity, respectively. Arrange these plants in the order (faster to slowest) in which they will dry up.

A. (*i*), (*ii*), (*iii*) B. (*ii*), (*i*), (*iii*)

C. (*iii*), (*ii*), (*i*) D. (*iii*), (*i*), (*ii*)

80. Many population colonising a new habitat show a logistic population growth pattern over time, as shown in the figure below.

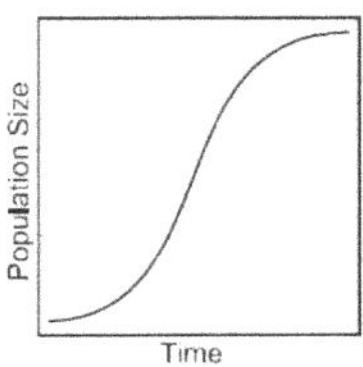

In such a population, the POPULATION growth rate

A. stays constant over time

B. increases and then reaches an asymptote

C. decreases over time

D. increases to a maximum and then decreases

ANSWERS

1	2	3	4	5	6	7	8	9	10
C	C	C	B	C	A	C	C	C	D
11	**12**	**13**	**14**	**15**	**16**	**17**	**18**	**19**	**20**
B	C	A	B	B	A	B	A	D	D
21	**22**	**23**	**24**	**25**	**26**	**27**	**28**	**29**	**30**
B	D	B	A	C	C	A	B	A	D
31	**32**	**33**	**34**	**35**	**36**	**37**	**38**	**39**	**40**
B	C	A	C	C	D	D	B	B	D
41	**42**	**43**	**44**	**45**	**46**	**47**	**48**	**49**	**50**
B	B	A	B	C	A	A	B	A	B
51	**52**	**53**	**54**	**55**	**56**	**57**	**58**	**59**	**60**
A	B	B	C	D	A	B	C	C	D
61	**62**	**63**	**64**	**65**	**66**	**67**	**68**	**69**	**70**
B	D	D	C	B	A	A	A	A	D
71	**72**	**73**	**74**	**75**	**76**	**77**	**78**	**79**	**80**
A	C	A	A	B	B	A	C	B	D

EXPLANATORY ANSWERS

1. Let three numbers are

$x + 1, y + 1, z + 1$

We, know that, AM $\geq$ GM

$$\frac{(x+1)+(y+1)+(z+1)}{3} \geq \{(x+1)(y+1)(z+1)\}^{1/3}$$

$$\left(\frac{13}{3}\right)^3 \geq xyz + xy + yz + zx + 11$$

$$\left(\frac{13}{3}\right)^3 - 11 \geq xyz + xy + yz + zx$$

equality hold when $x = y = z$, but $x + y + z = 10$ and x, y, z are integers.

So, maximum value when any two of x, y, z are equal to 3 and third is equal to 4.

$\therefore$ $x = y = 3$ and $z = 4$

So the maximum value of $xyz + xy + yz + zx$

$= 3 \times 3 \times 4 + 3 \times 3 + 3 \times 4 + 4 \times 3$

$= 36 + 9 + 12 + 12 = 69.$

2. $(b - a)(b + a) = 2013 = 3 \times 11 \times 61$

ab minimum when $b - a = 33$

$b + a = 61$

$a = 14$

$ab = 14 \times 47 = 658.$

3. Case-I $b + 5 = 3b - 2$

$\Rightarrow$ $b = \frac{7}{2}$

So, sides are $\frac{17}{2}, \frac{17}{2}, \frac{5}{2}$

Case-II $b + 5 = 6 - b = b = \frac{1}{2}$

Sides $\frac{11}{2}, \frac{-1}{2}, \frac{11}{2}$ Not possible

Case-III $3b - 2 = 6 - b$

$4b = 8$

$b = 2$

7, 4, 4, two cases are possible.

4. $ax^2 + (a + b)x + b = 0$

$(x + 1)(ax + b) = 0$ roots are $-1, \frac{-b}{a}$.

5. $a^3 + b^3 + c^3 - 3abc$

$= [a + b + c] [(a + b + c)^2 - 3(ab + bc + ca)]$

$= [7] [(7)^2 . 3(9)]$

$= 7(49 - 27) = 7 \times 22 = 154.$

6.

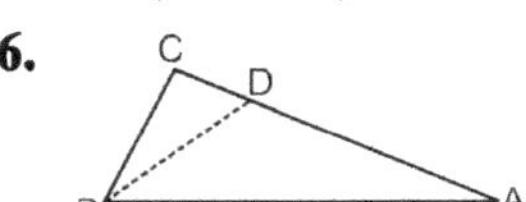

In ΔABD greatest angles is $\angle$D which is greater by $\angle$C. So, ΔABD is not similar to ΔABC.

7. PR and QR are two tangent of the circle, let the radius of circle is 'r'

$\angle OPQ = \theta$

$\therefore$ $\angle PRQ = \theta$

In ΔRCP $\Rightarrow$ $\cos\theta = \frac{4}{5}$

In ΔPCO $\Rightarrow$ $\cos\theta = \frac{3}{r}$

$\therefore$ $\frac{4}{5} = \frac{3}{r}$, $4r = 15$, $r = \frac{15}{4}$.

8.

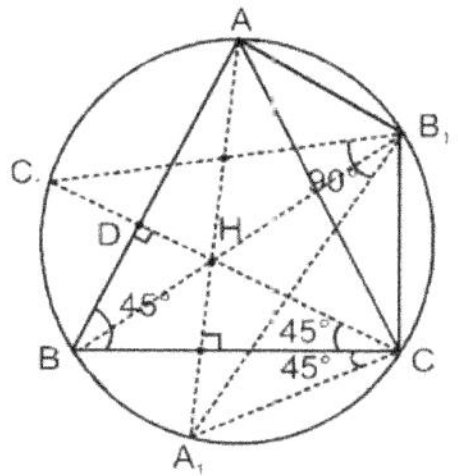

$\angle BCH = 45° = \angle BCA_1$

$\angle C_1CA_1 = \angle C_1B_1A_1 = 90°.$

9.

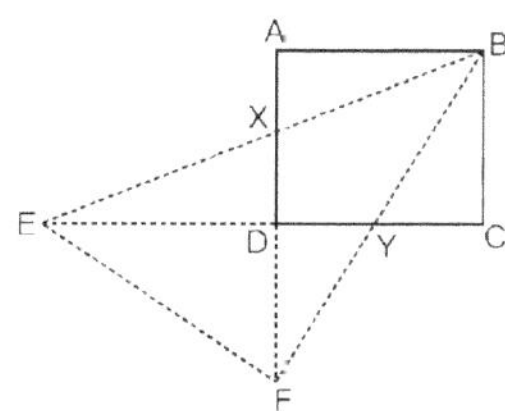

Let, $AB = x$, $BC = y$, $xy = 60$

$\Delta XED \simeq \Delta XBA$

and $\Delta DFY \simeq \Delta CBY$

$$\Delta BEF = \square BXDY + \Delta XED + \Delta DFY + \Delta DEF$$
$$= 60 + \Delta DEF$$
$$= 60 + \frac{1}{2} \times xy$$

$60 + 30 = 90.$

10. In ΔAPQ, $AP = AQ = \sqrt{2}$

$\angle APQ = 30°$

In ΔSRP, $SR = SP = 1$

$\angle RSP = 30°$

$\angle FAB = 120°$

$\angle BAS = \angle FAB - \angle FAS$

$= 120° - 90° = 30°$

$\angle SAR = \angle BAR - \angle BAS = 60°$

In ΔARS, $\cos 60° = \dfrac{1+1-SR^2}{2.1.1}$ $[\because AR = AS = 1]$

$\Rightarrow$ $SR = 1$

Now, $\angle RSP = \angle ASP - \angle ASR$

$= 90° - 60° = 30°$

$[\because$ ASR is equilateral$]$

Now, from $\Delta SRP \Rightarrow RP = \dfrac{\sqrt{3}-1}{2\sqrt{2}}$

In ΔAPR,

$$\cos \angle RAP = \frac{(\sqrt{2})^2 + 1^2 - PR^2}{2\sqrt{2}}$$

$\Rightarrow$ $\cos \angle RAP = 15°$

$\angle PAQ = \angle RAQ - \angle RAP = 45° - 15° = 30°$

$$\text{Now, } \frac{ar(\Delta APQ)}{ar(\Delta SRP)} = \frac{\frac{1}{2} \times \sqrt{2} \times \sqrt{2} \sin 30°}{\frac{1}{2} \times 1 \times 1 \times \sin 30°} = 2.$$

11. $\theta = \dfrac{2\pi}{40} \times 15 = 2\pi - \dfrac{2\pi}{n} \times 15$

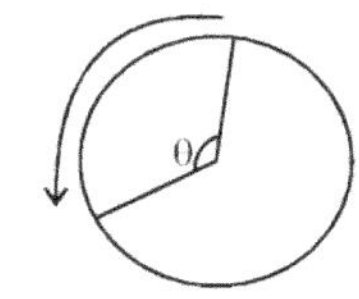

$\therefore$ $\dfrac{3}{8} = 1 - \dfrac{15}{n}$

$\Rightarrow$ $n = 24.$

12. $\sqrt{n+1} < 0.2 + \sqrt{n-1}$

squaring, $1.96 < .4\sqrt{n-1}$

again squaring $(4.9)^2 + 1 < n.$

13. If $n = 1, 2, 4, 5$, $n! + 10$ is not a perfect square

If $n = 3$, $n! + 10$ is a perfect square

If $n > 5$

$n! + 10 = \underline{10}\ \dfrac{[3 \times 4 \times 6 \ldots .xn + 1]}{1}$

$\downarrow$ even; $[3 \times 4 \times 6 \ldots .xn + 1]$ is odd

than exponent of 2 is one so it is not a perfect square.

14.

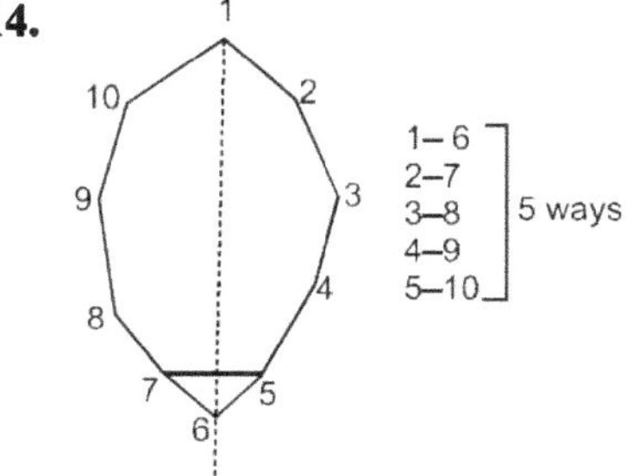

15. Let total number of people with salary below ₹ 10000 per annum is x and salary is A. Let total number of people with salary above ₹ 10000 per annum is y and salary is B then.

$$xA - yB < 0$$

$$\frac{\text{average after}}{\text{average before}} = \frac{x\left(\frac{105}{100}A\right) + y\left(\frac{95}{100}B\right)}{xA + yB}$$

$$= 1 + \frac{5}{100}\left(\frac{xA - yB}{xA + yB}\right).$$

17. As, $V_y = U_y - gt$

$V_y = -gt + U_y$

The slope of the curve is $-g$ and the curve will be shrink as time increases.

Hence, option (B) represents the graph.

19. From graph V first increases then decreases

Hence a is earlier positive then negative

$a = P - qt.$

20. ΔV = Const and ΔS increases with time.

21. $\mu(\lambda) = B + \dfrac{C}{\lambda^2} + \ldots$

$\mu_2 > \mu_1 > \mu_3.$

22.

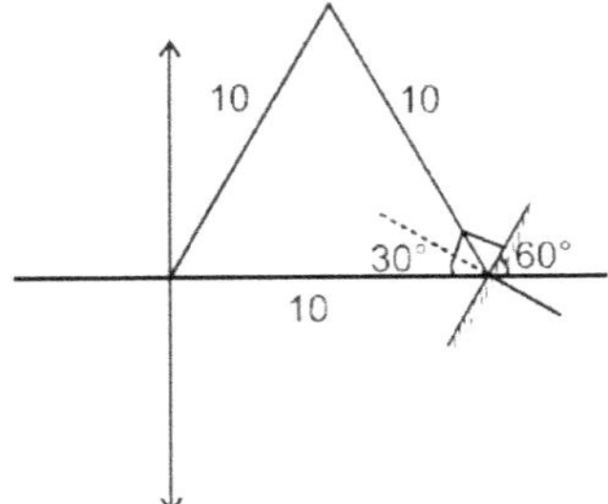

23.

$$u = -10 \text{ m}$$
$$R = 1.5 \text{ m}$$
$$\frac{1}{v} + \frac{1}{u} = \frac{2}{R}$$
$$\frac{1}{v} - \frac{1}{10} = \frac{2}{1.5}$$
$$v = \frac{30}{43}$$
$$m = -\frac{v}{u} = \frac{30}{43 \times 10} \simeq 0.07.$$

24. 

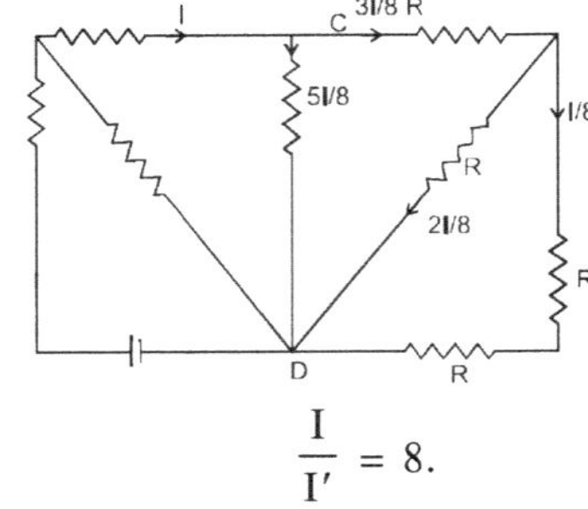

$$\frac{I}{I'} = 8.$$

25. No EMF induce if ring rotate about its own axis ($\because \Delta\phi = 0$)

Hence, I, II & IV are correct.

26.

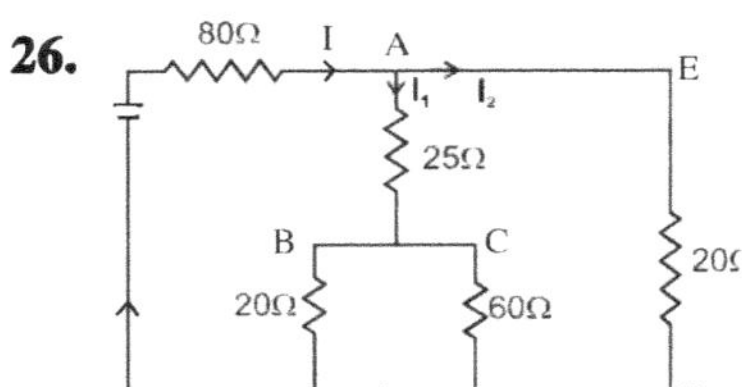

We have, $I_1 = 0.1$ A

$$V_{AD} = V_{EF} \text{ (parallel)}$$
$$0.1 \times \left(25 + \frac{20 \times 60}{20 + 60}\right) = I_2 \times 20$$
$$I_2 = 0.2 \text{ A}$$

Hence, I through 80 Ω, By Kirchoff junction rule at point A

$I = I_1 + I_2 = 0.1 + 0.2 = 0.3$ A.

27. E Radiated by Sun

$$E = 4\pi r^2 \times 1.4 \text{ kW} = mc^2$$
$$E = 4\pi \times (1.5 \times 10^{11})^2 \times 1.4 \times 10^3$$
$$= m.(3 \times 10^8)^2$$
$$m = \frac{4 \times 22 \times (1.5)^2 \times 1.4 \times 10^9}{7 \times 9} = 10^9 \text{ kg/s.}$$

28.

$$P = I^2R$$
$$\frac{\Delta P}{P} = \frac{2\Delta I}{I} = 6\%.$$

29.

$$\frac{P_1V_1}{n_1} = \frac{P_2V_2}{n_2}$$
$$\frac{P_1V}{n_1} = \frac{P_1.\frac{V}{3}}{n_2} \Rightarrow n_2 = \frac{n_1}{3}$$

Now, $\frac{2}{3}$ of Gas will come out to make the presence P_1. Hence, 66.66%.

30. $q\vec{E} + q(\vec{V} \times \vec{B}) = 0$

Hence, into the paper.

31. (*a*) $CH_3-\underset{\underset{O}{||}}{C}-CH_3$ (*b*) $CH_3-\underset{\underset{O}{||}}{C}-H$

(*c*) $CH_3-\underset{\underset{O}{||}}{C}-OH$ (*d*) $CH_3-\underset{\underset{O}{||}}{C}-O-\underset{\underset{O}{||}}{C}-CH_3$

$CH_3-\underset{\underset{O}{||}}{C}-H$ has formal group.

32.

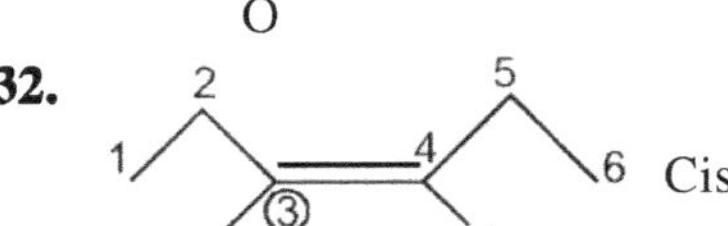

Cis-3-Hexene

33. $\overset{sp}{HC} \equiv \overset{sp}{C} - \overset{sp^3}{CH_2} - \underset{sp^2}{\overset{\overset{O}{||}}{C}} - \overset{sp^3}{CH_2} - \overset{sp^2}{CH} = \overset{sp^2}{CH_2}$.

36. CCl_4 has zero dipole moment due to its tetrahedral shape, all C–Cl bond moment cancel each other.

37. $C_t = C_0e^{-kt}$.

38.

$$\frac{r_{O_2}}{r_{H_2}} = \sqrt{\frac{M_{H_2}}{M_{O_2}}} ; \frac{r_{O_2}}{r_{H_2}} = \sqrt{\frac{2}{32}} = \frac{1}{4}$$

$$r_{O_2} : r_{H_2} = 1 : 4.$$

39. $2CH_3COOH + 2Na \longrightarrow 2CH_3COONa + H_2 \uparrow$

40.

$$K_c = \frac{[C_6H_6]}{[C_2H_2]^3}$$
$$4 = \frac{0.5}{[C_2H_2]^3}$$
$$[C_2H_2]^3 = \frac{0.5}{4} = \frac{1}{8}$$
$$[C_2H_2] = \frac{1}{2} = 0.5.$$

41. 3.42 gm sucrose in 100 gm solution

$$d = 1 \text{ gm ml}^{-1}$$

$$\because \quad d = \frac{\text{mass}}{\text{volume}}$$

$$\text{volume of solution} = \frac{100}{1} = 100 \text{ ml}$$

$$\text{Molarity} = \frac{n}{v} \times 1000$$

$$\text{Molarity} = \frac{3.42}{342 \times 100} \times 1000 = 0.1.$$

42. E^0_{red} = K < Mg < Zn < Au.

43. $-\underset{\underset{O}{\|}}{C}-O-\underset{\underset{O}{\|}}{C}-$; an hydride group.

44. E^0_{red} = Sn < Cu < Hg < Au.

45.
$$r = 0.529 \times \frac{n^2}{z}$$

$$r \,\alpha\, \frac{1}{z}$$

So, correct order is $r_H > r_{He^+} > r_{Li^{2+}}$.

46. In Bowman's capsule ultrafiltration of blood occur.

47. Parietal lobe is sensory lobe for touch, pain temperature.

48. Virus multiplies only in living cells.

49. Meiosis I – Reduction Division ($2n \longrightarrow n$), Separation of Homologous Chromosomes results in reduction of chromosome ploidy to half.

Meiosis II – Similar to mitosis sister chromatids separate.

50. Melanin pigment synthesized from Tyrosine amino acid impart colour to skin.

51. Image is formed before retina in short sightedness.

53. Mitochondria have circular DNA.

54. Guanine and Cytosine are nitrogenous bases of DNA.

55. Conjugation involves transfer of DNA from one microbe to another. (*e.g.* Bacteria).

57. pH stomach = 1.5 – 2.5

Intestine = 7.4 – 7.6.

58. NH_3 is converted to urea in hepatocytes.

59. Thick cuticle prevent loss of water.

61.
$$a = C - 2D$$
$$b = C - D$$
$$c = C$$
$$d = C + D$$
$$e = C + 2D$$
$$a + b + c + d + e = 5C = \lambda^3$$
$$b + c + d = 3C = \mu^2$$
$$\Rightarrow \quad 3\lambda^3 = 5\mu^2$$
$$\frac{\lambda^3}{5} = \frac{\mu^2}{3} \text{ least possibility}$$
$$\lambda = 5 \times 3, \ \mu = 5 \times 3 \times 3$$
$$\lambda = 15, \ \mu = 45$$
$$C = \frac{(45)^2}{3} = 15 \times 45 = 675.$$

62.
$$2(a + b) + ab = 16 \quad \text{... } (i)$$
$$2(b + c) + bc = 24 \quad \text{... } (ii)$$
$$2(c + a) + ca = 31 \quad \text{... } (iii)$$

From equation (*ii*) and equation (*iii*)

$$\Rightarrow \quad (a - b)(2 + c) = 7 \quad \text{... } (iv)$$

From equation (*ii*) and equation (*iv*)

$$\Rightarrow \quad 4a = 2 + 5b \quad \text{... } (v)$$

Solve equations (*i*) and (*v*)

$$b = 2, \ a = 3, \ c = 5$$

Volume = 30.

63.
$$CP = \frac{2}{3}a$$ 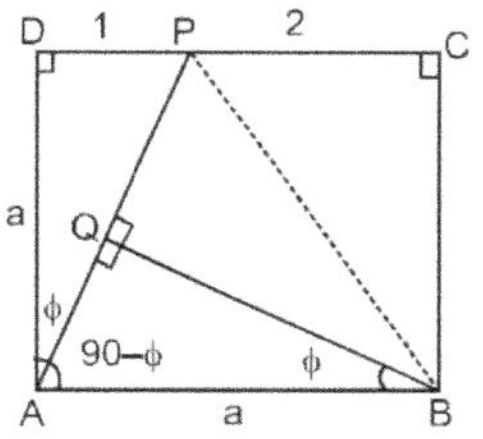
$$PD = \frac{a}{3}$$

Let, $\angle PAD = \phi$

$$\tan\phi = \frac{1}{3} (\text{In } \Delta APD)$$

Now, $\angle DAP = \angle QBA = \phi$

$$\text{Required ratio} = \frac{\text{area of PQBC}}{a^2}$$

$$= \frac{a^2 - (\text{area of } \Delta ADP + \text{area of } \Delta AQB)}{a^2}$$

$$\Rightarrow 1 - \left(\frac{1}{6} + \frac{3}{20}\right) = \frac{41}{60}.$$

64.
$$\frac{1}{3}(x^2)y = \frac{1}{3}x^2\left(\frac{100+p}{100}\right)^2\left(\frac{100-p}{100}\right)$$

$$\Rightarrow p^2 + 100p - 100^2 = 0$$

$$p = \sqrt{12500} - 50$$

$$60 < p < 65.$$

65. After one operation amount of x, y, z in J, respectively are

$$90 + 10 \times \left(\frac{1}{11}\right)^2, \ 100\left(\frac{1}{11}\right)^2, \ \frac{100}{11}$$

Similarly we can find after four operations amount of x, y, z in J_1.

66.

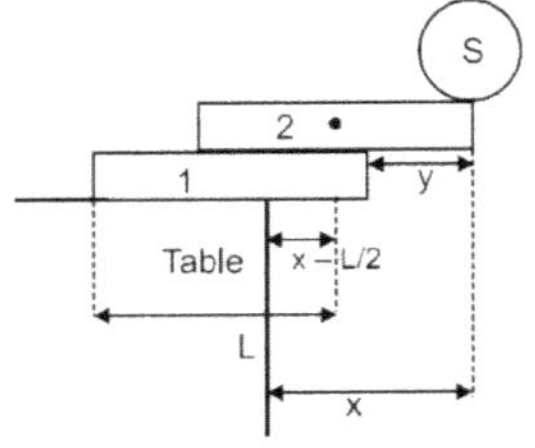

2 + S System lie above edge of 1.

$$\frac{M}{2}y - M\left(\frac{L}{2} - y\right) = 0$$

$$\frac{y}{2} + y = \frac{L}{2}$$

$$y = \frac{L}{3}$$

Now, 1 + 2 + S centre of mass will be above the table

$$\frac{3M}{2}\left(x - \frac{L}{3}\right) + M\left(x - \frac{L}{3} - \frac{L}{2}\right) = 0$$

$$\frac{3x}{2} - \frac{L}{2} + x - \frac{L}{3} - \frac{L}{2} = 0$$

$$\frac{5x}{2} = \frac{4L}{3}$$

$$x = \frac{8L}{15}.$$

67. (i) Let initial distance between P and Q is x.

At $t_1 = \frac{x}{2}$ a receive the ball.

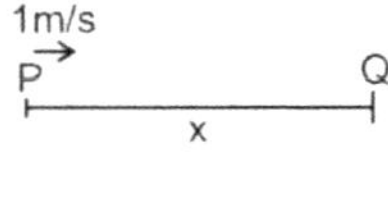

Next ball, $t_2 = \frac{x-5}{2} + 5$

$$\Delta t = \frac{5}{2}$$

(ii) In second case

1m/s
P
Q
x

At t = 0 P throws the ball.

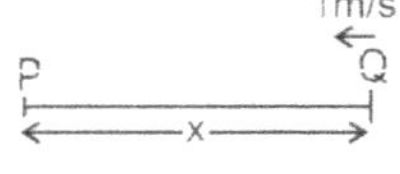

$$t_1 = \frac{x}{3}$$

Next ball, $t_2 = \frac{x-5}{3} + 5$

$$\Delta t = \frac{10}{3}.$$

68.

$$Pt = m_w S_w \Delta T + m_c s_c \Delta T$$

$$10 \times 15 \times 60 = 0.5 \times 4200 \times 3 + m_c s_c \times 3$$

$$9000 = 6300 + m_c s_c \times 3$$

$$m_c s_c = 900 \text{ J/k}.$$

Now, for oil

$$10 \times 20 \times 60 = 2 \times S_0 \times 2 + 900 \times 2$$

$$12000 - 1800 = 4 S_0$$

$$S_0 = \frac{10200}{4} = 2.51 \times 10^3 \text{ Jk}^{-1}\text{kg}^{-1}.$$

69.

$$S_1 = \frac{\pi}{4} - r$$

$$S_2 = \pi - 2r$$

$$S_3 = \frac{\pi}{4} - r$$

$$S = S_1 + S_2 + S_3$$

$$= \frac{3\pi}{2} - 4r.$$

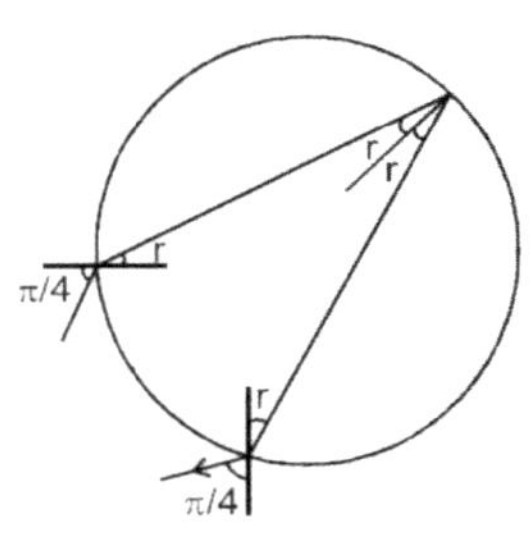

70.

$$qV = \frac{1}{2}mv^2$$

$$V = \frac{1}{2}\frac{mv^2}{q}$$

$$V = \frac{1}{2} \times \frac{9 \times 10^{-31} \times (4 \times 10^6)^2}{1.6 \times 10^{-19}} = 45\text{V}$$

45 V from higher to lower potential.

71.

$$C = 0.1 \text{ M}$$

$$K_a = 10^{-5}$$

$$K_a = \alpha^2 C$$

$$10^{-5} = \alpha^2 \times 0.1$$

$$\alpha^2 = 10^{-4}$$

$$\alpha = 10^{-2}.$$

72.

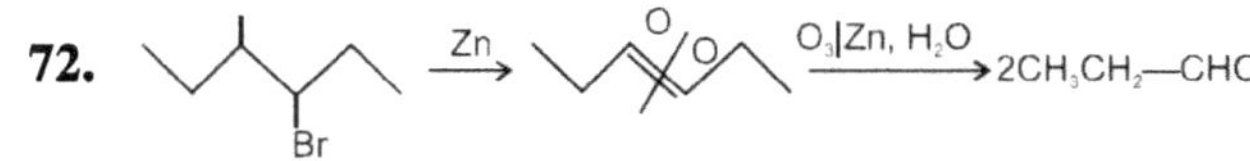

73. $Zn + 2OH^- + 2H_2O \rightarrow [Zn(OH_4)]^{2-} + H_2$

2 gm (1 mole) H_2 is given by 65.4 gm of Zn

1 gm is given by $\frac{65.4}{2}$ gm of Zn.

74. Percentage of C_2F_4 of Molar mass 100

$$= \frac{1}{100} \times \frac{1}{100} \times 100 = 0.01\%.$$

Percentage of C_2F_4 of Molar mass 102

$$= \frac{99}{100} \times \frac{99}{100} \times 100 = 98.01\%$$

Percentage of C_2F_4 of Molar mass 101

$$= 100 - (0.01 + 98.01) = 1.98\%.$$

75.

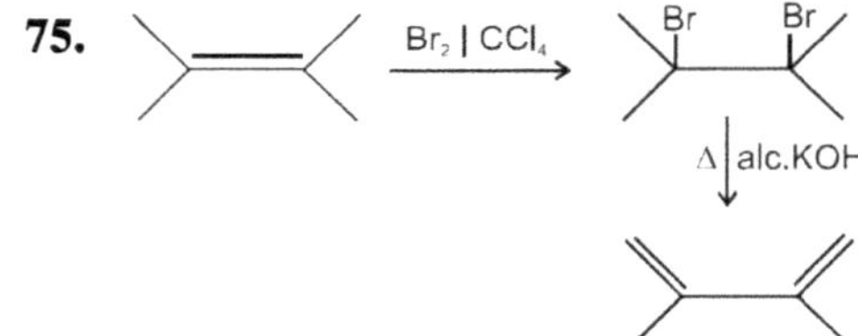

77. Insulin lowers blood sugar level and in this case brain is getting inadequate sugar/ glucose.

78. Infants have higher heart rate.

Kishore Vaigyanik Protsahan Yojana (KVPY)

STREAM – SA

Part-I

Mathematics

1. Let $f(x)$ be a quadratic polynomial with $f(2) = 10$ and $f(-2) = -2$. Then the coefficient of x in $f(x)$ is:

A. 1 B. 2
C. 3 D. 4

2. The square-root of $\frac{(0.75)^3}{1-(0.75)} + (0.75 + (0.75)^2 + 1)$ is:

A. 1 B. 2
C. 3 D. 4

3. The sides of a triangle are distinct positive integers in an arithmetic progression. If the smallest side is 10, the number of such triangles is:

A. 8 B. 9
C. 10 D. infinitely many

4. If a, b, c, d are positive real numbers such that $\frac{a}{3} = \frac{a+b}{4} = \frac{a+b+c}{5} = \frac{a+b+c+d}{6}$, then $\frac{a}{b+2c+3d}$ is:

A. $\frac{1}{2}$ B. 1
C. 2 D. not determinable

5. For $\frac{2^2+4^2+6^2+...+(2n)^2}{1^2+3^2+5^2+...+(2n-1)^2}$ to exceed 1.01, the maximum value of n is:

A. 99 B. 100
C. 101 D. 150

6. In triangle ABC, let AD, BE and CF be the internal angle bisectors with D, E and F on the sides BC, CA and AB respectively. Suppose AD, BE and CF concur at I and B, D, I, F are concyclic, then $\angle$IFD has measure

A. 15° B. 30°
C. 45° D. any value ≤ 90°

7. A regular octagon is formed by cutting congruent isosceles right-angled triangles from the corners of a square. If the square has side-length 1, the side-length of the octagon is:

A. $\frac{\sqrt{2}-1}{2}$ B. $\sqrt{2}-1$
C. $\frac{\sqrt{5}-1}{4}$ D. $\frac{\sqrt{5}-1}{3}$

8. A circle is drawn in a sector of a larger circle of radius, r, as shown in the adjacent figure. The smaller circle is tangent to the two bounding radii and the arc of the sector. The radius of the small circle is:

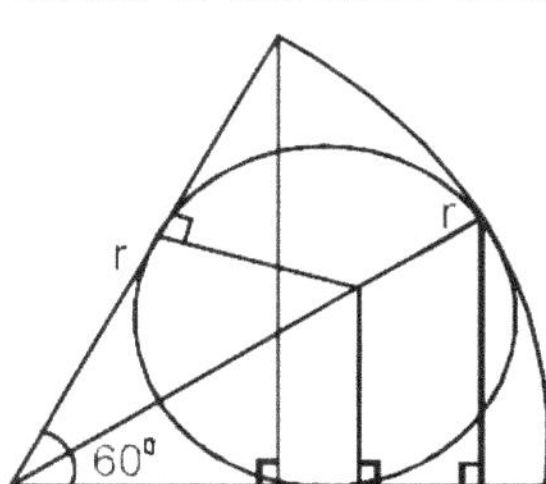

A. $\frac{r}{2}$ B. $\frac{r}{3}$
C. $\frac{2\sqrt{3}r}{5}$ D. $\frac{r}{\sqrt{2}}$

9. In the figure, AKHF, FKDE and HBCK are unit squares; AD and BF intersect in X. Then the ratio of the areas of triangles AXF and ABF is:

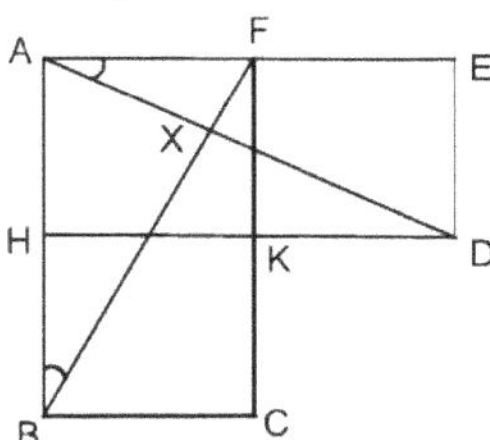

A. $\frac{1}{4}$ B. $\frac{1}{5}$
C. $\frac{1}{6}$ D. $\frac{1}{8}$

10. Suppose Q is a point on the circle with centre P and radius 1, as shown in the figure; R is a point outside the circle such that QR = 1 and ∠QRP = 2°. Let S be the point where the segment RP intersects the given circle. Then measure of ∠RQS equals:

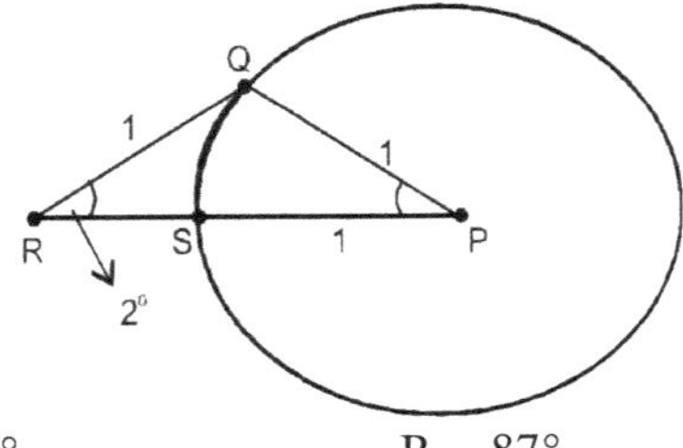

A. 86° B. 87°
C. 88° D. 89°

11. Observe that, at any instant, the minute and hour hands of a clock make two angles them whose sum is 360°. At 6:15 the difference between these two angles is
A. 165° B. 170°
C. 175° D. 180°

12. Two workers A and B are engaged to do a piece of work. Working alone, A takes 8 hours more to complete the work than if both worked together. On the other hand, working alone, B would need $4\frac{1}{2}$ hours more to complete the work than if both worked together. How much time would they take to complete the job working together?
A. 4 hours B. 5 hours
C. 6 hours D. 7 hours

13. When a bucket is half full, the weight of the bucket and the water is 10 kg. When the bucket is two-thirds full, the total weight is 11 kg. What is the total weight, in kg, when the bucket is completely full?

A. 12 B. $12\frac{1}{2}$

C. $12\frac{2}{3}$ D. 13

14. How many ordered pairs of (m, n) integers satisfy $\frac{m}{12} = \frac{12}{n}$?
A. 30 B. 15
C. 12 D. 10

15. Let S = {1, 2, 3, ..., 40} and let A be a subset of S such that no two elements in A have their sum divisible by 5. What is the maximum number of elements possible in A?
A. 10 B. 13
C. 17 D. 20

Physics

16. A clay ball of mass m and speed v strikes another metal ball of same mass m, which is at rest. They stick together after collision. The kinetic energy of the system after collision is:
A. $mv^2/2$ B. $mv^2/4$
C. $2\,mv^2$ D. mv^2

17. A ball falls vertically downward and bounces off a horizontal floor. The speed of the ball just before reaching the floor (u_1) is equal to the speed just after leaving contact with the floor (u_2); $u_1 = u_2$. The corresponding magnitudes of accelerations are denoted respectively by a_1 and a_2. The air resistance during motion is proportional to speed and is not negligible. If g is acceleration due to gravity, then:
A. $a_1 < a_2$ B. $a_1 = a_2 \neq g$
C. $a_1 > a_2$ D. $a_1 = a_2 = g$

18. Which of the following statements is true about the flow of electrons in an electric circuit?
A. Electrons always flow from lower to higher potential
B. Electrons always flow from higher to lower potential
C. Electrons flow from lower to higher potential except through power sources
D. Electrons flow from higher to lower potential, except through power sources

19. A boat crossing a river moves with a velocity v relative to still water. The river is flowing with a velocity $v/2$ with respect to the bank. The angle with respect to the flow direction with which the boat should move to minimize the drift is:
A. 30° B. 60°
C. 150° D. 120°

20. In the Arctic region hemispherical houses called Igloos are made of ice. It is possible to maintain inside an Igloo as high as 20ºC because:
A. ice has high thermal conductivity
B. ice has low thermal conductivity
C. ice has high specific heat
D. ice has higher density than water

21. In the figure below, PQRS denotes the path followed by a ray of light as it travels three media in succession. The absolute refractive indices of the media are μ_1, μ_2 and μ_3 respectively. (The line segment RS′ in the figure is parallel to PQ). Then:

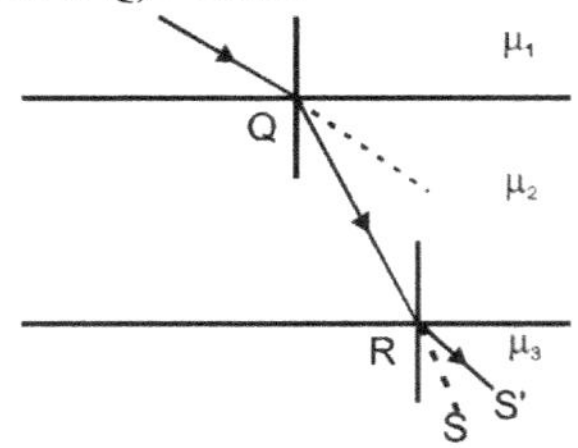

A. $\mu_1 > \mu_2 > \mu_3$ B. $\mu_1 < \mu_2 < \mu_3$
C. $\mu_1 = \mu_3 < \mu_2$ D. $\mu_1 < \mu_3 < \mu_2$

22. A ray of white light is incident on a spherical water drop whose centre is C as shown below. When observed from the opposite side, the emergent light:

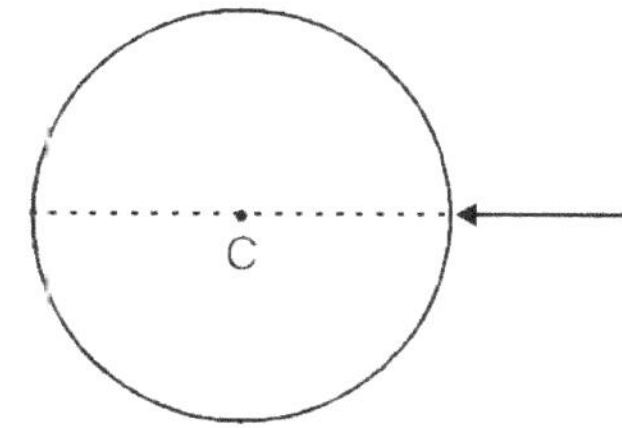

A. will be white and will emerge without deviating
B. will be internally reflected
C. will split into different colours such that the angles of deviation will be different for different colours
D. will split into different colours such that the angles of deviation will be same for all colours

23. A convex lens of focal length 15 cm is placed infront of a plane mirror at a distance 25 cm from the mirror. Where on the optical axis and from the centre of the lens should a small object be placed such that the final image coincides with the object:
A. 15 cm and on the opposite side of the mirror
B. 15 cm and between the mirror and the lens
C. 7.5 cm and on the opposite side of the mirror
D. 7.5 cm and between the mirror and the lens

24. Following figures show different combinations of identical bulb(s) connected to identical battery(ies). Which option is correct regarding the total power dissipated in the circuit?

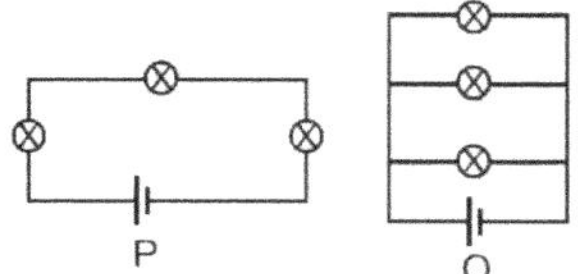

A. P < Q < R < S B. R < Q < P < S
C. P < Q < R = S D. P < R < Q < S

25. A circular metallic ring of radius R has a small gap of width d. The coefficient of thermal expansion of the metal is α in appropriate units. If we increase the temperature of the ring by an amount ΔT, then width of the gap:
A. will increase by an amount $d\alpha\Delta T$
B. will not change
C. will increase by an amount $(2\pi R - d)\alpha\Delta T$
D. will decrease by an amount $d\alpha\Delta T$

26. A girl holds a book of mass m against a vertical wall with a horizontal force F using her finger so that the book does not move. The frictional force on the book by the wall is:
A. F and along the finger but pointing towards the girl
B. μF upwards where μ is the coefficient of static friction
C. mg and upwards
D. equal and opposite to the resultant of F and mg

27. A solid cube and a solid sphere both made of same material are completely submerged in water but to different depths. The sphere and the cube have same surface area. The buoyant force is:
A. greater for the cube than the sphere
B. greater for the sphere than the cube
C. same for the sphere and the cube
D. greater for the object that is submerged deeper

28. ${}^{238}_{92}U$ atom disintegrates to ${}^{214}_{84}Po$ with a half life of 4.5×10^9 years by emitting six alpha particle and n electrons. Here n is:
A. 6 B. 4
C. 10 D. 7

29. Which statement about the Rutherford model of the atom is NOT true?
A. There is a positively charged centre in an atom called the nucleus
B. Nearly all the mass of an atom resides in the nucleus
C. Size of the nucleus is comparable to the atom
D. Electrons occupy the space surrounding the nucleus

30. A girl brings a positively charged rod near a thin neutral stream of water from a tap. She observes that the water stream bends towards her. Instead, if she were to bring a negatively charged rod near to the stream, it will:
A. bend in the same direction
B. bend in the opposite direction
C. not bend at all
D. bend in the opposite direction above and below the rod

Chemistry

31. The weight of calcium oxide formed by burning 20 g of calcium in excess oxygen is:
A. 36 g B. 56 g
C. 28 g D. 72 g

32. The major products in the reaction
$Br_3CCHO \xrightarrow{NaOH}$ are:

A. $CHBr_3$ + H–C(=O)–ONa
B. NaBr + (H)(HO)C=C(Br)(Br)
C. NaOBr + D–C(=O)–H
D. Br_3C–CH_2–OH + Br_3C–C(=O)–ONa

33. The number of electrons plus neutrons in ${}^{40}_{19}K^{+}$ is:

A. 38 B. 59
C. 39 D. 40

34. Among the following, the most basic oxide is:

A. Al_2O_3 B. P_2O_5
C. SiO_2 D. Na_2O

35. By dissolving 0.35 mole of sodium chloride in water, 1.30 L of salt solution is obtained. The molarity of the resulting solution should be reported as:

A. 0.3 B. 0.269
C. 0.27 D. 0.2692

36. Among the quantities, density (ρ), temperature (T), enthalpy (H), heat capacity (C_p), volume (V) and pressure (P), a set of intensive variables are:

A. (ρ, T, H) B. (H, T, V)
C. (V, T, C_p) D. (ρ, T, P)

37. The value of 'x' in $KAl(SO_4)_x$, $12H_2O$ is:

A. 1 B. 2
C. 3 D. 4

38. Among the following substituted pyridines, the most basic compound is:

A. 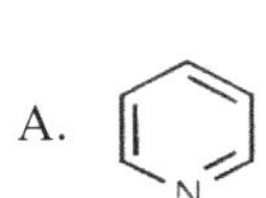

B. 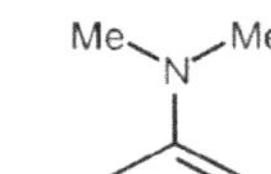

C. 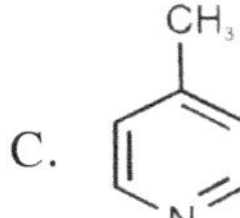

D. Cl-substituted pyridine (Cl at 4-position, N)

39. The major product in the following reaction is:

$H_3C - C \equiv C - H + HBr$ (excess)

A. $CH_2=C(CH_3)Br$ B. $H_3C-CBr_2-CH_3$
C. $H_3C-CH(Br)-CH_2Br$ D. $H_3C-CH_2-CHBr_2$

40. The major product in the following at 25°C is:

$CH_3COOH \xrightarrow{CH_3CH_2NH_2}$

A. $CH_3CONHCH_2CH_3$
B. $CH_3CH=NCH_2CH_3$
C. $NH_3^{+}CH_2CH_3.CH_3COO^{-}$
D. $CH_3CON=CHCH_3$

41. A reaction with reaction quotient Q_C and equilibrium constant K_C, will proceed in the direction of the products when:

A. $Q_C = K_C$ B. $Q_C < K_C$
C. $Q_C > K_C$ D. $Q_C = 0$

42. Acetylsalicylic acid is a pain killer and is commonly known as:

A. paracetamol B. aspirin
C. ibuprofen D. penicillin

43. The molecule which does not exhibit strong hydrogen bonding is:

A. methyl amine B. acetic acid
C. diethyl ether D. glucose

44. The following two compounds are:

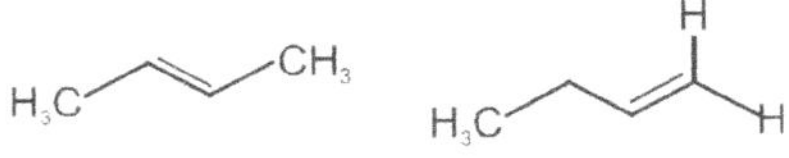

A. geometrical isomers
B. positional isomers
C. functional group isomers
D. optical isomers

45. The graph that does not represent the behaviour of an ideal gas is:

A. 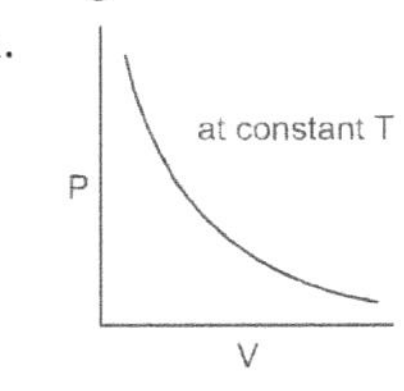

B. 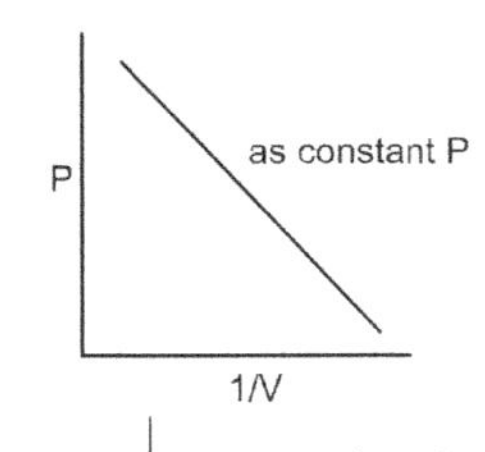

C. 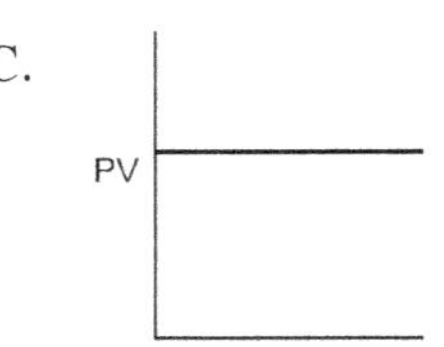

D. 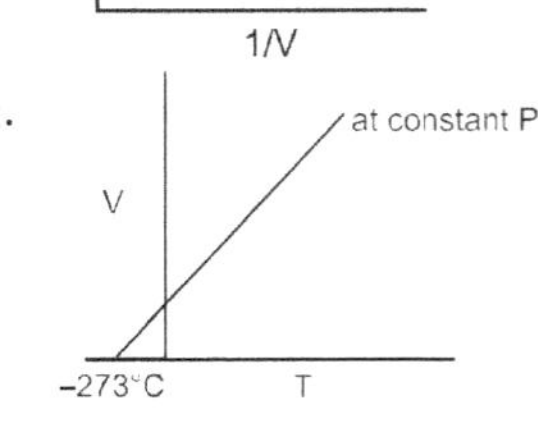

Biology

46. A smear of blood from a healthy individual is stained with a nuclear stain called hematoxylin and then observed under a light microscope. Which of the following cell type would be highest in number?

A. neutrophils
B. lymphocytes
C. eosinophils
D. monocytes

47. Which of the following biological phenomenon involves a bacteriophage?

A. transformation B. conjugation
C. translocation D. transduction

48. In which compartment of cell does the process of glycolysis takes place?

A. Golgi complex B. cytoplasm
C. mitochondria D. ribosome

49. Huntingtion's disease is disease of the:
A. nervous system B. circulatory system
C. respiratory system D. excretory system

50. A cell will experience the highest level of endosmosis when it is kept in:
A. distilled water B. sugar solution
C. salt solution D. protein solution

51. When the leaf of the 'touch-me-not' (chui-mui, *Minosa pudica*) plant is touched, the leaf droops because:
A. a nerve signal passes through the plant
B. the temperature of the plant increases
C. water is lost from the cell at the base of the leaf
D. the plant dies

52. If you are seeing mangroves around you, which part to India are you visiting?
A. Western Ghats B. Thar desert
C. Sunderbans D. Himalayas

53. Myeloid tissue is a type of:
A. haematopoietic tissue B. cartilage tissue
C. muscular tissue D. areolar tissue

54. The heart of an amphibian is usually:
A. two chambered B. three chambered
C. four chambered D. three and half chambered

55. Gigantism and acromegaly are due to defects in the function of the following gland:
A. adrenals B. thyroid
C. pancreas D. pituitary

56. The pH of 10^{-8} M HCl solution is:
A. 8 B. close to 7
C. 1 D. 0

57. Which one of the following organelles can synthesize some of its own proteins?
A. lysosome B. Golgi apparatus
C. vacuole D. mitochondrion

58. Maltose is a polymer of:
A. one glucose and one fructose molecule
B. one glucose and galactose molecule
C. two glucose molecules
D. two fructose molecules

59. The roots of some higher plants get associated with a fungal partner. The roots provide food to the fungus while the fungus supplies water to the roots. The structure so formed is known as:
A. lichen B. anabaena
C. mycorrhiza D. rhizobium

60. Prehistoric forms of life are found in fossils. The probability of finding fossils of more complex organisms:
A. increases from lower to upper strata
B. decreases from lower to upper strata
C. remains constant in each stratum
D. uncertain

Part-II

Mathematics

61. Let a, b, c be positive integers such that $\frac{a\sqrt{2}+b}{b\sqrt{2}+c}$ is a rational number, then which of the following is always an integer?
A. $\frac{2a^2+b^2}{2b^2+c^2}$ B. $\frac{a^2+b^2-c^2}{a+b-c}$
C. $\frac{a^2+2b^2}{b^2+2c^2}$ D. $\frac{a^2+b^2+c^2}{a+c-b}$

62. The number of solutions (x, y, z) to the system of equations $x + 2y + 4z = 9$, $4yz + 2xz + xy = 13$, $xyz = 13$, such that at least two of x, y, z are integers is:
A. 3 B. 5
C. 6 D. 4

63. In a triangle ABC, it is known that AB = AC. Suppose D is the mid-point of AC and BD = BC = 2. Then the area of the triangle ABC, is:
A. 2 B. $2\sqrt{2}$
C. $\sqrt{7}$ D. $2\sqrt{7}$

64. A train leaves Pune at 7:30 am and reaches Mumbai at 11:30 am. Another train leaves Mumbai at 9:30 am and reaches Pune at 1:00 pm. Assuming that the two trains travel at constant speeds, at what time do the two trains cross each other?
A. 10:20 am
B. 11:30 am
C. 10:26 am
D. data not sufficient

65. In the adjacent figures, which has the shortest path?

A. 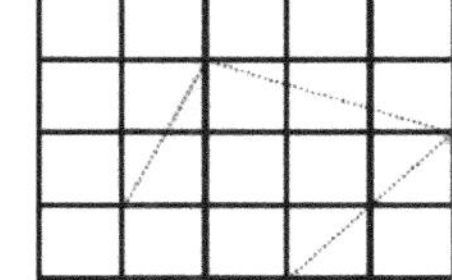

B. 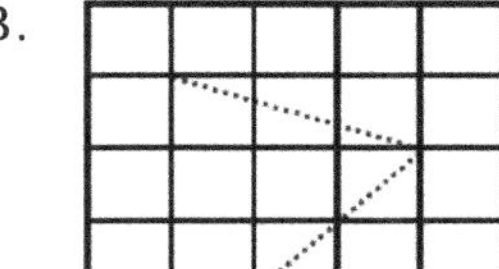

C. 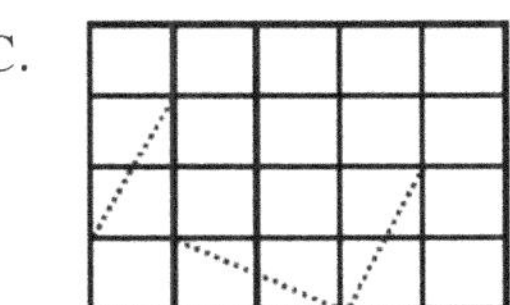

D. 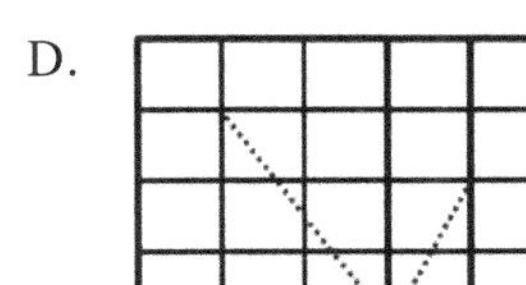

Physics

66. In the circuit shown, n identical resistors R are connected in parallel ($n > 1$) and the combination in series to another resistor R_0. In the adjoining circuit n resistors of resistance R are all connected in series along with R_0.

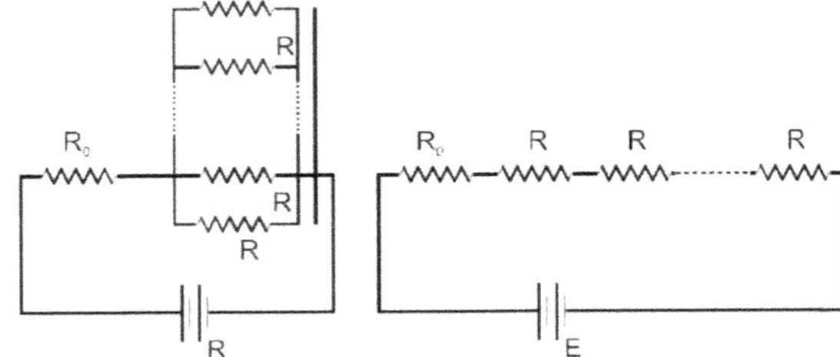

The batteries in both circuits are identical and net power dissipated in the n resistors in both circuit is same. The ratio R_0/R is:

A. 1 B. n
C. n^2 D. $1/n$

67. A firecracker is thrown with velocity of 30 ms^{-1} in a direction which makes an angle of 75° with the vertical axis. At some point on its trajectory, the firecracker split into two identical pieces in such a way that one piece falls 27 m far from the shooting point. Assuming that all trajectories are contained in the same plane, how far will the other piece fall from the shooting point? (Take g = 10 ms^{-2} and neglect air resistance)

A. 63 m or 144 m B. 28 m or 72 m
C. 72 m or 99 m D. 63 m or 117 m

68. A block of mass m is sliding down an inclined plane with constant speed. At a certain instant t_0, its height above the ground is h. The coefficient of kinetic friction between the block and the plane is μ. If the block reaches the ground at a later instant t_g, then the energy dissipated by friction in the time interval $(t_g - t_0)$ is:

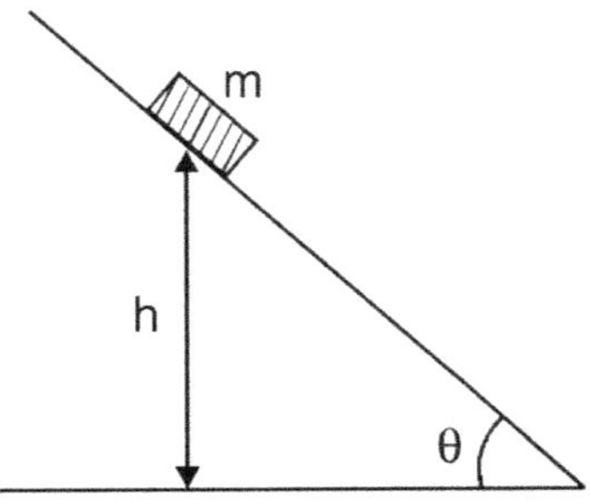

A. μmgh B. mgh
C. $\mu mgh/\sin\theta$ D. $\mu mgh/\cos\theta$

69. A circular loop of wire is in the same plane as an infinitely long wire carrying a constant current i. Four possible motions of the loop are marked by N, E, W and S as shown:

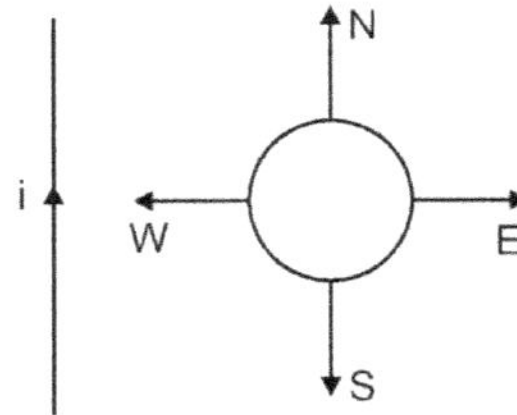

A clockwise current is induced in the loop when loop is pulled towards:

A. N B. E
C. W D. S

70. 150 g of ice is mixed with 100 g of water at temperature 80°C. The latent heat of ice is 80 cal/g and the specific heat of water is 1 cal/g-°C. Assuming no heat loss to the environment, the amount of ice which does not melt is:

A. 100 g B. 0 g
C. 150 g D. 50 g

Chemistry

71. Upon fully dissolving 2.0 g of a metal in sulphuric acid, 6.8 g of the metal suphfate is formed. The equivalent weight of the metal is:

A. 13.6 g B. 20.0 g
C. 4.0 g D. 10.0 g

72. Upon mixing equal volumes of aqueous solutions of 0.1 M HCl and 0.2 M H_2SO_4, the concentration of H^+ in the resulting solution is:

A. 0.30 mol/L
B. 0.25 mol/L
C. 0.15 mol/L
D. 0.10 mol/L

73. The products X and Y in the following reaction sequence are:

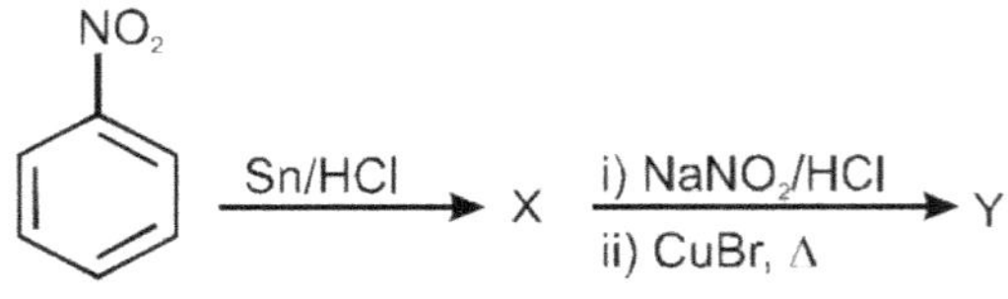

$C_6H_5NO_2 \xrightarrow{Sn/HCl} X \xrightarrow[\text{ii) CuBr, }\Delta]{\text{i) NaNO}_2\text{/HCl}} Y$

A. X: C_6H_5NO Y: C_6H_5Cl

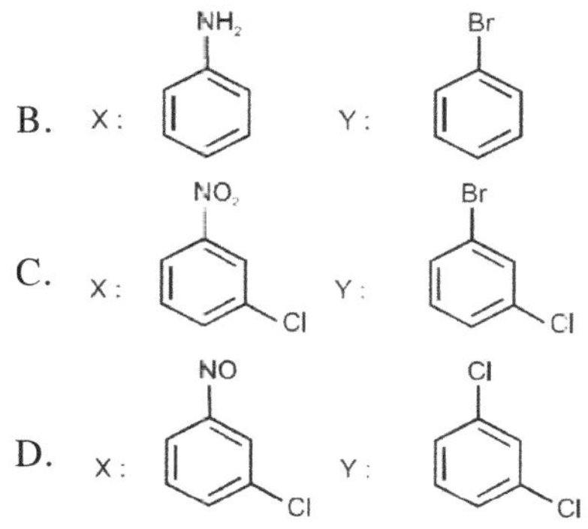

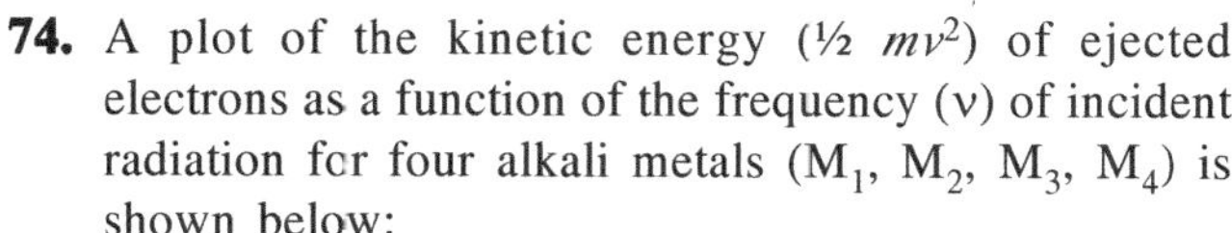

74. A plot of the kinetic energy ($\frac{1}{2}\ mv^2$) of ejected electrons as a function of the frequency (ν) of incident radiation for four alkali metals (M_1, M_2, M_3, M_4) is shown below:

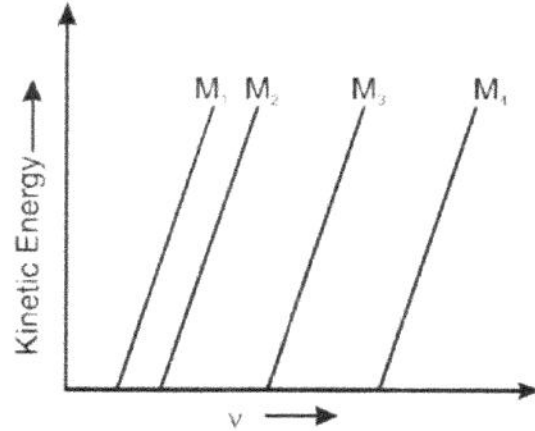

The alkali metals M_1, M_2, M_3 and M_4 are, respectively:

A. Li, Na, K, and Rb B. Rb, K, Na, and Li
C. Na, K, Li, and Rb D. Rb, Li, Na, and K

75. The number of moles of Br_2 produced when two moles of potassium permanganate are treated with excess potassium bromide in aqueous acid medium is:

A. 1 B. 3
C. 2 D. 4

Biology

76. A baby is born with the normal number and distribution of rods, but no cones in his eyes. We would expect that the baby would be

A. colour blind
B. night blind
C. blind in both eyes
D. blind in one eye

77. In mammals, pleural membranes cover the lungs as well as insides of the rib cage. The pleural fluid in between the two membranes

A. dissolves oxygen for transfer to the alveoli
B. dissolves CO_2 for transfer to the blood
C. provides partial pressure
D. reduces the friction between the ribs and the lungs

78. At which phase of the cell cycle, DNA polymerase activity is at its highest?

A. Gap 1 (G1) B. Mitotic (M)
C. Synthetic (S) D. Gap 2 (G2)

79. Usain Bolt, an Olympic runner, at the end of a 100 meter sprint, will have more of the following in his muscles

A. ATP B. Pyruvic acid
C. Lactic acid D. Carbon dioxide

80. Desert temperature often varies between 0 to 50°C. The DNA polymerase isolated from a Camel living in the desert will be able to synthesize DNA most efficiently at:

A. 0°C B. 37°C
C. 50°C D. 25°C

ANSWERS

1	**2**	**3**	**4**	**5**	**6**	**7**	**8**	**9**	**10**
C	B	B	A	D	B	B	B	B	B
11	**12**	**13**	**14**	**15**	**16**	**17**	**18**	**19**	**20**
A	C	D	A	C	B	A	C	D	B
21	**22**	**23**	**24**	**25**	**26**	**27**	**28**	**29**	**30**
D	A	A	D	A	C	B	B	C	A
31	**32**	**33**	**34**	**35**	**36**	**37**	**38**	**39**	**40**
C	A	C	D	C	D	B	B	B	C
41	**42**	**43**	**44**	**45**	**46**	**47**	**48**	**49**	**50**
B	B	C	B	B	A	D	B	A	A
51	**52**	**53**	**54**	**55**	**56**	**57**	**58**	**59**	**60**
C	C	A	B	D	C	D	C	C	A
61	**62**	**63**	**64**	**65**	**66**	**67**	**68**	**69**	**70**
D	B	C	C	C	A	D	B	B	D
71	**72**	**73**	**74**	**75**	**76**	**77**	**78**	**79**	**80**
B	B	B	B	B	A	D	C	C	B

EXPLANATORY ANSWERS

1. $$f(x) = ax^2 + bx + c$$
$$10 = 4a + 2b + c \quad ...(i)$$
$$-2 = 4a - 2b + c \quad ...(ii)$$
$$12 = 4b \Rightarrow b = 3.$$

2. $$\frac{(.75)^3 + (1-0.75)(.75+(0.75)^2+1)}{1-(0.75)} = \frac{1}{.25} = 4$$
$$[\because (a-b)(a^2+b^2+ab) = a^3 - b^3]$$
Square-root = 2.

3.

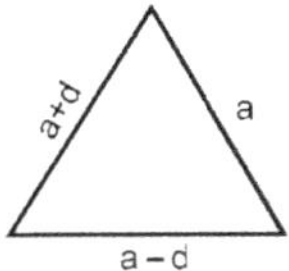

10, 10 + d, 10 + 2d, $d \in$ I, $d \geq$ I
$$10 + 2d < 10 + 10 + d$$
$$d < 10$$
$$\therefore \quad d = 1, 2, 3, ... 9$$
9 triangles are possible.

4. $$a = 3k$$
$$b = k$$
$$c = 5k - 4k = k$$
$$d = 6k - 5k = k$$
$$\frac{a}{b+2c+3d} = \frac{3k}{k+2k+3k} = \frac{1}{2}.$$

5. $$\frac{2^2[1^2+2^2+...+n^2]}{[1^2+3^2+5^2+...+(2n-1)^2]}$$
$$1^2 + 2^2 + 3^2 + ... + (2n)^2 = \frac{2n(2n+1)(4n+1)}{6}$$
$$[1^2 + 3^2 ... + (2n-1)^2 + 2^2]\,[1^2 + 2^2 ... + n^2] = \frac{2n(2n+1)(4n+1)}{6}$$
$$S + 4\frac{n(n+1)(2n+1)}{6} = \frac{2n(2n+1)(4n+1)}{6}$$
$$S + \frac{2n(2n+1)(4n+1)}{6} - \frac{4n(n+1)(2n+1)}{6}$$
$$= 2n\left(\frac{2n+1}{6}\right)[4n+1-2n-2]$$
$$= \frac{2n(2n+1)(2n-1)}{6}$$
$$\text{Ratio} = \frac{4n(n+1)(2n+1)}{6} \times \frac{6}{2n(2n+1)(2n-1)}$$
$$= \frac{2n+2}{2n-1}$$
$$\frac{2n+2}{2n-1} > \frac{101}{100}$$
$$200n + 200 > 202n - 101$$
$$2n < 301$$
$$n < \frac{301}{2}$$
$\Rightarrow$ Maximum value = 150.

6. $$\angle ADB = 180° - \left(\frac{A}{2} + B\right)$$
$$\angle BFC = 180° - \left(\frac{C}{2} + B\right)$$
$$180° - \frac{A}{2} - B + 180° - \frac{C}{2} - B = 180°$$
$$180° = \frac{A+C}{2} + 2B$$
$$\Rightarrow 360° = A + C + 4B$$
$$360° = A + B + C + 3B$$
$$\Rightarrow B = 60°$$
$$\angle IFD = \angle IBD = \frac{B}{2} = 30°.$$

7.

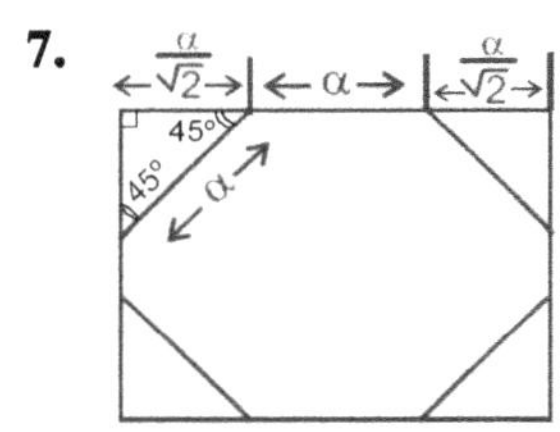

$$\alpha + \frac{\alpha}{\sqrt{2}} + \frac{\alpha}{\sqrt{2}} = 1$$
$$a + \sqrt{2}\alpha = 1$$
$$\alpha = \frac{1}{\sqrt{2}+1} = \sqrt{2} - 1.$$

8. $$\frac{R}{\alpha} = \frac{1}{2}$$
$$\Rightarrow \quad \alpha = 2R$$
Now $$\alpha + R = r$$
$$3R = r$$
$$R = \frac{r}{3}.$$

9.

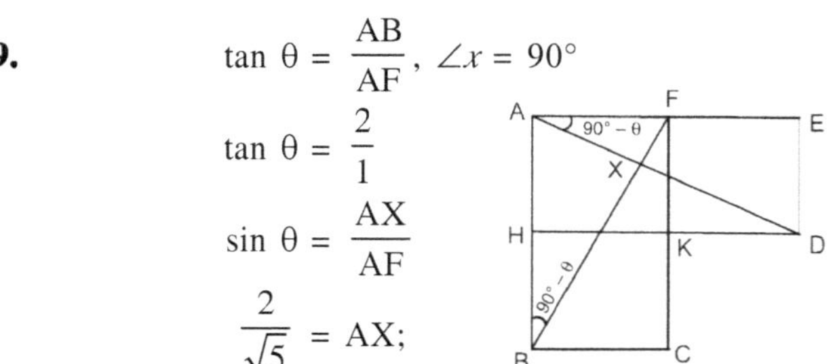

$$\tan\theta = \frac{AB}{AF}, \ \angle x = 90°$$
$$\tan\theta = \frac{2}{1}$$
$$\sin\theta = \frac{AX}{AF}$$
$$\frac{2}{\sqrt{5}} = AX;$$

$$XF = \frac{1}{\sqrt{5}}$$

$$\frac{\text{Area of } \Delta AXF}{\text{Area of } \Delta ABF} = \frac{\frac{1}{2} \times (AX) \times (XF)}{\frac{1}{2}(AB \times AF)}$$

$$= \frac{\frac{1}{2} \times \frac{2}{\sqrt{5}} \times \frac{1}{\sqrt{5}}}{\frac{1}{2} \times 2 \times 1} = \frac{1}{5}.$$

10. $\angle RQP = 176°$

$\angle SPQ = 2°$

$\angle SQP = 89°$ (SP = PQ)

$\angle SQR = 176 - 89 = 87°$.

11.

$$\alpha = 90 + 15 \times \left(\frac{1}{2}\right)^{\circ} = \frac{195°}{2}$$

$$\beta = 360 - \frac{195}{2} = \frac{720 - 195}{2} = \frac{525}{2}$$

$$\text{Difference} = \frac{525 - 195}{2} = \frac{330}{2} = 165°.$$

12. Let A take x hour and B take y hour.

A and B together complete the work in 1 hour

$$= \left(\frac{1}{x} + \frac{1}{y}\right)$$

Let A and B work together 't' hours.

Then, $$t\left(\frac{1}{x} + \frac{1}{y}\right) + 8 = \frac{t + 8}{x}$$

$$\frac{t}{y} = \frac{8}{x}$$

$$t\left(\frac{1}{x} + \frac{1}{y}\right) = \frac{t + 4.5}{y}$$

$$\frac{t}{x} = \frac{4.5}{y}$$

$$\frac{x}{y} = \frac{8}{t};\ \frac{x}{y} = \frac{t}{4.5}$$

$$\frac{8}{t} = \frac{t}{4.5}$$

$\Rightarrow$ $t^2 = 36$

$t = 6$ hours.

13. Let weight of bucket be α and weight of water is β

$\Rightarrow$ $2a + b = 20$ ...(*i*)

and $3a + 2b = 33$ ...(*ii*)

$\alpha = 7$

$\beta = 6$

total weight $= \alpha + \beta = 13$.

16. Apply conservation of Momentum.

$$mv = (m + m)v$$

$$v' = \frac{v}{2}$$

$$K.E. = \frac{1}{2} \times 2m\left(\frac{v}{2}\right)^2 = mv^2/4.$$

17. Down: $mg - F = ma_1$

$$a_1 = g - \frac{F}{m}$$

Up: $mg + F = ma_2$

$$a_2 = g + \frac{F}{m}$$

$a_2 > a_1$.

19.

$\theta = 30° + 90°$

$= 120°$.

22. $i = r = 0$

So, $\delta = 0$

No dispersion.

23.

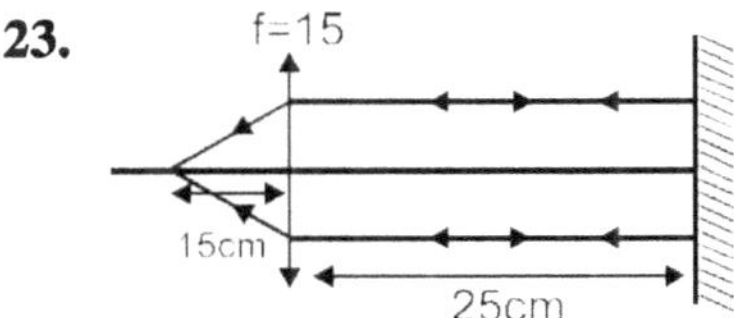

24. In $P = \frac{v^2}{3R}$

In $Q = \frac{3v^2}{R}$

In $R = \frac{v^2}{R}$

In $S = \frac{4v^2}{R}$

So, $P < R < Q < S$.

25. In length $2\pi R$ change $\rightarrow 2\pi R\alpha\Delta T$

$1 \rightarrow \alpha\Delta T$

In $d \rightarrow d\alpha\Delta T$.

26. $f_s = mg$

F

mg

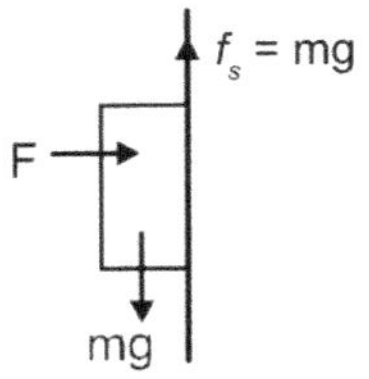

$f_s = mg$.

27.
$$6a^2 = 4\pi r^2$$
$$\frac{a}{r} = \sqrt{\frac{4\pi}{6}}$$
$$B_S = \frac{4}{3}\pi r^3 \rho g$$
$$B_C = a^3 \rho g$$
$$\frac{B_S}{B_C} = \frac{4\pi}{3}\frac{r^3}{a^3} = \frac{4\pi}{3}\cdot\frac{6}{4\pi}\sqrt{\frac{6}{4\pi}} = 2\sqrt{\frac{3}{2\pi}} > 1$$
$$B_S > B_C.$$

28. ${}^{238}_{92}U \rightarrow {}^{214}_{84}Po + 6a + ne$

${}^{238}_{92}U \rightarrow {}^{214}_{84}Po + 6_2He^4 + ne$

So, $n = 4$.

30. Due to attraction in both case bend in the same direction.

31. $2Ca + \underset{(excess)}{O_2} \xrightarrow{\Delta} 2CaO$

$\frac{20}{40} = \frac{1}{2}$ mole

$\frac{1}{2}$ mole of CaO will be formed *i.e.,* $\frac{1}{2} \times 56 = 28$ g.

32. It is an example of bromoform reaction (similar to Iodoform reaction).

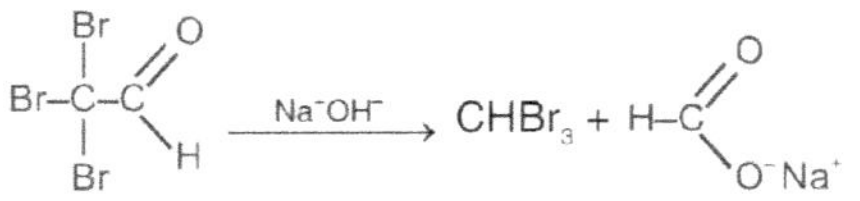

$CBr_3-CHO \xrightarrow{Na^+OH^-} CHBr_3 + HCOO^-Na^+$

33. ${}^{40}_{19}K^+$

e^- s = 19 – 1 = 18

N = 40 – 19 = 21

∴ Electrons + Neutrons = 18 + 21 = 39.

34. Na_2O is most basic Oxide as it will form NaOH on dissolving in water which is strong base.

35. Molarity = $\frac{\text{moles of solute}}{\text{lit. of solution}}$

or $\frac{0.35}{1.3} = 0.269$ M = 0.27 M.

36. Density (ρ), temperature (T) and pressure (p) are intensive variables because they donot depend upon mass.

37. Potash alum is $K_2SO_4.Al_2(SO_4)_3.24H_2O$

∴ Empirical formula is $KAl(SO_4)_2.12H_2O$

38. [Resonance structures of protonated 4-dimethylaminopyridine: Me_2N–pyridine $\xrightarrow{H^+}$ ... $\longrightarrow$ ... $\longrightarrow$ ... $\longrightarrow$ $Me_2N^{\oplus}$=pyridine–N–H]

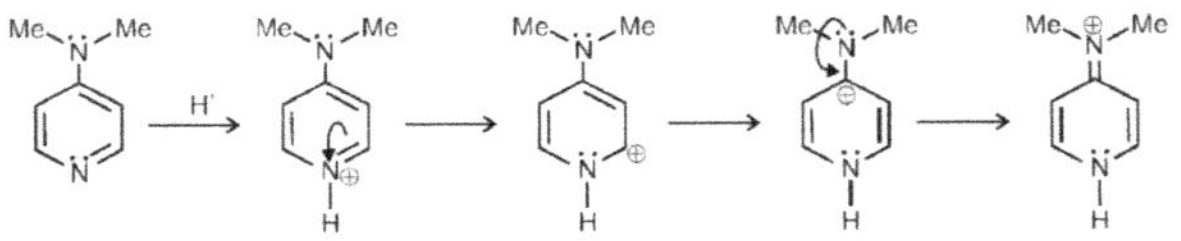

The conjugate acid is resonance stabilized.

39. It is example of electrophilic addition reaction following the Markownikov rule.

40. At room temperature, it is a simple acid-base reaction resulting in the formation of salt.

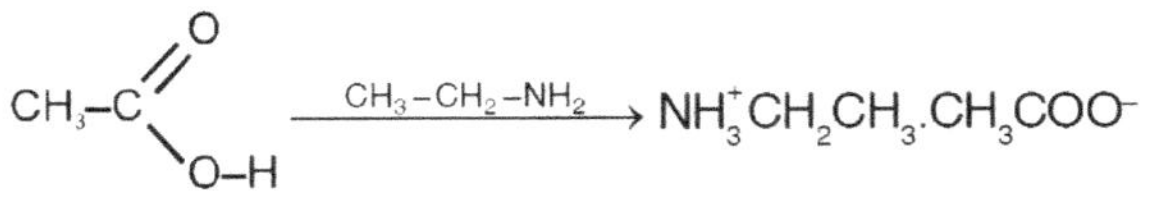

$CH_3-COOH \xrightarrow{CH_3-CH_2-NH_2} NH_3^+CH_2CH_3.CH_3COO^-$

41. If $Q_C < K_C$ then reaction will move in forward direction.

42. Acetyl salicylic acid is commonly known as aspirin.

43. There is not any acidic proton in diethyl ether, hence it does not exhibit strong hydrogen bonding.

Or

For H–bonding in molecule highly electronegative element and H should be directly connected. In $(C_2H_5)_2O$, H is connected to carbon.

44. Both A and B differs in position of double bond, hence they are positional isomers.

45. (B) [Graph: P vs 1/V, straight line through origin] (C) [Graph: PV vs T, horizontal line]

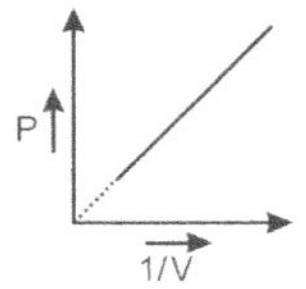

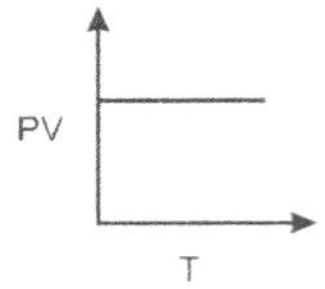

61.
$$\frac{a\sqrt{2}+b}{b\sqrt{2}+c} \times \frac{b\sqrt{2}-c}{b\sqrt{2}-c} = \frac{2ab-\sqrt{2}ac+b^2\sqrt{2}-bc}{2b^2-c^2}$$
$$= \frac{2ab-bc+\sqrt{2}(b^2-ac)}{2b^2-c^2}$$

⇒ $b^2 = ac$, number are a, ar, ar^2

A. $\frac{2a^2+b^2}{2b^2+c^2} = \frac{2a^2+ac}{2ac+c^2} = \frac{a(2a+c)}{c(2a+c)} = \frac{a}{c} = \frac{1}{r^2}$

may or may not be integer.

B. $\frac{a^2+2b^2}{b^2+2c^2} = \frac{a^2+2a^2r^2}{a^2r^2+2a^2r^4} = \frac{a^2(2r^2+1)}{a^2r^2(2r^2+1)} = \frac{1}{r^2}$

C. $\dfrac{a^2+b^2-c^2}{a+b-c} = \dfrac{a^2+a^2r^2-a^2r^4}{a+ar-ar^2} = a\left(\dfrac{1+r^2-r^4}{1+r-r^2}\right)$

D. $\dfrac{a^2+b^2+c^2}{a+c-b} = \dfrac{a^2(1+r^2+r^4)}{a(r^2-r+1)}$

$= a(r^2 + r + 1) = a + b + c =$ Integer.

62. $z = \dfrac{3}{xy}, \quad x+2y+4\times\dfrac{3}{xy} = 9$

$x+2y+\dfrac{3(4-3xy)}{xy} = 0$

$xy(x + 2y - 9) = -12$

C-I $xy = 1,\ x + 2y = -3$

$x+\dfrac{2}{x}+3 = 0 \qquad (-1, -1, 3)$

$x^2 + 3x + 2 = 0 \qquad -1, -2 \quad \left(-2, \dfrac{-1}{2}, 3\right)$

C-II $xy = -1,\ x + 2y = 21$

$\Rightarrow \quad x = \dfrac{21 \pm \sqrt{449}}{2}$

$x+\dfrac{2(-1)}{x} = 3$

$x^2 - 3x - 2 = 0$

$x = \dfrac{3\pm\sqrt{9-4(-2)}}{2} = \dfrac{3\pm\sqrt{17}}{2}$

C-III $xy = 2,\ x + 2y = -6 + 9 = 3$

$x+2.\dfrac{2}{x} = 3$

$\Rightarrow \quad x^2 - 3x + 4 = 0$

$D = 9 - 4.1.4 < 0$

C-IV $xy = -2, \quad x + 2y - 9 = 6$

$x + 2y = 15, \quad x^2 - 15x - 4 = 0$

$x+2\left(\dfrac{-2}{x}\right) = 15, \quad 15^2 + 4.1.4$

C-V $xy = 3,\ x + 2y = 9 - 4$

$x + 2y = 5$

$x+2.\dfrac{3}{x} = 5 \quad \Rightarrow x^2 - 5x + 6 = 0$

$\Rightarrow x = 2, 3$

$x = 2,\ y = \dfrac{3}{2},\ z = 1 \ \left(2, \dfrac{3}{2}, 1\right)$

$x = 3,\ y = 1,\ z = 1 \ (3, 1, 1)$

C-VI $xy = -3,\ x + 2y - 9 = 4$

$x + 2y = 13$

$x+\dfrac{2(-3)}{x} = 13$

$x^2 - 13x - 6 = 0 \qquad D = 13^2 + 4 \times 6 = 193$

C-VII $xy = 4$

$x + 2y - 9 = -3$

$x + 2y = 6$

$x+2.\dfrac{4}{x} = 6$

$\Rightarrow \quad x^2 - 6x + 8 = 0$

$x = 2, 4$

$x = 2,\ y = 4,\ z = \dfrac{3}{4} \ \left(2, 4, \dfrac{3}{4}\right)$

$x = 4,\ y = 1,\ z = \dfrac{3}{4} \ \left(4, 1, \dfrac{3}{4}\right).$

63.

$AB = AC$

$\Delta ABC \sim \Delta BDC$

$\dfrac{AB}{BD} = \dfrac{BC}{DC} = \dfrac{AC}{BC}$

$\cos A = \dfrac{x^2+x^2-2^2}{2xx} = \dfrac{2^2+2^2-\left(\dfrac{x}{2}\right)^2}{2.2.2}$

$\dfrac{2x^2-4}{x^2} = \dfrac{8-\dfrac{x^2}{4}}{4}$

$8x^2 - 16 = 8x^2 - \dfrac{x^4}{4}$

$x^4 = 64$

$x = 2\sqrt{2}$

$s = \dfrac{2\sqrt{2}+2\sqrt{2}+2}{2} = 2\sqrt{2}+1$

Area of $\Delta ABC = \sqrt{\left(2\sqrt{2}+1\right)\left(2\sqrt{2}-1\right)(1)(1)} = \sqrt{7}.$

64. Let distance between Pune and Mumbai be ℓ

Speed of first train $= \dfrac{\ell}{4}$

Speed of second train $= \dfrac{\ell}{3\frac{1}{2}} = \dfrac{2\ell}{7}$

Distance covered by first train in 2 hours

$= \dfrac{\ell}{4}\times 2 = \dfrac{\ell}{2}$

at 9:30 relative distance to be covered $= \dfrac{\ell}{2}$

Let they meet at time t

$$\frac{\ell}{2} = \left(\frac{\ell}{4} \times t\right) + \frac{2\ell}{7} t$$

$$\frac{\ell}{2} = \ell t\left(\frac{7+8}{28}\right)$$

$$\Rightarrow \qquad t = \frac{14}{15} \text{ hours or } 56$$

$\therefore$ Ans. 9:30 + 56 min = 10:26.

65. Applying pythagorus theorem.

$$\text{Path} = \sqrt{2^2+2^2} + \sqrt{3^2+1^2} = \sqrt{8} + \sqrt{10}$$

Option (B) is correct.

66. In parallel combination

$$I = \left(\frac{E}{R_0 + \frac{R}{n}}\right)$$

$$P_1 = \left(I^2 . \frac{R}{n}\right) = \left(\frac{E}{R_0 + \frac{R}{n}}\right)^2 . \frac{R}{n}$$

In series combination

$$I = \frac{E}{R_0 + nR}$$

$$P_2 = \left(\frac{E}{R_0 + nR}\right)^2 .nR$$

But, $P_1 = P_2$

$$\left(\frac{E}{R_0 + \frac{R}{n}}\right)^2 . \frac{R}{n} = \left(\frac{E}{R_0 + nR}\right)^2 .nR$$

$$\frac{n}{nR_0 + R} = \left(\frac{n}{R_0 + nR}\right)$$

$$R_0 + nR = nR_0 + R$$

$$R_0(1 - n) = R(1 - n)$$

$$\frac{R_0}{R} = 1.$$

67.

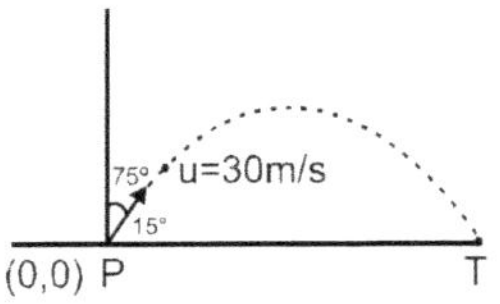

75°
u=30m/s
15°
(0,0) P
T

$$R = \frac{u^2 \sin 2\theta}{g} = \frac{30^2 \sin 30°}{10} = 90 \times \frac{1}{2} = 45 \text{ m}$$

Conservation of momentum of firecracker at 45 m from projection point

$$X_{cm} = \frac{m_1 r_1 + m_2 r_2}{m_1 + m_2}$$

$$45 = \frac{\frac{m}{2}(27) + \frac{m}{2} r_2}{m}$$

$$90 = 27 + r_2$$

$$r_2 = 90 - 27 = 64 \text{ m}$$

If $\quad r_2 = -27$ m, then

$$90 = -27 + r_2$$

$$r_2 = 117 \text{ m.}$$

68. Using, *w.f.t.*

$$K_f - K_i = W_g + W_f$$

$$\frac{1}{2}mu^2 - \frac{1}{2}mu^2 = mgh + W_f$$

$$W_f = -mgh$$

Which is equal to energy loss in process.

69. Magnetic field due to wire is inwards when loop moves towards E current is clockwise.

70. Heat given by water = 100 × 1 × 80 = 8000 cal

Heat taken by ice = 8000 cal = m × 80

m = 100 gm

So, amount of ice which does not melt

= 150 – 100 = 50 gm

71. Metal + $H_2SO_4 \rightarrow$ Metal sulphate

No. of Eq. of metal = No. of eq. of metal sulphate

$$\frac{2}{E} = \frac{6.8}{\left(E + \frac{96}{2}\right)}$$

E = 20.

72. $$[x^+]_f = \frac{V \times 0.1 + V \times 0.2 \times 2}{2V} = \frac{0.5V}{2V} = 0.25\text{M}.$$

73.

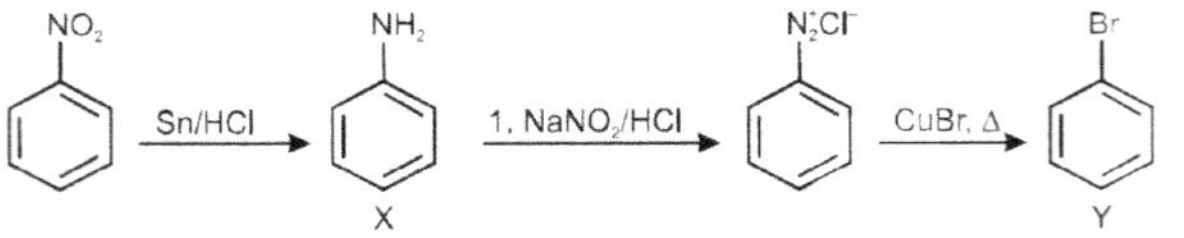

NO2
Sn/HCl
NH2
X
1. NaNO2/HCl
N2Cl
CuBr, Δ
Br
Y

74. $$\frac{1}{2}mv^2 = h\nu - W$$

High is the threshold frequency of metal greater will be the work function.

So, $M_1 \rightarrow$ Rb; $M_2 \rightarrow$ K; $M_3 \rightarrow$ Na; $M_4 \rightarrow$ Li.

Previous Paper (Solved), 2011

Kishore Vaigyanik Protsahan Yojana (KVPY)

STREAM – SA

Part-I

Mathematics

1. Suppose a, b, c are three distinct real numbers. Let $P(x) = \frac{(x-b)(x-c)}{(a-b)(a-c)} + \frac{(x-c)(x-a)}{(b-c)(b-a)} + \frac{(x-a)(x-b)}{(c-a)(c-b)}$.
When simplified, P(x) becomes

A. 1
B. x
C. $\frac{x^2+(a+b+c)(ab+bc+ca)}{(a-b)(b-c)(c-a)}$
D. 0

2. Let a, b, x, y be real numbers such that $a^2 + b^2 = 81$, $x^2 + y^2 = 121$ and $ax + by = 99$. Then the set of all possible values of $ay - bx$ is:

A. $\left(0, \frac{9}{11}\right]$ B. $\left(0, \frac{9}{11}\right)$
C. $\{0\}$ D. $\left[\frac{9}{11}, \infty\right)$

3. If $x+\frac{1}{x} = a$, $x^2+\frac{1}{x^3} = b$, then $x^3+\frac{1}{x^2}$ is:

A. $a^3 + a^2 - 3a - 2 - b$
B. $a^3 - a^2 - 3a + 4 - b$
C. $a^3 - a^2 + 3a - 6 - b$
D. $a^3 + a^2 + 3a - 16 - b$

4. Let a, b, c, d be real numbers such that $|a - b| = 2$, $|b - c| = 3$, $|c - d| = 4$. Then the sum of all possible values of $|a - d|$ is:

A. 9 B. 18
C. 24 D. 30

5. Below are four equations in x. Assume that $0 < r < 4$. Which of the following has the largest solution for x?

A. $5\left(1+\frac{r}{\pi}\right)^x = 9$ B. $5\left(1+\frac{r}{17}\right)^x = 9$
C. $5(1 + 2r)^x = 9$ D. $5\left(1+\frac{1}{r}\right)^x = 9$

6. Let ABC be a triangle with $\angle B = 90°$. Let AD be the bisector of $\angle A$ with D on BC. Suppose AC = 6 cm and the area of the triangle ADC is 10 cm^2. Then the length of BD in cm is equal to:

A. $\frac{3}{5}$ B. $\frac{3}{10}$
C. $\frac{5}{3}$ D. $\frac{10}{3}$

7. A piece of paper in the shape of a sector of a circle (see Fig. 1) is rolled up to form a right-circular cone (see Fig. 2). The value of the angle θ is:

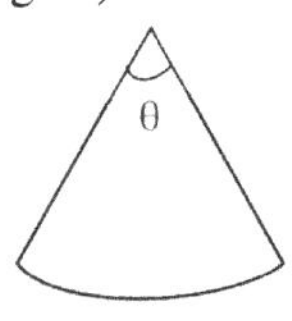

Fig.1

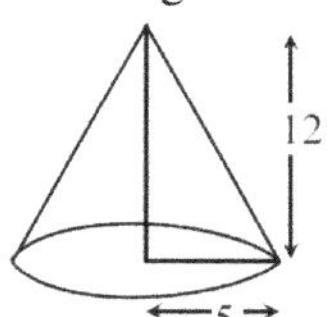

Fig.2

A. $\frac{10\pi}{13}$ B. $\frac{9\pi}{13}$
C. $\frac{5\pi}{13}$ D. $\frac{6\pi}{13}$

8. In the adjoining figure AB = 12 cm, CD = 8 cm, BD = 20 cm; $\angle ABD = \angle AEC = \angle EDC = 90°$. If BE = x, then:

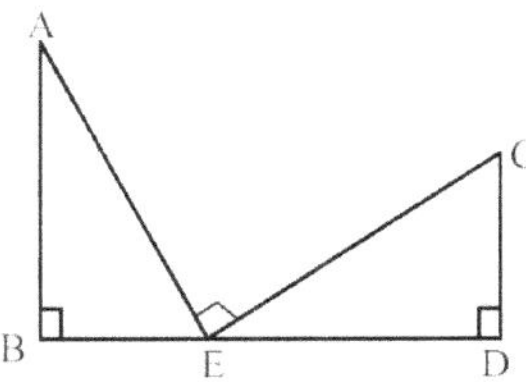

A. x has two possible values whose difference is 4
B. x has two possible values whose sum is 28
C. x has only one value and $x \geq 12$
D. x cannot be determined with the given information

9. Three circles each of radius 1, touch one another externally and they lie between two parallel lines. The minimum possible distance between the lines is:

A. $2+\sqrt{3}$ B. $3+\sqrt{3}$

C. 4 D. $2+\frac{1}{\sqrt{3}}$

10. The number of distinct prime divisors of the number $512^3 - 253^3 - 259^3$ is:

A. 4 B. 5

C. 6 D. 7

11. Consider an incomplete pyramid of balls on a square base having 18 layers; and having 13 balls on each side of the top layer. Then the total number N of balls in that pyramid satisfies:

A. $9000 < N < 10000$ B. $8000 < N < 9000$

C. $7000 < N < 8000$ D. $10000 < N < 12000$

12. A man wants to reach a certain destination. One-sixth of the total distance is muddy while half the distance is tar road. For the remaining distance he takes a boat. His speed of travelling in mud, in water, on tar road is in the ratio 3 : 4 : 5. The ratio of the durations he requires to cross the patch of mud, stream and tar road is:

A. $\frac{1}{2}:\frac{4}{3}:\frac{5}{2}$ B. 3 : 8 : 15

C. 10 : 15 : 18 D. 1 : 2 : 3

13. A frog is presently located at the origin (0, 0) in the xy-plane. It always jumps from a point with integer coordinates to a point with integer coordinates moving a distance of 5 units in each jump. What is the minimum number of jumps required for the frog to go from (0, 0) to (0, 1)?

A. 2 B. 3

C. 4 D. 9

14. A certain 12-hour digital clock displays the hour and the minute of a day. Due to a defect in the clock whenever the digit 1 is supposed to be displayed it displays 7. What fraction of the day will the clock show the correct time?

A. $\frac{1}{2}$ B. $\frac{5}{8}$

C. $\frac{3}{4}$ D. $\frac{5}{6}$

15. There are 30 questions in a multiple–choice test. A student gets 1 mark for each unattempted question, 0 mark for each wrong answer and 4 marks for each correct answer. A student answered x question correctly and scored 60. Then the number of possible value of x is:

A. 15 B. 10

C. 6 D. 5

Physics

16. A simple pendulum oscillates freely between points A and B.

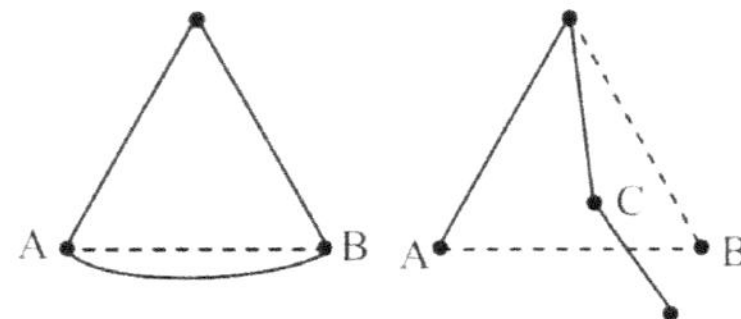

We now put a peg (nail) at some point C as shown. As the pendulum moves from A to the right, the string will bend at C and the pendulum will go to its extreme points D. Ignoring friction, the point D.

A. will lie on the line AB
B. will lie above the line AB
C. will lie below the line AB
D. will coincide with B

17. A small child tries to move a large rubber toy placed on the ground. The toy does not move but gets deformed under her pushing force ($\vec{F}$) which is obliquely upward as shown. Then:

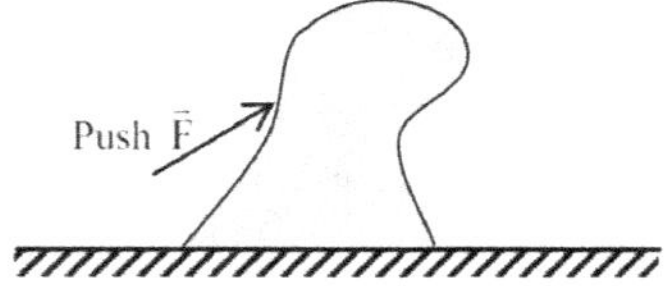

A. the resultant of the pushing force ($\vec{F}$), weight of the toy, normal force by the ground on the toy and the frictional force is zero
B. the normal force by the ground is equal and opposite to the weight of the toy
C. the pushing force ($\vec{F}$) of the child is balanced by the equal and opposite frictional force
D. the pushing force ($\vec{F}$) of the child is balanced by the total internal force in the toy generated due to deformation

18. A juggler tosses a ball up in the air with initial speed u. At the instant it reaches its maximum height H, he tosses up a second ball with the same initial speed. The two balls will collide at a height:

A. $\frac{H}{4}$ B. $\frac{H}{2}$

C. $\frac{3H}{4}$ D. $\sqrt{\frac{3}{4}}H$

19. On a horizontal frictionless frozen lake, a girl (36 kg) and a box (9 kg) are connected to each other by means of a rope. Initially they are 20 m apart. The girl exerts a horizontal force on the box, pulling it towards her. How far has the girl travelled when she meets the box?

A. 10 m
B. Since there is no friction, the girl will not move

C. 16 m
D. 4 m

20. The following three objects (1) a metal tray, (2) a block of wood, and (3) a woollen cap are left in a closed room overnight. Next day the temperature of each is recorded as T_1, T_2 and T_3 respectively. The likely situation is:
A. $T_1 = T_2 = T_3$ B. $T_3 > T_2 > T_1$
C. $T_3 = T_2 > T_1$ D. $T_3 > T_2 = T_1$

21. We sit in the room with windows open. Then:
A. air pressure on the floor of the room equals the atmospheric pressure but the air pressure on the ceiling is negligible
B. air pressure is nearly the same on the floor, the walls and the ceiling
C. air pressure on the floor equals the weight of the air column inside the room (from floor to ceiling) per unit area
D. air pressure on the walls is zero since the weight of air acts downward

22. A girl standing at point P on a beach wishes to reach a point Q in the sea as quickly as possible. She can run at 6 km h^{-1} on the beach and swim at 4 km h^{-1} in the sea. She should take the path:

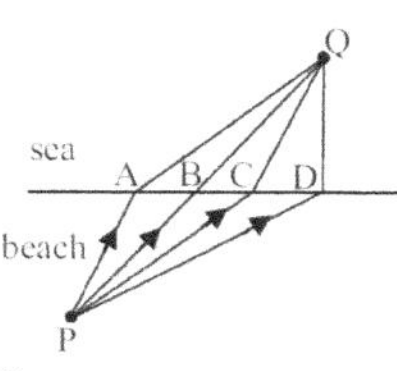

A. PAQ B. PBQ
C. PCQ D. PDQ

23. Light enters an isosceles right triangular prism at normal incidence through face AB and undergoes total internal reflection at face BC as shown below.

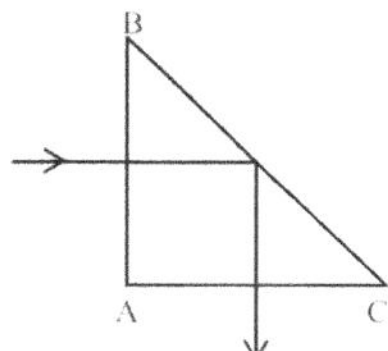

The minimum value of the refractive index of the prism is close to:
A. 1.10 B. 1.55
C. 1.42 D. 1.72

24. A convex lens is used to form an image of an object on a screen. If the upper half of the lens is blackened so that it becomes opaque, then:
A. only half of the image will be visible
B. the image position shifts towards the lens
C. the image position shifts away from the lens
D. the brightness of the image reduces

25. A cylindrical copper rod has length L and resistance R. If it is melted and formed into another rod of length 2L, the resistance will be:
A. R B. 2R
C. 4R D. 8R

26. Two charges + Q and –2Q are located at points A and B on a horizontal line as shown below:

The electric field is zero at a point which is located at a finite distance:
A. on the perpendicular bisector of AB
B. left of A on the line
C. between A and B on the line
D. right of B on the line

27. A 750 W motor drives a pump which lifts 300 litres of water per minute to a height of 6 meters. The efficiency of the motor is nearly (take acceleration due to gravity to be 10 m/s^2):
A. 30% B. 40%
C. 50% D. 20%

28. Figure below shows a portion of an electric circuit with the currents in amperes and their directions. The magnitude and direction of the current in the portion PQ is:

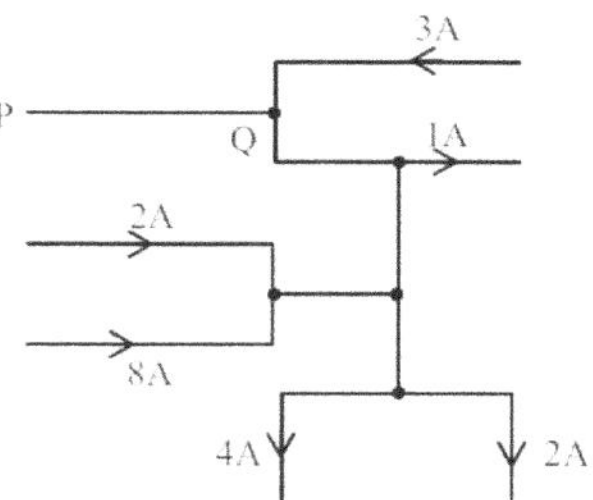

A. 0 A B. 3 A from P to Q
C. 4 A from Q to P D. 6 A from Q to P

29. A nucleus of lead Pb^{214}_{82} emits two electrons followed by an alpha particle. The resulting nucleus will have:
A. 82 protons and 128 neutrons
B. 80 protons and 130 neutrons
C. 82 protons and 130 neutrons
D. 78 protons and 134 neutrons

30. The number of air molecules in a (5 m × 5 m × 4 m) room at standard temperature and pressure is of the order of:
A. 6×10^{23} B. 3×10^{24}
C. 3×10^{27} D. 6×10^{30}

Chemistry

31. Two balloons A and B containing 0.2 mole and 0.1 mole of helium at room temperature and 2.0 atm, respectively, are connected. When equilibrium is established, the final pressure of He in the system is:
A. 1.0 atm B. 1.5 atm
C. 0.5 atm D. 2.0 atm

32. In the following set of aromatic compounds

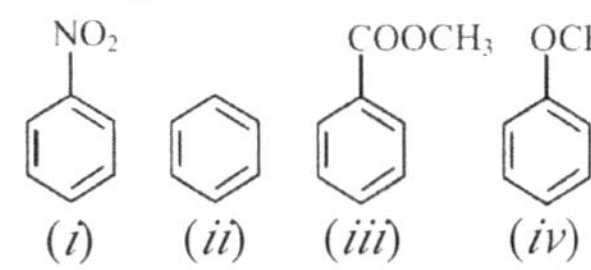

the correct order of reactivity toward Friedel-Crafts alkylation is:

A. (*i*) > (*ii*) > (*iii*) > (*iv*) B. (*ii*) > (*iv*) > (*iii*) > (*i*)
C. (*iv*) > (*ii*) > (*iii*) > (*i*) D. (*iii*) > (*i*) > (*iv*) > (*ii*)

33. The set of principal (n), azimuthal (ℓ) and magnetic (m_l) quantum numbers that is not allowed for the electron in H-atom is:

A. $n = 3, \ell = 1, m_l = -1$
B. $n = 3, \ell = 0, m_l = 0$
C. $n = 2, \ell = 1, m_l = 0$
D. $n = 2, \ell = 2, m_l = -1$

34. At 298 K, assuming ideal behaviour, the average kinetic energy of a deuterium molecule is:

A. two times that of a hydrogen molecule
B. four times that of a hydrogen molecule
C. half of that of a hydrogen molecule
D. same as that of a hydrogen molecule

35. As isolated box, equally partitioned contains two ideal gases A and B as shown.

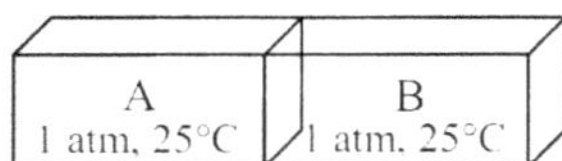

When the partition is removed, the gases mix. The changes in enthalpy (ΔH) and entropy (ΔS) in the process, respectively, are:

A. zero, positive B. zero, negative
C. positive, zero D. negative, zero

36. The gas produced from thermal decomposition of $(NH_4)_2Cr_2O_7$ is:

A. oxygen B. nitric oxide
C. ammonia D. nitrogen

37. The solubility curve of KNO_3 in water is shown below.

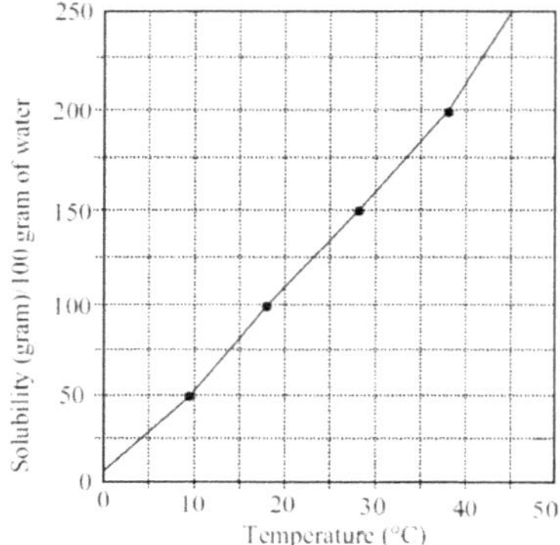

The amount of KNO_3 that dissolves in 50 g of water at 40 °C is closest to:

A. 100 g B. 150 g
C. 200 g D. 50 g

38. A compound that shows positive iodoform test is:

A. 2-pentanone B. 3-pentanone
C. 3-pentanol D. 1-pentanol

39. After 2 hours the amount of a certain radioactive substance reduces to 1/16th of the original amount (the decay process follows first-order kinetics). The half-life of the radioactive substance is:

A. 15 min B. 30 min
C. 45 min D. 60 min

40. In the conversion of zinc ore to zinc metal, the process of roasting involves:

A. $ZnCO_3 \rightarrow ZnO$ B. $ZnO \rightarrow ZnSO_4$
C. $ZnS \rightarrow ZnO$ D. $ZnS \rightarrow ZnSO_4$

41. The number of P–H bond(s) in H_3PO_2, H_3PO_3 and H_3PO_4, respectively, is:

A. 2, 0, 1 B. 1, 1, 1
C. 2, 0, 0 D. 2, 1, 0

42. When chlorine gas is passed through an aqueous solution of KBr, the solution turns orange brown due to the formation of:

A. KCl B. HCl
C. HBr D. Br_2

43. Among

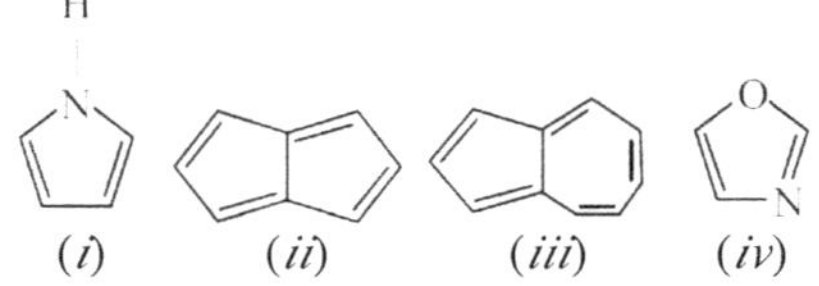

the compound which is not aromatic is:

A. (*i*) B. (*ii*)
C. (*iii*) D. (*iv*)

44. Among the following compounds

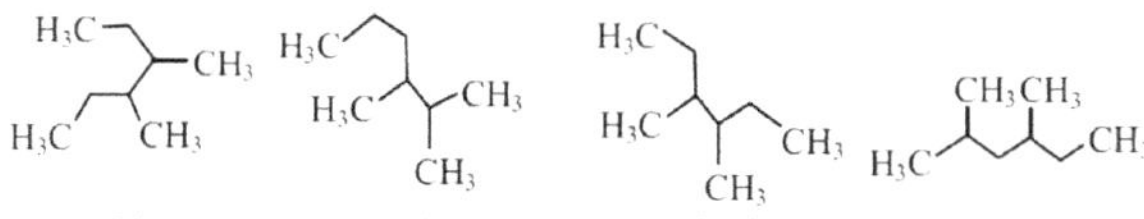

(*i*) (*ii*) (*iii*) (*iv*)

2, 3-dimethylhexane is:

A. (*i*) B. (*ii*)
C. (*iii*) D. (*iv*)

45. The major product formed in the reaction

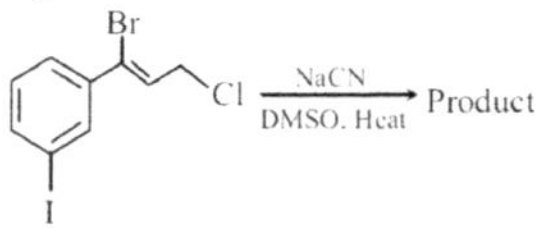

$\xrightarrow[\text{DMSO, Heat}]{\text{NaCN}}$ Product is:

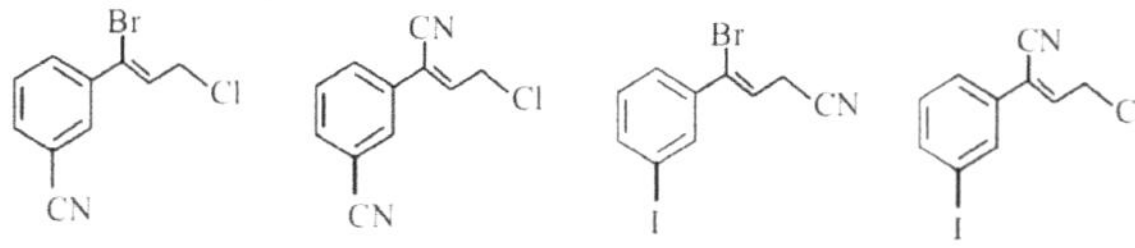

(*i*) (*ii*) (*iii*) (*iv*)

A. (*i*) B. (*ii*)
C. (*iii*) D. (*iv*)

Biology

46. If parents have free ear lobes and the offspring has attached ear lobes, then the parents must be:
A. homozygous B. heterozygous
C. co-dominant D. nullizygous

47. During meiosis there is:
A. one round of DNA replication and one division
B. two rounds of DNA replication and one division
C. two rounds of DNA replication and two division
D. one round of DNA replication and two division

48. Blood clotting involves the conversion of:
A. prothrombin to thromboplastin
B. thromboplastin to prothrombin
C. fibrinogen to fibrin
D. fibrin to fibrinogen

49. The gall bladder is involved in:
A. synthesizing bile
B. storing and secreting bile
C. degrading bile
D. producing insulin

50. Which one of the following colours is the LEAST useful for plant life?
A. red B. blue
C. green D. violet

51. At rest the volume of air that moves in and out per breath is called:
A. resting volume B. vital capacity
C. lung capacity D. tidal volume

52. How many sex chromosomes does a normal human inherit from father?
A. 1 B. 2
C. 23 D. 46

53. In the 16th century, sailors who travelled long distances had diseases related to malnutrition, because they were not able to eat fresh vegetables and fruits for months at a time. Scurvy is a result of deficiency of:
A. carbohydrates B. proteins
C. Vitamin C D. Vitamin D

54. The following structure is NOT found in plant cells:
A. vacuole B. nucleus
C. centriole D. endoplasmic reticulum

55. The cell that transfers information about pain to the brain is called a:
A. neuron B. blastocyst
C. histoblast D. haemocyte

56. The presence of nutrients in the food can be tested. Benedict's test is used to detect:
A. sucrose B. glucose
C. fatty acid D. vitamin

57. Several minerals such as iron, iodine, calcium and phosphorous are important nutrients. Iodine is found in:
A. thyroxine B. adrenaline
C. insulin D. testosterone

58. The principle upon which a lactometer works is:
A. viscosity B. density
C. surface tension D. presence of protein

59. Mammalian liver cells will swell when kept in:
A. hypertonic solution B. hypotonic solution
C. isotonic solution D. isothermal solution

60. The form of cancer called 'carcinoma' is associated with:
A. lymph cells B. mesodermal cells
C. blood cells D. epithelial cells

Part-II

Mathematics

61. Let $f(x) = ax^2 + bx + c$, where a, b, c are integers. Suppose $f(1) = 0$, $40 < f(6) < 50$, $60 < f(7) < 70$, and $1000t < f(50) < 1000(t+1)$ for some integer t. Then the value of t is:
A. 2 B. 3
C. 4 D. 5 or more

62. The expression $\frac{2^2+1}{2^2-1}+\frac{3^2+1}{3^2-1}+\frac{4^2+1}{4^2-1}+...+\frac{(2011)^2+1}{(2011)^2-1}$ lies in the interval:
A. $\left(2010, 2010\frac{1}{2}\right)$
B. $\left(2011-\frac{1}{2011}, 2011-\frac{1}{2012}\right)$
C. $\left(2011, 2011\frac{1}{2}\right)$
D. $\left(2012, 2012\frac{1}{2}\right)$

63. The diameter of one of the bases of a truncated cone is 100 mm. If the diameter of this base is increased by 21% such that it still remains a truncated cone with the height and the other base unchanged, the volume also increases by 21%. The radius of the other base (in mm) is:
A. 65 B. 55
C. 45 D. 35

64. Two friends A and B are 30 km apart and they start simultaneously on motorcycles to meet each other. The speed of A is 3 times that of B. The distance between them decreases at the rate of 2 km per minute. Ten minutes after they start, A's vehicle breaks down and A stops and waits for B to arrive. After how much time (in minutes) A started riding, does B meet A?

A. 15 B. 20

C. 25 D. 30

65. Three taps A, B, C fill up a tank independently in 10 hr, 20 hr, 30 hr, respectively. Initially the tank is empty and exactly one pair of taps is open during each hour and every pair of taps is open at least for one hour. What is the minimum number of hours required to fill the tank?

A. 8 B. 9

C. 10 D. 11

Physics

66. An object with uniform density ρ is attached to a spring that is known to stretch linearly with applied force as shown below.

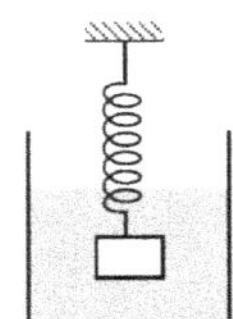

When the spring-object system is immersed in a liquid of density ρ_1 as shown in the figure, the spring stretches by an amount $x_1 (\rho > \rho_1)$. When the experiment is repeated in a liquid of density $\rho_2 < \rho_1$, the spring stretches by an amount x_2. Neglecting any buoyant force on the spring, the density of the object is:

A. $\rho = \dfrac{\rho_1 x_1 - \rho_2 x_2}{x_1 - x_2}$ B. $\rho = \dfrac{\rho_1 x_2 - \rho_2 x_1}{x_2 - x_1}$

C. $\rho = \dfrac{\rho_1 x_2 + \rho_2 x_1}{x_1 + x_2}$ D. $\rho = \dfrac{\rho_1 x_1 + \rho_2 x_2}{x_1 + x_2}$

67. A body of 0.5 kg moves along the positive x-axis under the influence of a varying force F (in Newtons) as shown below.

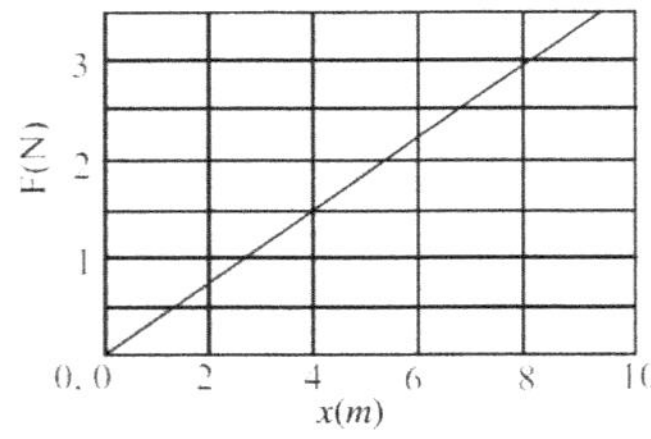

If the speed of the object at $x = 4$ m in 3.16 ms^{-1} then its speed at $x = 8$ m is:

A. 3.16 ms^{-1} B. 9.3 ms^{-1}

C. 8 ms^{-1} D. 6.8 ms^{-1}

68. In a thermally isolated system, two boxes filled with an ideal gas are connected by a valve. When the valve is in closed position, states of the box 1 and 2, respectively, are (1 atm, V, T) and (0.5 atm, 4V, T). When the valve is opened, the final pressure of the system is approximately?

A. 0.5 atm B. 0.6 atm

C. 0.75 atm D. 1.0 atm

69. A student sees the top edge and the bottom center C of a pool simultaneously from an angle θ above the horizontal as shown in the figure. The refraction index of water which fills up to the top edge of the pool is 4/3. If $h/x = 7/4$ then $\cos\theta$ is:

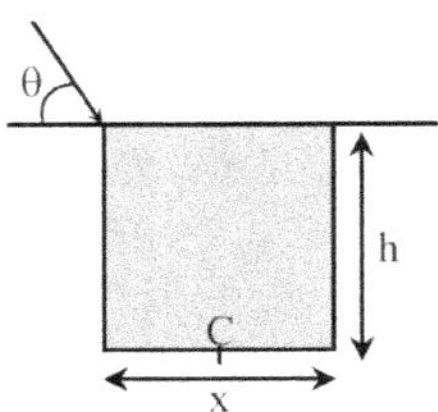

A. $\dfrac{2}{7}$ B. $\dfrac{8}{3\sqrt{45}}$

C. $\dfrac{8}{3\sqrt{53}}$ D. $\dfrac{8}{21}$

70. In the following circuit, the 1 Ω resistor dissipates power P. If the resistor is replaced by 9 Ω, the power dissipated in it is:

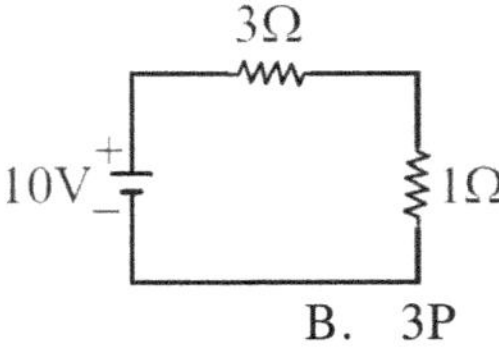

A. P B. 3P

C. 9P D. P/3

Chemistry

71. An aqueous buffer is prepared by adding 100 ml of 0.1 mol l^{-1} acetic acid to 50 ml of 0.2 mol l^{-1} of sodium acetate. If pK_a of acetic acid is 4.76, the pH of the buffer is:

A. 4.26 B. 5.76

C. 3.76 D. 4.76

72. The maximum number of structural isomers possible for the hydrocarbon having the molecular formula C_4H_6, is:

A. 12 B. 3

C. 9 D. 5

73. In the following reaction sequence, X and Y, respectively are:

A. H_2O_2; $LiAlH_4$
B. C_6H_5COOOH; $LiAlH_4$
C. C_6H_5COOOH; Zn/Hg.HCl
D. Alkaline $KMnO_4$; $LiAlH_4$

74. Among (*i*) $[Co(NH_3)_6]Cl_3$, (*ii*) $[Ni(NH_3)_6]Cl_2$, (*iii*) $[Cr(H_2O)_6]Cl_3$, (*iv*) $[Fe(H_2O)_6]Cl_2$ the complex which is diamagnetic is:

A. (*i*) B. (*ii*)
C. (*iii*) D. (*iv*)

75. At 783 K in the reaction $H_2(g) + I_2(g) \rightleftharpoons 2HI\ (g)$, the molar concentrations (mol^{-1}) of H_2, I_2 and HI at some instant of time are 0.1, 0.2 and 0.4, respectively. If the equilibrium constant is 46 at the same temperature, then as the reaction proceeds:

A. the amount of HI will increase
B. the amount of HI will decrease
C. the amount of H_2 and I_2 will increase
D. the amount of H_2 and I_2 will not change

Biology

76. You remove four fresh tobacco leaves of similar size and age. Leave "leaf 1" as it is, smear "leaf 2" with vaseline on the upper surface, "leaf 3" on the lower surface and "leaf 4" on both the surfaces. Hang the leaves for a few hours and you observe that leaf 1 wilts the most, leaf 2 has wilted, leaf 3 wilted less than leaf 2 and leaf 4 remains fresh. Which of the following conclusion is most logical?

A. tobacco leaf has more stomata on the upper surface
B. tobacco leaf has more stomata on the lower surface
C. stomata are equally distributed in upper and lower surfaces
D. no conclusion on stomatal distribution can be drawn from this experiment

77. Vestigial organs such as the appendix exist because:

A. they had an important function during development which is not needed in the adult
B. they have a redundant role to play if an organ with similar function fails
C. nature cannot get rid of structures that have already formed
D. they were inherited from an evolutionary ancestor in which they were functional

78. Mendel showed that unit factors, now called alleles, exhibit a dominant/recessive relationship. In a monohybrid cross, the .... trait disappears in the first filial generation:

A. dominant B. co-dominant
C. recessive D. semi-dominant

79. If a man with an X-linked dominant disease has six sons with a woman having a normal complement of genes, then the sons will:

A. not show any symptoms of the disease
B. show strong symptoms of the disease
C. three will show a disease symptom, while three will not
D. five will show a disease symptom, while one will not

80. In evolutionary terms, an Indian school boys is more closely related to:

A. an Indian frog B. an American snake
C. a Chinese horse D. an African shark

ANSWERS

1	**2**	**3**	**4**	**5**	**6**	**7**	**8**	**9**	**10**
A	C	A	B	B	D	A	A	A	C
11	**12**	**13**	**14**	**15**	**16**	**17**	**18**	**19**	**20**
B	C	B	A	C	A	A	C	D	A
21	**22**	**23**	**24**	**25**	**26**	**27**	**28**	**29**	**30**
B	C	C	D	C	B	B	D	A	C
31	**32**	**33**	**34**	**35**	**36**	**37**	**38**	**39**	**40**
D	C	D	D	A	D	A	A	B	C
41	**42**	**43**	**44**	**45**	**46**	**47**	**48**	**49**	**50**
D	D	B	B	C	B	D	C	B	C
51	**52**	**53**	**54**	**55**	**56**	**57**	**58**	**59**	**60**
D	A	C	C	A	B	A	B	B	D
61	**62**	**63**	**64**	**65**	**66**	**67**	**68**	**69**	**70**
C	C	B	D	A	B	D	B	C	A
71	**72**	**73**	**74**	**75**	**76**	**77**	**78**	**79**	**80**
D	C	B	A	A	B	D	C	A	C

EXPLANATORY ANSWERS

1. $P(x) = \dfrac{(x-b)(x-c)}{(a-b)(a-c)} + \dfrac{(x-c)(x-a)}{(b-c)(b-a)} + \dfrac{(x-a)(x-b)}{(c-a)(c-b)}$

Let, $P(a) = 1 + 0 + 0 = 1$

$P(b) = 0 + 1 + 0 = 1$

$P(c) = 0 + 0 + 1 = 1$

$\therefore\ P(x) = 1$ for all $x \in R$.

2. $a^2 + b^2 = 81$

$x^2 + y^2 = 121$

$ax + by = 99$

$(a^2 + b^2)(x^2 + y^2) = (81)(121)$ ...(*i*)

and $(ax + by)^2 = (99)^2$ ...(*ii*)

(*i*) – (*ii*) $(ay - bx)^2 = 0$

$ay - bx = 0.$

3. $x + \dfrac{1}{x} = a$ and $x^2 + \dfrac{1}{x^3} = b$

$$\left(x + \frac{1}{x}\right)^2 = a^2$$

$\Rightarrow\ x^2 + \dfrac{1}{x^2} + 2 = a^2$ ...(*i*)

and $\left(x + \dfrac{1}{x}\right)^3 = a^3$

$\Rightarrow\ x^3 + \dfrac{1}{x^3} + 3x.\dfrac{1}{x}\left(x + \dfrac{1}{x}\right) = a^3$ ...(*ii*)

adding (*i*) and (*ii*)

$$\left(x^2 + \frac{1}{x^3}\right) + \left(x^3 + \frac{1}{x^2}\right) + 2 + 3\left(x + \frac{1}{x}\right) = a^2 + a^3$$

$$b + \left(x^3 + \frac{1}{x^2}\right) + 2 + 3a = a^2 + a^3$$

$\therefore\ x^3 + \dfrac{1}{x^2} = a^3 + a^2 - 3a - 2 - b.$

4. $|a - b| = 2 \Rightarrow a - b = \pm 2$

$|a - c| = 3 \Rightarrow b - c = \pm 3$

$|c - d| = 4 \Rightarrow c - d = \pm 4$

Possible values of $a - d$ are $\pm 9, \pm 5, \pm 3, \pm 1$

$|a - d| = 9, 5, 3, 1$

Sum = 18.

5. Given $0 < r < 4$

in the given options

$(\text{Base})^x = \dfrac{9}{5}$

for largest value of x, base should be minimum.

$\therefore$ in option B base $\left(1 + \dfrac{r}{17}\right)$ is minimum for $0 < r < 4$.

6. From angle bisector theorem

$\dfrac{r}{6} = \dfrac{p}{q}$

$q\,r = 6\,p$ ...(*i*)

Area of ΔADC = 10 cm²

$\dfrac{1}{2}(DC)(AB) = 10$

$\dfrac{1}{2}(q)(r) = 10$

$q\,r = 20$

From (*i*) $\Rightarrow$ $20 = 6p$

$p = \dfrac{20}{6} = \dfrac{10}{3}.$

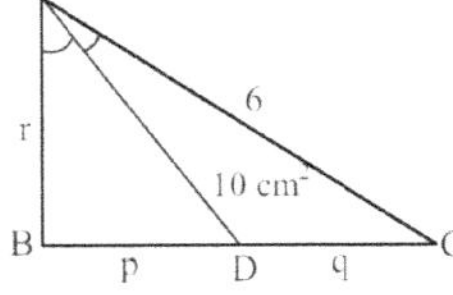

7. Slant height = 13

$\theta = \dfrac{S}{r}$

$\Rightarrow\ S = r\,\theta$

$\Rightarrow\ 2\pi(5) = 13\,\theta$

$\Rightarrow\ \theta = \dfrac{10\pi}{13}.$

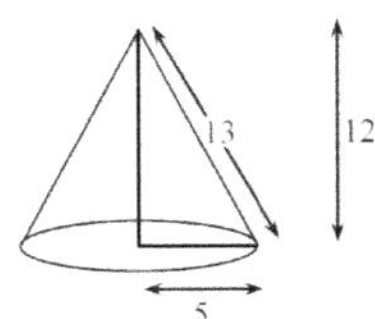

8.

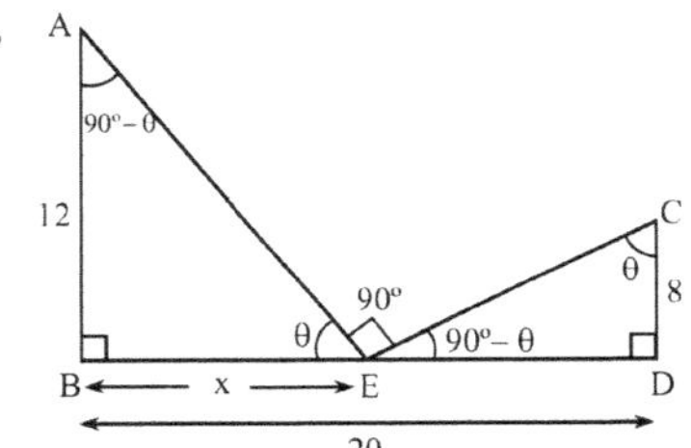

$\dfrac{12}{x} = \dfrac{20 - x}{8}$

$\Rightarrow x^2 - 20x + 96 = 0$

$\Rightarrow\ x = 8, 12.$

9.

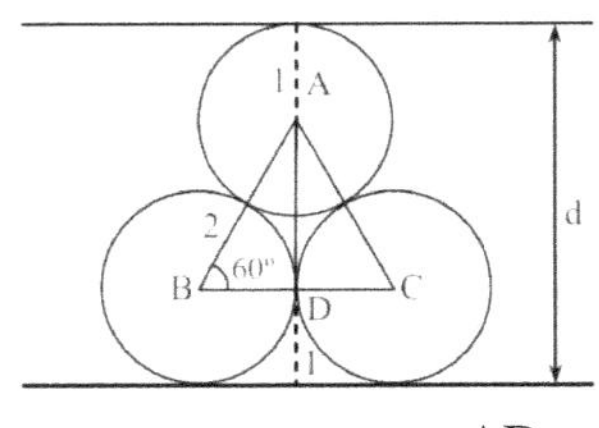

$\sin 60° = \dfrac{AD}{2}$

$AD = 2 \sin 60° = \dfrac{2\sqrt{3}}{2} = \sqrt{3}$

$d = 1 + AD + 1$

$d = 2 + \sqrt{3}.$

10. $(512)^3 - 253^3 - 259^3$

$= (512)^3 - [(253^3) + (259)^3]$

$= (512)^3 - (253 + 259)(253^2 + 259)^2 - (253)(259)$

$= (512)^3 - (512)[(253 + 259)^2 - 2(253)(259) - (253)(259)]$
$= 512 [(512)^2 - \{(512)^2 - 3 (253)(259)\}]$
$= (512) [3 (253)(259)]$
$= 2^9 \cdot 3 \cdot (253)(259)$
$= 2^9 \cdot 3 (11)(23)(7)(37)$
6 prime divisors.

11. Top layer has (13 × 13) balls similarly are layer below top layer will have (14 × 14) balls
We have 18 layer
So, total number of balls

$$N = (13)^2 + (14)^2 + ... + (30)^2$$
$$N = \frac{30 \times 31 \times 61}{6} - \frac{12 \times 13 \times 25}{6}$$
$$N = 8805.$$

12. Let distance is $6x$

	mud	:	tar	:	stream
distance	x	:	$3x$	:	$2x$
speed	$3v$	:	$5v$	:	$4v$
time	$\frac{x}{3v}$	:	$\frac{3x}{5v}$	:	$\frac{2x}{4v}$
	10	:	18	:	15

13.

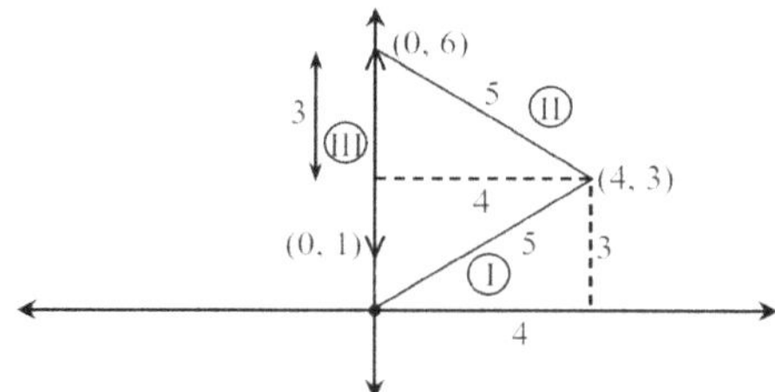

3 steps.

14. The clock will show the incorrect time (between 1–2, 10–11, 11–12 , 12–1 day and night both)
∴ incorrect time 8 × 60 = 480 (each minute it will display 1)
Remaining 20 hours it will show the incorrect time 16 × 15 = 240
Total incorrect time = 240 + 480 = 720
correct time = 1 – incorrect time

$$= 1 - \frac{720}{24 \times 60} = 1/2.$$

15.

Right (4 marks)	Wrong (0 mark)	Unattempted (1 mark)
15	15	0
14		4
13		8
12		12
11		16
10		20

6 cases.

16.

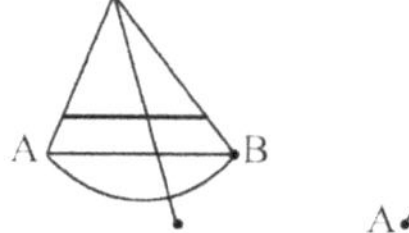

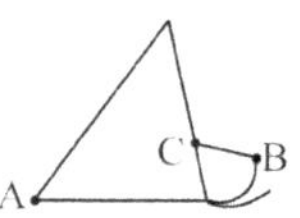

According to law of conservation of mechanical energy

$$K_i + U_i = K_f + U_f$$
$$0 + U_i = 0 + U_f$$
$$h_i = h_f$$

Point D is at line AB.

17. $\because \quad \sum F_{ext} = 0$
$\therefore \quad a_{system} = 0.$

18. $H - h = \frac{1}{2}gt^2$

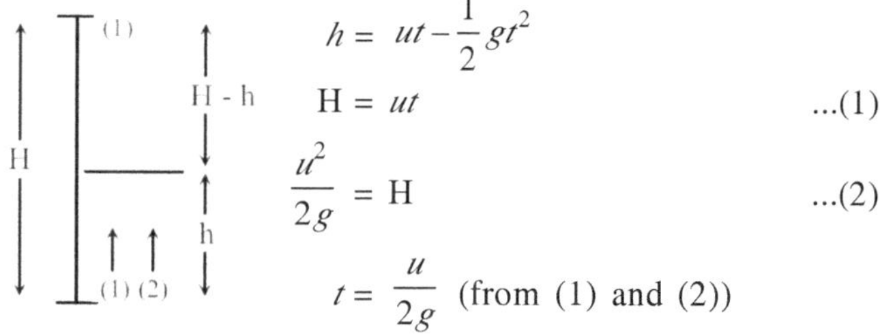

$$h = ut - \frac{1}{2}gt^2$$
$$H = ut \quad ...(1)$$
$$\frac{u^2}{2g} = H \quad ...(2)$$
$$t = \frac{u}{2g} \text{ (from (1) and (2))}$$
$$\therefore \quad h = u \times \frac{u}{2g} - \frac{1}{2}g \times \frac{u^2}{4g^2} = \frac{3u^2}{8g} = \frac{3H}{4}.$$

19.

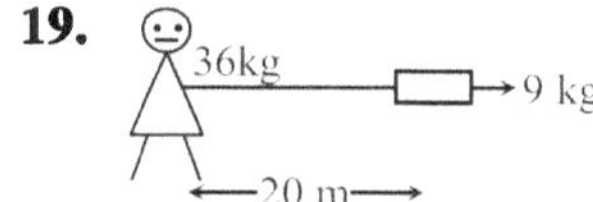

∵ external force does not work on system
So, according to concept of mass

$$36\,x = 9 \times (20 - x)$$
$$x = 4 \text{ m}.$$

20. All the three object will be in thermal equilibrium then % $T_1 = T_2 = T_3$.

21. Pressure of gas is app. same everywhere in the vessel.

22.

Sea

beach

In beach velocity is higher
∴ beach is rarer and sea is denser medium.
So, when it go from rarer to denser medium it bend toward normal to reach in minimum time.

23. $i = 45° \geq C$
For minimum refractive index C = 45°

$$\mu \sin 45° = 1$$
$$\mu = \sqrt{2} = 1.42.$$

24.

Only half part of the lens will be used so its intensity will be decreased.

25. Applying volume conservation

$$A \times L = A' \times 2L$$

$$A' = \frac{A}{2}$$

$$R = \frac{\rho L}{A}$$

$$R' = \frac{\rho \times 2L}{A'} = \frac{\rho \times 4L}{A}$$

$$R' = 4R.$$

26. E_1 E_2 Q −2Q

27.

$$mgh = 300 \times 10 \times 6$$

$$P_i = \frac{mgh}{t} = \frac{300 \times 10 \times 6}{60} = 300 \text{ W}$$

$$P_0 = 750 \text{ W}$$

$$\eta = \frac{300}{750} \times 100 = 40\%.$$

28.

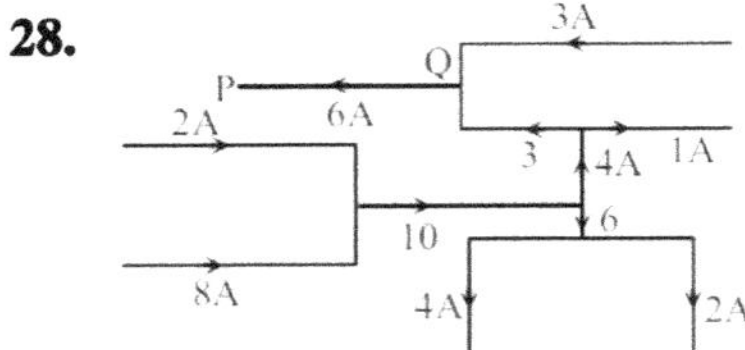

29. $Pb^{214}_{82} \xrightarrow[2e^- + {}_2He^4]{} {}^{210}_{82}X$

82 → Proton

210 − 82 = 128 Neutron.

30.

$$PV = N \times K \times T$$

where K is Boltzmann constant

$$10^5 \times 100 = N \times 1.38 \times 10^{23} \times 273$$

$$N \approx 3 \times 10^{27}.$$

31. Since pressure of the gases are same in both the containers. Therefore the final pressure will not change.

32. $-OCH_3$ is activating group.

order of deactivating is $-\overset{O}{\overset{||}{C}}-O-CH_3 < -NO_2$.

33. n is always greater than ℓ

and $m = -\ell \ldots\ldots\ 0 \ \ldots\ldots + \ell$

If $n = 2$, then $\ell = 0, 1$

and $m_\ell = 0, \{-1, 0, +1\}$.

34. $(K.E.)_{average} = \frac{3}{2}kT$

i.e., average kinetic energy depends only on temperature.

35. According to KTG

Force of attraction and repulsion amongst molecules of ideal gas are negligible

So, $\Delta H = 0$

and randomness increases due to increase in volume so $\Delta S = +ve$.

36. $(NH_4)_2Cr_2O_7 \xrightarrow{\Delta} N_2 + Cr_2O_3 + 4H_2O$.

37. At 40°C solubility is 200 gm per 100 ml (approx)

i.e., 100 ml of water contains = 200 gm of KNO_3 (approx)

50 ml of water contains = 100 gm (approx).

38. A. $CH_3-\overset{O}{\overset{||}{C}}-CH_2-CH_2-CH_3$ → Show iodoform test

B. $CH_3-CH_2-\overset{O}{\overset{||}{C}}-CH_2-CH_3$

C. $CH_3-CH_2-\underset{OH}{\underset{|}{CH}}-CH_2-CH_3$

D. $CH_3-CH_2-CH_2-CH_2-CH_2-OH$

39.

$$\frac{0.693}{t_{1/2}} = \frac{2.303}{2 \times 60} \log \frac{a}{a/16}$$

$$t_{1/2} = 30 \text{ min.}$$

40. $2ZnS + 3O_2 \xrightarrow{950°C} 2ZnO + 2SO_2$

$ZnS + 2O_2 \xrightarrow{950°C} ZnSO_4$

then, $2ZnSO_4 \xrightarrow{950°C} 2ZnO + 2SO_2 + O_2$.

41. $H-\overset{O}{\overset{||}{\underset{H}{\underset{|}{P}}}}-OH$ $H-\overset{O}{\overset{||}{\underset{OH}{\underset{|}{P}}}}-OH$ $HO-\overset{O}{\overset{||}{\underset{OH}{\underset{|}{P}}}}-OH$

So, H_3PO_2, H_3PO_3 and H_3PO_4 contains 2, 1 and zero P–H bonds.

42. $2KBr + Cl_2 \rightarrow 2KCl + Br_2$ (brown).

43. (*i*) and (*iv*) are heteroaromatic compound.

(*ii*) is non aromatic.

(*iii*) → aromatic

44. H_3C 6 5 4 3 2 1 CH_3 H_3C CH_3

45. Given reaction → SN^2

Br Cl + $CN^{(-)}$ → Br CN
I I

47. DNA replication occur in S phase just before to meiosis-I only it will not replicates in between meiosis-I & meiosis-II.

52. Either X or Y chromosome.

54. Centriole or centrosome is only present in animal.

56. Only reducing sugar give the test with benedict solution.

59. Endo-osmosis occur in cell, when cell is placed in Hypotonic solution.

61. $f(x) = ax^2 + bx + c$

given $f(1) = 0$

$\Rightarrow \quad a + b + c = 0$

and $\quad 40 < f(6) < 50$

$\Rightarrow \quad 40 < 36a + 6b + c < 50$

$\Rightarrow \quad 40 < 35a + 5b < 50$

$\Rightarrow \quad 8 < 7a + b < 10$

$7a + b = \text{integer} = 9 \qquad ...(i)$

and $\quad 60 < f(7) < 70$

$\Rightarrow \quad 60 < 49a + 7b + c < 70$

$\Rightarrow \quad 60 < 48a + 6b < 70$

$\Rightarrow \quad 10 < 8a + b < 11.6$

$8a + b = \text{integer} = 11 \qquad ...(ii)$

Solving (*i*) & (*ii*)

$a = 2, b = -5, c = 3$

$\therefore \quad f(x) = 2x^2 - 5x + 3$

$f(50) = 4753$

$1000\, t < f(50) < 1000(t + 1)$

$(1000 \times 4) < 4753 < 1000(4 + 1)$

$\therefore \quad t = 4.$

62. $\dfrac{2^2+1}{2^2-1}+\dfrac{3^2+1}{3^2-1}+\dfrac{4^2+1}{4^2-1}+...+\dfrac{(2011)^2+1}{(2011)^2-1}$

$$\Rightarrow \sum_{r=2}^{2011}\frac{r^2+1}{r^2-1} = \sum_{r=2}^{2011}\left[1+\frac{2}{(r+1)(r-1)}\right]$$

$$= \sum_{r=2}^{2011}\left[1+\frac{1}{r-1}-\frac{1}{r+1}\right]$$

$$= 2010+\left[1-\frac{1}{3}+\frac{1}{2}-\frac{1}{4}+\frac{1}{3}-\frac{1}{5}+...+\frac{1}{2010}-\frac{1}{2012}\right]$$

$$= 2010+1+\frac{1}{2}-\frac{1}{2012}-\frac{1}{2011}$$

$$= 2011+\frac{1}{2}-\left[\frac{1}{2011}+\frac{1}{2012}\right]$$

lies between $\left(2011, 2011\frac{1}{2}\right)$.

63. Let initially 2 bases have radii 5 cm and r cm.

Finally base have radii (1.21×5) and r

Ratios of volumes $= \dfrac{V_2}{V_1} = 1.21$

$$V_2 = \frac{\pi h}{3}[(6.05)^2+(6.05)r+r^2]$$

$$V_1 = \frac{\pi h}{3}[5^2+5r+r^2]$$

$$\frac{V_2}{V_1} = 1.21$$

$$\Rightarrow \frac{(6.05)^2+(6.05)r+r^2}{5^2+5r+r^2} = 1.21$$

$$\Rightarrow r^2 = \frac{6.3525}{21}$$

$$\Rightarrow r = \frac{11}{2}\text{ cm} = 55\text{ mm}.$$

64. Speed of B = V km/hr

Speed of A = 3 V km/hr

Given 4 V = 2 × 60 km/hr

$\Rightarrow$ V = 30 km/hr

Distance covered by then after 10 min

= 2 × 10 = 20 km

So, remaining distance = (30 – 20) km = 10 km

Time taken by B to cover 10 km $= \dfrac{10}{30/60} = 20$ min.

Total time = 20 +10 = 30 min.

65. A 10 hr

B 20 hr

C 30 hr

Exactly are pair of taps is open during each hour and every pair of taps is open at least for one hour.

First A and B are open for 1 hour then B and C and then C and A

$$\left(\frac{1}{10}+\frac{1}{20}\right)+\left(\frac{1}{20}+\frac{1}{30}\right)+\left(\frac{1}{30}+\frac{1}{10}\right)=\frac{22}{60}$$

first second third

In three hours the tank will be filled $\left(\dfrac{22}{60}\right)^{th}$ part.

Now, for minimum time the rest tank must be filled with A and B taps

$\left(\dfrac{1}{10}+\dfrac{1}{20}=\dfrac{9}{60}\right)$. So, the rest $\left(\dfrac{38}{60}\right)^{th}$ part of tank will take 5 hours more. So, the tank will be filled in 8th hour.

66.

m

F.B.D.

$\rho_1 Vg$ kx_1 m ρVg $\qquad$ $\rho_2 Vg$ kx_2 m ρVg

$$kx_1 + \rho_1 Vg = \rho Vg \qquad ...(i)$$

$$kx_2 + \rho_2 Vg = \rho Vg \qquad ...(ii)$$

From (*i*) and (*ii*)

$$\rho = \frac{\rho_2 x_1 - \rho_1 x_2}{x_1 - x_2} = \frac{\rho_1 x_2 - \rho_2 x_1}{x_2 - x_1}.$$

67. According to work-energy principle

$$W_C + W_{nc} + W_{ext} = \Delta KE$$

$$\int_4^8 F\,dx = \frac{1}{2}mv_f^2 - \frac{1}{2}mv_i^2$$

$$\frac{1}{2}\times 3\times 8 - \frac{1}{2}\times 1.5\times 4 = \frac{1}{2}\times\frac{1}{2}[v_f^2 - (3.16)^2]$$

$$v_f = 6.8 \text{ m/s.}$$

68. 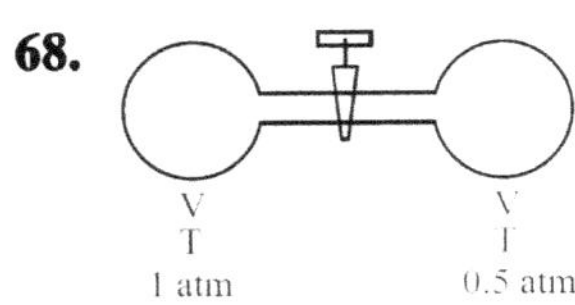

After opening of at equilibrium temperature and pressure of whole gas is T_1 and P_1

$$n_1 = \frac{1\times V}{RT},\ n_2 = \frac{0.5\times V\times 4}{RT}$$

$$n_1 + n_2 = n$$

$$\frac{V}{RT} + \frac{V\times 4}{2RT} = \frac{5VP_1}{RT_1}$$

$$\frac{3V}{RT} = \frac{5VP_1}{RT_1}$$

$$\frac{P_1}{T_1} = \frac{0.6}{T}$$

$$\Delta Q = 0,\ \Delta W = 0$$

$$\therefore \quad \Delta U = 0$$

$$n_1C_VT + n_2C_VT = (n_1 + n_2)C_VT_1$$

$$T_1 = T$$

$$\frac{P_1}{T} = \frac{0.6}{T}$$

$$P_1 = 0.6 \text{ atm.}$$

69. $1 \times \sin i = \mu \sin r$

$$\sin(90 - \theta) = \frac{4}{3}\sin r$$

$$\tan r = \frac{x}{2h} = \frac{4}{7\times 2} = \frac{2}{7}$$

$$\sin r = \frac{2}{\sqrt{53}}$$

$$\cos\theta = \frac{4}{3}\times\frac{2}{\sqrt{53}} = \frac{8}{3\sqrt{53}}.$$

70. $10 = 4i$

$$i = \frac{5}{2}$$

$$P_i = i^2R = \left(\frac{5}{2}\right)^2 \times 1 = \frac{25}{4}$$

$$P_f = \left(\frac{10}{12}\right)^2 \times 9 = \frac{100}{12\times 12}\times 9 \Rightarrow P_f = P_i$$

71. Meq of $CH_3COOH = 100 \times 0.1 \times 1 = 10$

Meq of $CH_3COONa = 50 \times 0.2 \times 1 = 10$

$$pH = pK_a + \log\frac{[CH_3COO^-]}{[CH_3COOH]}$$

$$pH = 4.76 + \log\frac{10}{10}$$

$$pH = 4.76 + \log 1$$

$$pH = 4.76.$$

72. Possible structural isomers are nine.

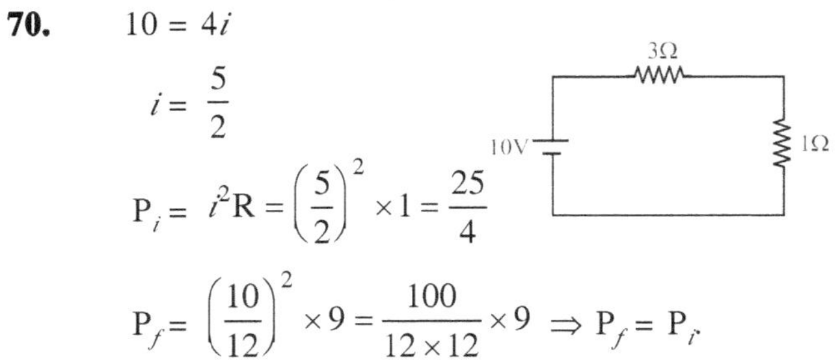

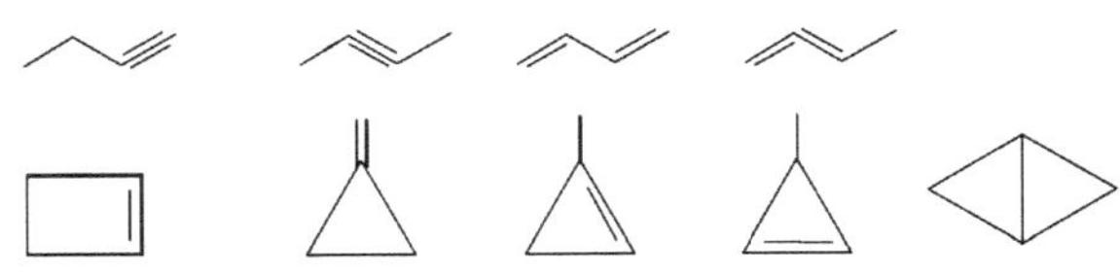

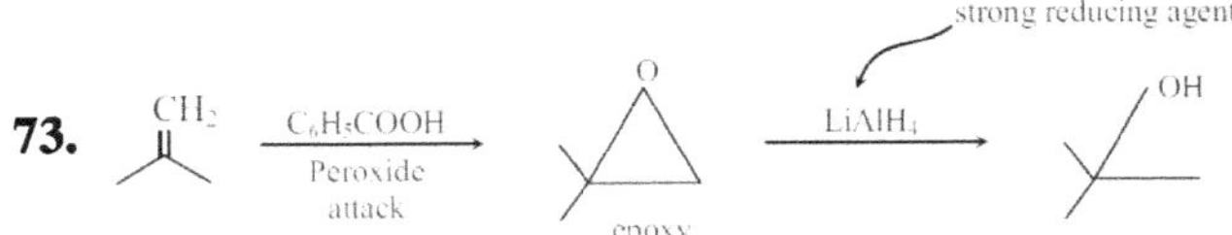

73. CH_2 —(C_6H_5COOH, Peroxide attack)→ epoxy —($LiAlH_4$, strong reducing agent)→ OH

74. (*i*) Co^{+3} = [Ar] $3d^6\ s^0$

NH_3 is a strong field ligand

(*ii*) Ni^{+2} = [Ar] $3d^8\ 4s^0$

NH_3 is a strong field ligand

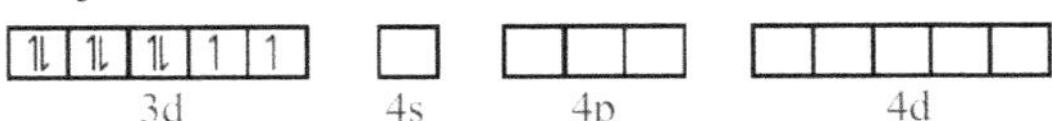

(*iii*) Cr^{+3} = [Ar] $3d^3\ 4s^0$

H_2O is a weak field ligand

(*iv*) Fe^{+2} = [Ar] $3d^6\ 4s^0$

H_2O is a weak field ligand.

So, $[Co(NH_3)_6]Cl_3$ will be diamagnetic.

75. Reaction quotient

$$Q = \frac{[HI]^2}{[H_2][I_2]} = \frac{0.4\times 0.4}{0.1\times 0.2}$$

$$Q = 8$$

$$Q < K$$

So, reaction will proceeds in forward direction.

Hence, amount of HI increases.

78. Recessive allele does not express itself in presence of dominant allele.

79. Son get their X chromosome from mother.

80. Human & horse both belongs to mammalia.

Previous Paper (Solved), 2010

Kishore Vaigyanik Protsahan Yojana (KVPY)

STREAM – SA

Part-I

Mathematics

1. A student notices that the roots of the equation $x^2 + bx + a = 0$ are each 1 less than the roots of the equation $x^2 + ax + b = 0$. Then $a + b$ is:

A. Possibly any real number
B. –2
C. –4
D. –5

2. If x, y are real numbers such that $3^{\frac{x}{y}+1} - 3^{\frac{x}{y}-1} = 24$, then the value of $(x + y) / (x - y)$ is:

A. 0 B. 1
C. 2 D. 3

3. The number of positive integers n in the set $\{1, 2, 3, \ldots, 100\}$ for which the number $\dfrac{1^2 + 2^2 + 3^2 + \ldots + n^2}{1 + 2 + 3 + \ldots + n}$ is an integer is:

A. 33 B. 34
C. 50 D. 100

4. The three different face diagonals of a cuboid (rectangular parallelopiped) have lengths 39, 40, 41. The length of the main diagonal of the cuboid which joins a pair of opposite corners is:

A. 49 B. $49\sqrt{2}$
C. 60 D. $60\sqrt{2}$

5. The sides of a triangle ABC are positive integers. The smallest side has length 1. Which of the following statements is true?

A. The area of ABC is always a rational number
B. The area of ABC is always an irrational number
C. The perimeter of ABC is an even integer
D. The information provided is not sufficient to conclude any of the statements A, B or C above

6. Consider a square ABCD of side 12 and let M, N be the midpoints of AB, CD respectively. Take a point P on MN and let AP = r, PC = s. Then the area of the triangle whose sides are r, s, 12 is:

A. 72 B. 36
C. $\dfrac{rs}{2}$ D. $\dfrac{rs}{7}$

7. A cow is tied to a corner (vertex) of a regular hexagonal fenced area of side a metres by a rope of length $5a/2$ metres in a grass field. (The cow cannot graze inside the fenced area.) What is the maximum possible area of the grass field to which the cow has access to graze?

A. $5\pi a^2$ B. $\dfrac{5}{2}\pi a^2$
C. $6\pi a^2$ D. $3\pi a^2$

8. A closed conical vessel is filled with water fully and is placed with its vertex down. The water is let out at a constant speed. After 21 minutes, it was found that the height of the water column is half of the original height. How much more time in minutes does it require to empty the vessel?

A. 21 B. 14
C. 7 D. 3

9. I carried 1000 kg of watermelon in summer by train. In the beginning, the water content was 99%. By the time I reached the destination, the water content had dropped to 98%. The reduction in the weight of the watermelon was:

A. 10 kg B. 50 kg
C. 100 kg D. 500 kg

10. A rectangle is divided into 16 sub-rectangles as in the figure, the number in each sub-rectangle represents the area of that sub-rectangle. What is the area of the rectangle KLMN?

10	4		
N M	12	15	
		25	

K L

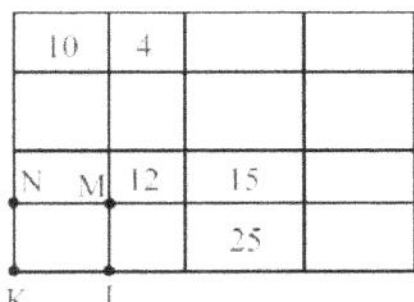

A. 20 B. 30
C. 40 D. 50

Physics

11. A hollow pendulum bob filled with water has a small hole at the bottom through which water escapes at a constant rate. Which of the following statements describes the variation of the time period (T) of the pendulum as the water flows out?
A. T decreases first and then increases
B. T increases first and then decreases
C. T increases throughout
D. T does not change

12. A block of mass M rests on a rough horizontal table. A steadily increasing horizontal force is applied such that the block starts to slide on the table without toppling. The force is continued even after sliding has started. Assume the coefficients of static and kinetic friction between the table and the block to be equal. The correct representation of the variation of the frictional force, *f*, exerted by the table on the block with time *t* is given by:

A. 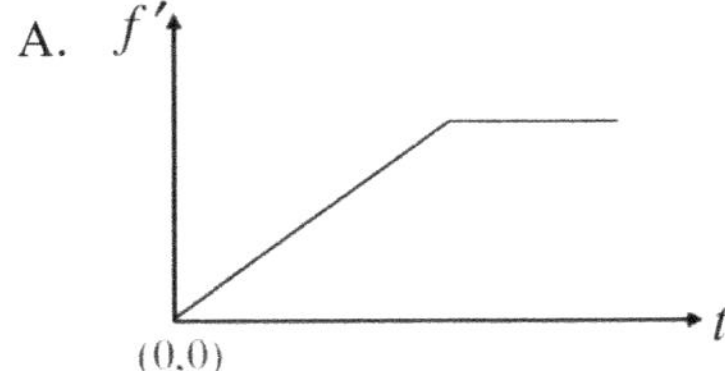

B. 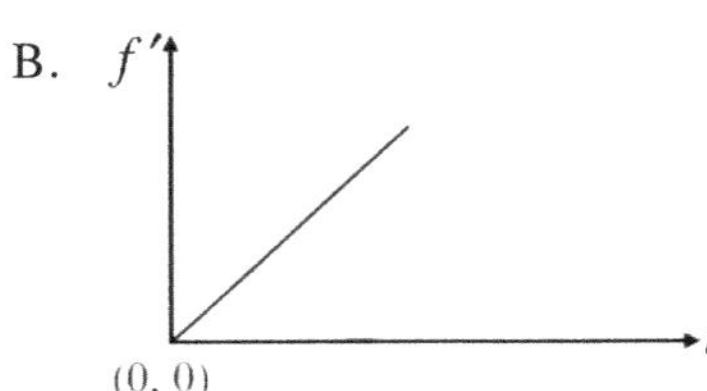

C. 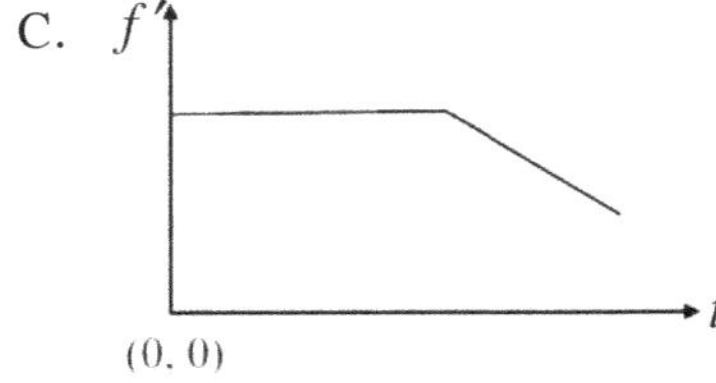

D. 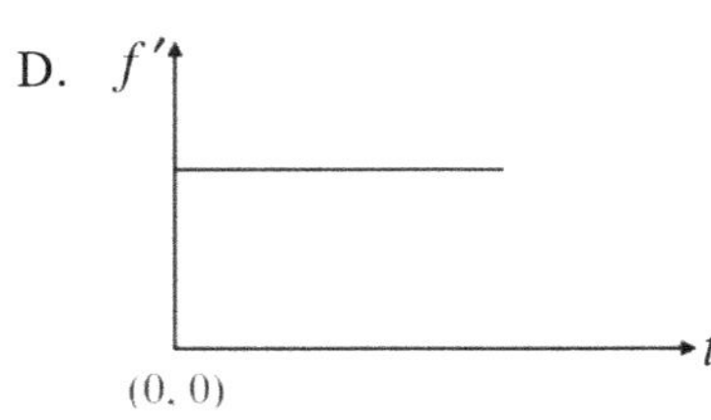

13. A soldier with a machine gun, falling from an airplane gets detached from his parachute. He is able to resist the downward acceleration if he shoots 40 bullets a second at the speed of 500 m/s. If the weight of a bullet is 49 gm, what is the weight of the man with the gun? Ignore resistance due to air and assume the acceleration due to gravity $g = 9.8$ ms^{-2}:

A. 50 kg B. 75 kg
C. 100 kg D. 125 kg

14. A planet of mass *m* is moving around a star of mass M and radius R in a circular orbit of radius *r*. The star abruptly shrinks to half its radius without any loss of mass. What change will be there in the orbit of the planet?
A. The planet will escape from the star
B. The radius of the orbit will increase
C. The radius of the orbit will decrease
D. The radius of the orbit will not change

15. Figure (*a*) below shows a Wheatstone bridge in which P, Q, R, S are fixed resistances, G is a galvanometer and B is a battery. For this particular case the galvanometer shows zero deflection. Now, only the positions of B and G are interchanged, as shown in figure (*b*). The new deflection of the galvanometer:

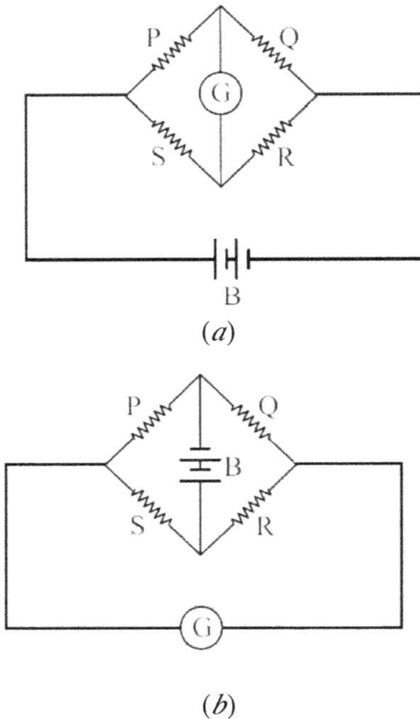

A. is to the left
B. is to the right
C. is zero
D. depends on the values of P, Q, R, S

16. 12 positive charges of magnitude *q* are placed on a circle of radius R in a manner that they are equally spaced. A charge +Q is placed at the centre. If one of the charges *q* is removed, then the force on Q is:
A. zero
B. $\frac{qQ}{4\pi\varepsilon_0 R^2}$ away from the position of the removed charge

C. $\frac{11qQ}{4\pi\varepsilon_0 R^2}$ away from the position of the removed charge

D. $\frac{qQ}{4\pi\varepsilon_0 R^2}$ towards the position of the removed charge

17. An electric heater consists of a nichrome coil and runs under 220 V, consuming 1 kW power. Part of its coil burned out and it was reconnected after cutting off the burnt portion. The power it will consume now is:
A. more than 1 kW
B. less than 1 kW, but not zero
C. 1 kW
D. 0 kW

18. White light is split into a spectrum by a prism and it is seen on a screen. If we put another identical inverted prism behind it in contact, what will be seen on the screen?
A. Violet will appear where red was
B. The spectrum will remain the same
C. There will be no spectrum, but only the original light with no deviation
D. There will be no spectrum, but the original light will be laterally displaced

19. Two identical blocks of metal are at 20°C and 80°C, respectively. The specific heat of the material of the two blocks increases with temperature. Which of the following is true about the final temperature T_f when the two blocks are brought into contact (assuming that no heat is lost to the surroundings):
A. T_f will be 50°C
B. T_f will be more than 50°C
C. T_f will be less than 50°C
D. T_f can be either more than or less than 50°C depending on the precise variation of the specific heat with temperature

20. A new temperature scale uses X as a unit of temperature, where the numerical value of the temperature t_x in this scale is related to the absolute temperature T by $t_x - 3T + 300$. If the specific heat of a material using this unit is 1400 J $kg^{-1}X^{-1}$ its specific heat in the S.I. system of units is:
A. 4200 J $kg^{-1}X^{-1}$
B. 1400 J $kg^{-1}X^{-1}$
C. 466.7 J $kg^{-1}X^{-1}$
D. impossible to determine from the information provided

Chemistry

21. The boiling points of 0.01 M aqueous solutions of sucrose, NaCl and $CaCl_2$ would be:
A. the same
B. highest for sucrose solution
C. highest for NaCl solution
D. highest for $CaCl_2$ solution

22. The correct electronic configuration for the ground state of silicon (atomic number 14) is:
A. $1s^2\ 2s^2\ 2p^6\ 3s^2\ 3p^2$
B. $1s^2\ 2s^2\ 2p^6\ 3p^4$
C. $1s^2\ 2s^2\ 2p^4\ 3s^2\ 3p^4$
D. $1s^2\ 2s^2\ 2p^6\ 3s^1\ 3p^3$

23. The molar mass of $CaCO_3$ is 100 g. The maximum amount of carbon dioxide that can be liberated on heating 25 g of $CaCO_3$ is:
A. 11 g   B. 55 g
C. 22 g   D. 2.2 g

24. The atomic radii of the elements across the second period of the periodic table:
A. decrease due to increase in atomic number
B. decrease due to increase in effective nuclear charge
C. decrease due to increase in atomic weights
D. increase due to increase in the effective nuclear charge

25. Among NH_3, BCl_3, Cl_2 and N_2 the compound that does not satisfy the octet rule is:
A. NH_3 B. BCl_3
C. Cl_2 D. N_2

26. The gas produced on heating MnO_2 with conc. HCl is:
A. Cl_2 B. H_2
C. O_2 D. O_3

27. The number of covalent bonds in $C_4H_3Br_2$ is:
A. 12
B. 10
C. 13
D. 11

28. An aqueous solution of HCl has a pH of 2.0. When water is added to increase the pH to 5.0, the hydrogen ion concentration:
A. remains the same
B. decreases three-fold
C. increases three-fold
D. decreases thousand-fold

29. Consider two sealed jars of equal volume. One contains 2 g of hydrogen at 200 K and the other contains 28 g of nitrogen at 400 K. The gases in the two jars will have:

A. the same pressure
B. the same average kinetic energy
C. the same number of molecules
D. the same average molecular speed

30. Identify the stereoisomeric pair from the following choices:

A. $CH_3CH_2CH_2OH$ and $CH_3CH_2OCH_3$
B. $CH_3CH_2CH_2Cl$ and $CH_3CHClCH_3$
C. $CH_3-CH=CH-CH_3$ and $CH_3-CH_2-CH_2-CH_3$ (structures drawn with H atoms)
D. methylcyclopentane (CH_3 on a pentagon) and cyclohexane

Biology

31. Which of the following is a water-borne disease?
A. Tuberculosis B. Chickenpox
C. Malaria D. Cholera

32. In his seminal work on genetics, Gregor Mendel described the physical traits in the pea plant as being controlled by two 'factors'. What term is used to define these factors today?
A. Chromosomes B. Alleles
C. Genes D. Hybrids

33. A majority of the tree species of peninsular Indian origin fruit in the months of:
A. April – May B. December – January
C. August – September D. All months of the year

34. In frogs, body proportions do not change with their growth. A frog that is twice as long as another will be heavier by approximately:
A. Two-fold B. Six-fold
C. Four-fold D. Eight-fold

35. Which of the following has the widest angle of binocular vision?
A. Rat B. Duck
C. Eagle D. Owl

36. The two alleles of a locus which an offspring receives from the male and female gametes are situated on:
A. Two different homologs of the same chromosome
B. Two different chromosomes
C. Sex chromosomes
D. A single chromosome

37. Ants locate sucrose by:
A. Using a strong sense of smell
B. Using a keen sense of vision
C. Physical contact with sucrose
D. Sensing the particular wavelength of light emitted/reflected by sucrose

38. The interior of a cow-dung pile kept for a few days is quite warm. This is mostly because:
A. Cellulose present in the dung is a good insulator
B. Bacterial metabolism inside the dung releases heat
C. Undigested material releases heat due to oxidation by air
D. Dung is dark and absorbs a lot of heat

39. Which one of these is the correct path for a reflex action?
A. Receptor-Motor Neuron-Spinal Cord-Sensory Neuron-Effector
B. Effector-Sensory Neuron-Spinal Cord-Motor Neuron-Receptor
C. Receptor-Sensory Neuron-Spinal Cord-Motor Neuron-Effector
D. Sensory Neuron-Receptor-Motor Neuron-Spinal Cord-Effector

40. Insectivorous plants digest insects to get an essential nutrient. Other plants generally get this nutrient from the soil. What is this nutrient?
A. Oxygen B. Carbon dioxide
C. Nitrogen D. Phosphates

Part-II

Mathematics

1. In a triangle ABC, D and E are points on AB, AC respectively such that DE is parallel to BC. Suppose BE, CD intersect at O. If the areas of the triangles ADE and ODE are 3 and 1 respectively, find the area of the triangle ABC, with justification.

2. Leela and Madan pooled their music CD's and sold them. They got as many rupees for each CD as the total number of CD's they sold. They share the money as follows Leela first takes 10 rupees, then Madan takes 10 rupees and they continue taking 10 rupees alternately till Madan is left out with less than 10 rupees to take. Find the amount that is left out for Madan at the end, with justification.

3. (*a*) Show that for every natural number n relatively prime to 10, there is another natural number m all of whose digits are 1's such that n divides m.

(*b*) Hence or otherwise show that every positive rational number can be expressed in the form $\frac{a}{10^b(10^c - 1)}$ for some natural numbers a, b, c.

Physics

4. Consider the two circuits P and Q, shown below, which are used to measure the unknown resistance R.

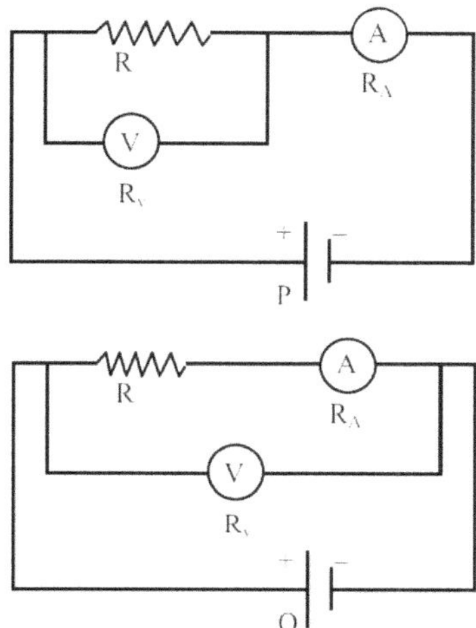

In each case, the resistance is estimated by using Ohm's law R_{est} = V/I, where V and I are the readings of the voltmeter and the ammeter respectively. The meter resistances, R_V and R_A are such that $R_A << R << R_V$. The internal resistance of the battery may be ignored. The absolute error in the estimate of the resistance is denoted by $\delta R = |R = R_{est}|$.

(*a*) Express δR_P in terms of the given resistance values

(*b*) Express δR_Q in terms of the given resistance values

(*c*) For what value of R will $\delta R_P \approx \delta R_Q$?

5. A point source is placed 20 cm to the left of a concave lens of focal length 10 cm.

(*a*) Where is the image formed?

(*b*) Where to the right of the lens would you place a concave mirror of focal length 5 cm so that the final image is coincident with the source?

(*c*) Where would the final image be formed if the concave mirror is replaced by a plane mirror at the same position?

6. A block of mass m is sliding on a fixed frictionless concave surface of radius R. It is released from rest at point P which is at a height of H < < R from the lowest point Q.

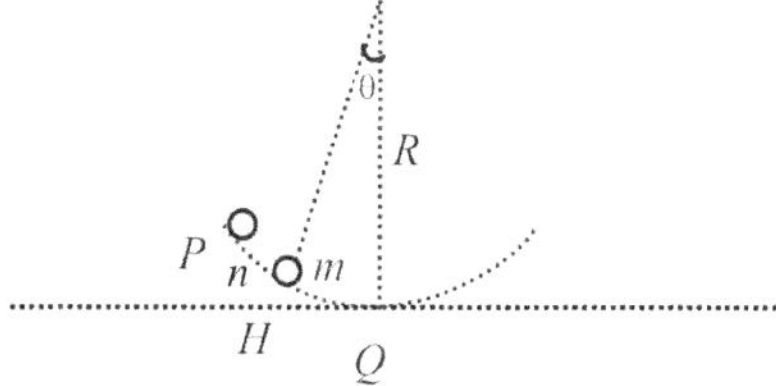

(*a*) What is the potential energy as a function of θ, taking the lowest point Q as the reference level for potential energy?

(*b*) What is the kinetic energy as a function of θ?

(*c*) What is the time taken for the particle to reach from point P to the lowest point Q?

(*d*) How much force is exerted by the block on the concave surface at the point Q?

Chemistry

7. Copper in an alloy is estimated by dissolving in conc. nitric acid. In this process copper is converted to cupric nitrate with the evolution of nitric oxide (NO). The mixture when treated with potassium iodide forms cupric iodide. Which is unstable and decomposes to cuprous iodide and iodine?

The amount of copper in the alloy is estimated by titrating the liberated iodine with sodium thiosulphate. The reactions are:

$a\,Cu + b\,HNO_3 \rightarrow c\,Cu(NO_3)_2 + d\,NO + e\,H_2O$

$f\,CuI_2 \rightarrow g\,Cu_2I_2 + h\,I_2$

$i\,Na_2S_2O_3 + j\,I_2 \rightarrow k\,Na_2S_4O_6 + l\,NaI$

(Fill up the blanks)

(*a*) The coefficients are: a = ____, b = ____, c = ____, d = ____ and e = ____.

(*b*) The coefficients are: f = ____, g = ____ and h = ____.

(*c*) The coefficients are: i = ____, j = ____, k = ____ and l = ____.

(*d*) If 2.54 g of I_2 is evolved from a 2.0 g sample of the alloy, what is the percentage of copper in the alloy?
(atomic weights of iodine and copper are 127 and 63.5, respectively)

8. You have been given four bottles marked A, B, C and D each containing one of the organic compounds given below:

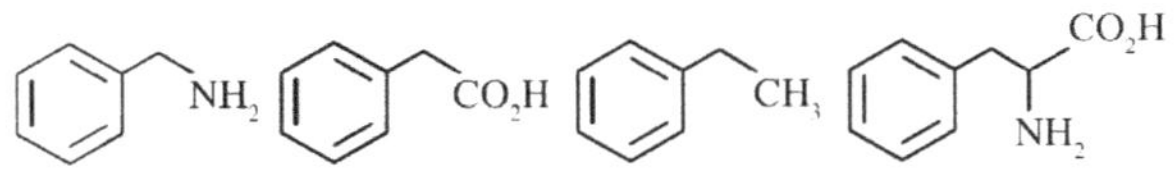

I II III IV

The following observations were made.

(*i*) The compound in the bottle A did not dissolve in either 1 N NaOH or 1 N HCl.

(*ii*) The compound in the bottle B dissolved in 1 N NaOH but not in 1 N HCl.

(*iii*) The compound in the bottle C dissolved in both 1 N NaOH and 1 N HCl.

(*iv*) The compound in the bottle D did not dissolved in 1 N NaOH but dissolved in 1 N HCl.

(Fill up the blanks)

(*a*) Indicate the compounds in: bottle A = ____ , bottle B = ____ , bottle C = ____ and bottle D = ____.

(*b*) The compound with the highest solubility in distilled water is ____.

9. Assume that a human body requires 2500 kcal of energy each day for metabolic activity and sucrose is the only source of energy, as per the equation

$C_{12}H_{22}O_{11}(s) + 12\ O_2(g) \rightarrow 12\ CO_2(g) + 11\ H_2O\ (l)$; $\Delta H = -\ 5.6 \times 10^6$ J.

(Fill up the blanks)

(*a*) The energy requirement of the human body per day is _____ kJ.

(*b*) The mass of sucrose required to provide this energy is _____ g and the volume of CO_2 (at STP) produced is _____ litres.

Biology

10. Mohini, a resident of Chandigarh went to Shimla with her parents. There she found the same plant that they have in their backyard, at home. However, she observed that while the plants in their backyard bore white flowers, those in Shimla had pink flowers. She brought home some seeds of the plant from Shimla and planted them in Chandigarh. Upon performing self breeding for several generations she found that the plant from Shimla produced only white flowers.

(*a*) According to you what might be the reason for this observation—genetic or environmental factors?

(*b*) Suggest a simple experiment to determine whether this variation is genetic in nature

(*c*) Suggest another experiment to check whether this variation in flower colour is due to environmental factors.

11. The break-down of glucose in a cell occurs in any of the following pathways:

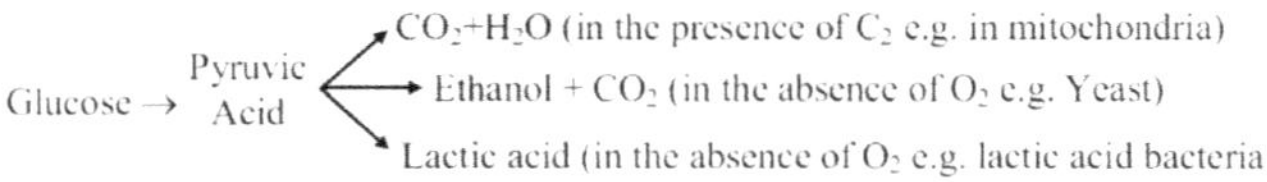

Three experiments (A, B, C) have been set up. In each experiment, a flask contains the organism in growth medium, glucose and a brown dye that changes its colour to yellow when the pH decreases. The mouth of the flask is attached to a test tube containing lime water (Calcium hydroxide; as shown in the figure). In C, but not in A and B, air is removed from the flask before beginning the experiment. After a period of growth, the following observations were made:

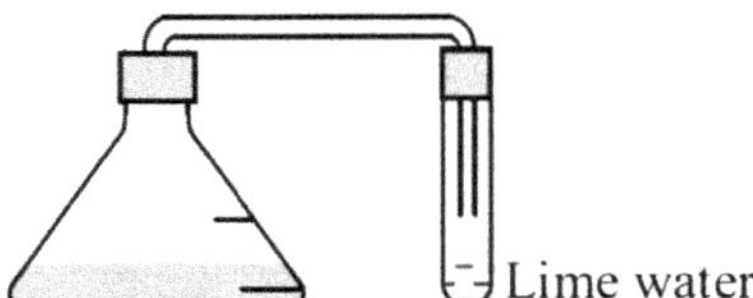

Organism in culture medium + Glucose + Dye

A : Lime water turns milky; the dye colour remains the same

B : The dye colour changes; lime water does not turn milky

C : Lime water turns milky ; the dye colour remains the same

(*a*) Question : Identify which of the reactions is the pathways depicted above is taking place in each experiment. Give reasons for your answer.

(*b*) Question : Identify which of the reactions in the pathways depicted above is expected to occur in Red Blood Cells (RBCs).

12. A scientist has a house just beside a busy highway. He collects leaves from some plants growing in his garden to do radio-carbon dating (to estimate the age of the plant by estimating the amount of a radioisotope of carbon in its tissues). Surprisingly the radio-carbon dating shows that the plant is a few thousand years old.

(*a*) Was the result of the radio-carbon dating wrong or can you propose a reason for such an observation?

(*b*) What simple experiment can be done to test the reason that you have proposed?

ANSWERS

Part-I

1	2	3	4	5	6	7	8	9	10
C	D	B	A	B	B	A	D	D	D
11	**12**	**13**	**14**	**15**	**16**	**17**	**18**	**19**	**20**
B	A	C	D	C	D	A	D	B	A
21	**22**	**23**	**24**	**25**	**26**	**27**	**28**	**29**	**30**
D	A	A	B	B	A	A	D	C	C
31	**32**	**33**	**34**	**35**	**36**	**37**	**38**	**39**	**40**
D	C	A	D	D	A	C	B	C	B

EXPLANATORY ANSWERS

1. $\alpha + \beta = -a$ and $\alpha\beta = a$

$\alpha + 1 + \beta + 1 = -a$

$\Rightarrow \quad \alpha + \beta + 2 = -a$

$\Rightarrow \quad -b + 2 = -a$

$b - a = 2 \quad ...(i)$

$(\alpha + 1)(\beta + 1) = b$

$\Rightarrow \quad \alpha\beta + \alpha + \beta + 1 = b$

$\Rightarrow \quad a + (-b) + 1 = b$

$2b - a = 1 \quad ...(ii)$

from (*i*) and (*ii*), $b = -1$

$a + b = -4.$

2. $3^{\frac{x}{y}+1} - 3^{\frac{x}{y}-1} = 24$

$\Rightarrow \quad 3^{\frac{x}{y}} \times 3 - \dfrac{3^{\frac{x}{y}}}{3} = 24$

$\Rightarrow \quad \dfrac{8}{3}\left(3^{x/y}\right) = 24$

$\Rightarrow \quad \dfrac{x}{y} = 2$

$\dfrac{x+y}{x-y} = 3.$

4. $\sqrt{a^2 + b^2} = 39 \quad ...(i)$

$\sqrt{b^2 + c^2} = 40 \quad ...(ii)$

$\sqrt{c^2 + a^2} = 41 \quad ...(iii)$

$\sqrt{a^2 + b^2 + c^2} = ?$

Square and add (*i*), (*ii*) and (*iii*)

$2(a^2 + b^2 + c^2) = 39^2 + 40^2 + 41^2 = 4802$

$a^2 + b^2 + c^2 = 2401$

$\Rightarrow \quad \sqrt{a^2 + b^2 + c^2} = 49.$

5. a = 1, b, c

$1 + b > c \Rightarrow c - b < 1$

$1 + c > b \Rightarrow b - c < 1$

$-1 < b - c < 1$

b, c are integers so $b - c = 0 \Rightarrow b = c$

semi perimeter, $S = \dfrac{2b+1}{2} = b + \dfrac{1}{2}$

area, $A = \sqrt{\left(b+\dfrac{1}{2}\right)\left(b+\dfrac{1}{2}-b\right)\left(b+\dfrac{1}{2}-c\right)\left(\dfrac{b}{2}+\dfrac{1}{2}-1\right)}$

$= \dfrac{1}{2}\sqrt{b^2 - \dfrac{1}{4}}$ = Irrational.

6.

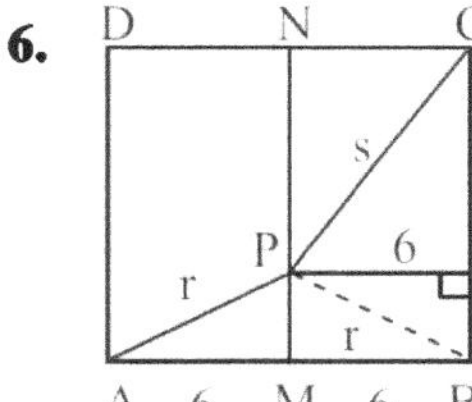

$PA = r$, $PC = s$

So, $PB = r$

Triangle with sides r, s and 12 is ΔPCB

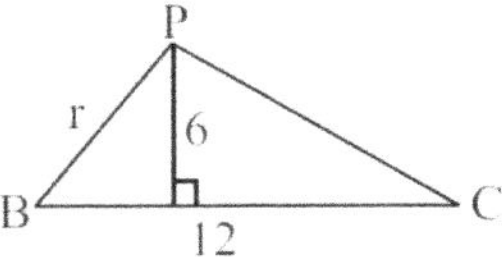

area $= \dfrac{1}{2}$ base × height

$= \dfrac{1}{2} \times 6 \times 12 = 36.$

7. Area

$$= 2\left[\frac{120}{360}\times\pi\left(\frac{5a}{2}\right)^2 + \frac{60}{360}\times\pi\left(\frac{3a}{2}\right)^2 + \frac{60}{360}\times\pi\left(\frac{a}{2}\right)^2\right]$$

$$= \frac{2\pi}{3}\left[\frac{25a^2}{4}+\frac{9a^2}{8}+\frac{a^2}{8}\right]$$

$$= \frac{2\pi}{3}\times\frac{30a^2}{4} = 5\pi a^2$$

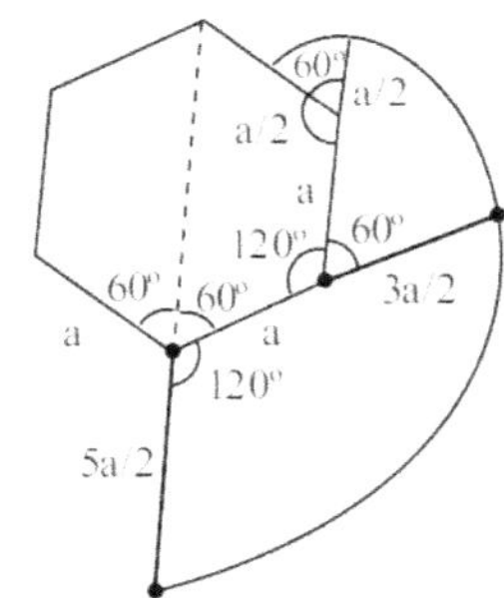

8. Rate of outflow of water

$$\Rightarrow \left(\pi r^2 h - \pi\left(\frac{r}{2}\right)^2\frac{h}{2}\right) \text{ litres in 21 minutes } i.e. \ \frac{7\pi r^2 h}{8}\text{L}$$

in 21 minutes.

Hence $\frac{\pi r^2 h}{8}$L in 3 min.

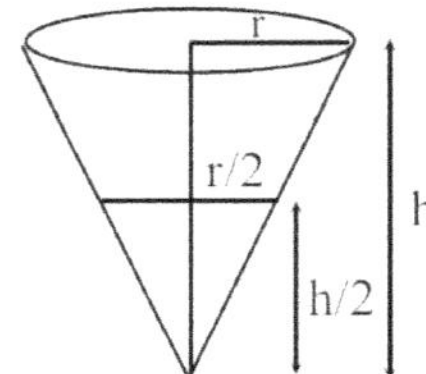

9. Initially 1000 kg [990 kg water + 10 kg rest]

Now x kg melon $\left[\frac{98x}{100}\text{water} + \frac{2x}{100}\text{rest}\right]$

Weight of solid part should remain same

$$\frac{2x}{100} = 10$$

$$\Rightarrow \qquad x = 500$$

Weight reduction = 1000 – 500 = 500 kg.

10. Area = 10 × 5 = 50 (from figure)
(assuming all sides to be integers).

11. Because initially the separation of centre of gravity from point of suspension increases & then finally decreases hence time period will initially increase & then decrease.

12. Initially when the block does not move the friction is static in nature and it will be equal (& opposite) to the magnitude of applied force so initially friction will increase. But once the body starts the motion the kinetic friction will come and it does not change with applied force.

13. To nullify the downward acceleration

$$(M_m + M_g)\ 9.8 = 40 \times 500 \times 49 \times 10^{-3}$$

$$\Rightarrow \qquad (M_m + M_g) = 100 \text{ kg.}$$

14. If radius of star is decreasing without any change in mass of star then it will not affect the force exerted by star on planet which is the required centripetal force. So radius of the orbit of planet with remain unaffected.

15.

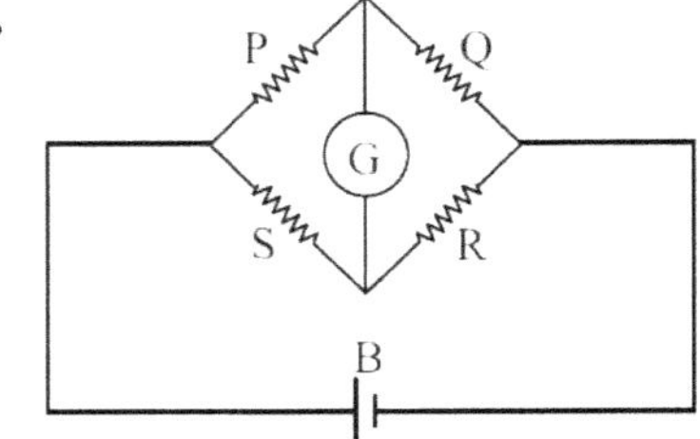

For null deflection

$$\frac{P}{Q} = \frac{S}{R}$$

or

$$\frac{P}{S} = \frac{Q}{R}$$

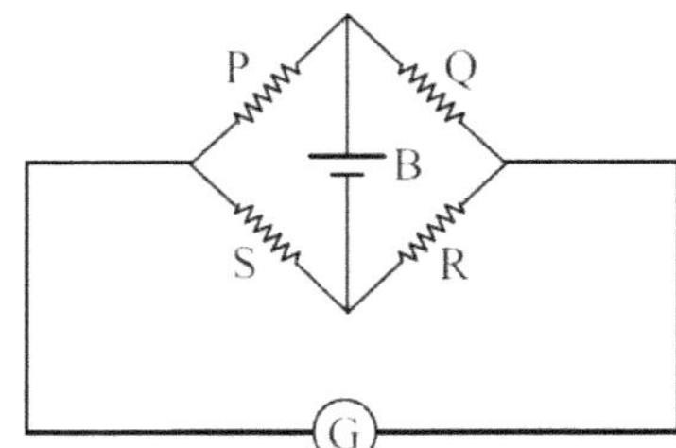

$$\frac{P}{Q} = \frac{S}{R} \text{ still valid}$$

∴ deflection is zero.

16.

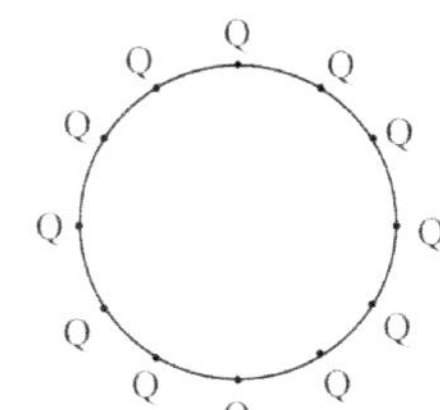

If one charge is removed then net force on Q is

$$\frac{q\times Q}{4\pi\varepsilon_0 R^2}$$

Towards the position of removed charge.

17. Part of coil turned then resistance decreases

∴ Power consumption will be more than 1 kW.

18.

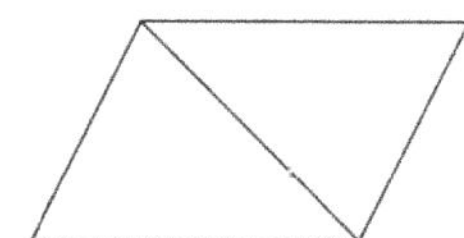

This system will behave as slab.

∴ No dispersion

No deviation.

19. If specific heat is constant, then

$$\text{Total heat gain} = 0$$
$$ms\,(T_f - 20) + ms\,(T_f - 80) = 0$$
$$T_f - 20 + T_f - 80 = 0$$
$$T_f = 50°C$$

Now T_f can be more than 50 or less than 50°C, depending on sp. heat variation with temperature.

20. $t_x = 3T + 300$

If in SI system the temperature has to be changed by one unit then in the given side the temperature has to be changed by three units

so specific heat in SI scale = 3(1400)

⇒ 4200 J/(kg – K).

21. ∵ Elevation of boiling point is proportional to the no. of foreign species.

$$CaCl_2 \rightarrow Ca^{2+} + 2Cl;\ 3$$
$$NaCl \rightarrow Na^+ + Cl;\ 2$$

Sucrose remains an dissociated mostly; 1.

23. 25g $CaCO_3$

$$\Rightarrow \quad \frac{25}{100} = \frac{1}{4} \text{ mole of } CaCO_3$$
$$CaCO_3 \rightarrow CaO + CO_2$$

∵ 1 mole $CaCO_3$ produce 1 mole CO_2

$$\therefore \frac{1}{4} \text{ mole } CaCO_3 \text{ produce } \frac{1}{4} \text{ mole } CO_2$$

and $\frac{1}{4}$ mole $CO_2 = \frac{1}{4} \times 44$ g of CO_2 = 11 g.

25. BCl_3 is electron deficient

:C̤̈l:B̤:C̤̈l:
 :C̤̈l:

Clearly B has only 6 *e*, Octet is not complete.

26. MnO_2 Oxidises Cl of HCl to Cl_2.

27.
```
 H      H
 H\     |
 H–C–C=C–C–Br
 H/  |  |  |
     H  H  H
```

12 bonds = 10 single + 1 double.

28. pH = 2 ⇒ $[H^+] = 10^{-2}$

pH = 5 ⇒ $[H^+] = 10^{-5}$

$$\therefore \quad \frac{[H^+]\text{ new}}{[H^+]\text{ old}} = \frac{10^{-5}}{10^{-2}} = 10^3.$$

29. 2 g H_2 ⇒ 1 mole gas at 200 K

28 g N_2 ⇒ 1 mole gas at 400 K

$$PV = nRT$$
$$\Rightarrow \quad P \propto nT.$$

30.
```
                                   H
                                   |
CH3 – C = C – CH3  and  CH3 – C = C – CH3
      |   |                   |
      H   H                   H
```

40. Insectivorous plant growing nitrogen deficient soil, so they get N_2 by trapping & digesting insect.

Part-II

1. We denote the area of triangle PQR by [PQR]. We see that [BOD] and [COE] are equal. Let the common value be x, and let [BOC] = t. Using the fact that the ratio of areas of two triangles having equal altitudes is the same as the ratio of their respective bases, we obtain.

$$\frac{x}{1} = \frac{BO}{OE} = \frac{t}{x}$$

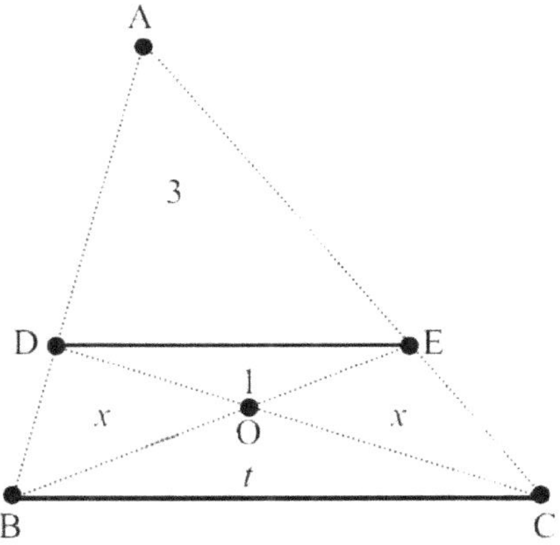

This gives $t = x^2$. Now ADE and ABC are similar so that

$$\frac{[ADE]}{ABC} = \frac{DE^2}{BC^2} = \frac{[ODE]}{[OBC]},$$

since ODE and OCB are also similar. This implies that

$$\frac{3}{4+2x+t} = \frac{1}{t},$$

which simplifies to $t = 2 + x$, using $t = x^2$ we get a quadratic in x : $x^2 - x - 2 = 0$. Its solution are $x = 2$ and $x = -1$. Since x cannot be negative, $x = 2$ and $t = 4$.

Thus [ABC] = 4 + 2x + t = 4 + 4 + 4 = 12.

2. Let t be the total number of CD's that Leela and Madan together sold. Then they obtain t^2 rupees together. Since Leela is the first one to take 10 rupees and also the last one to take 10 rupees, we must have

t^2 = 10(an old number) + (a number less than 10).

Suppose $t = 10q + r$, where r is the remainder when t is divided by 10.

Then $t^2 = 100q^2 + 20qr + r^2$.

Comparing, we conclude that

r^2 = 10 (an odd number) + (a number less than 10).

But we know that $0 \le r < 10$. Taking r = 0, 1, 2,.....9, we see that r = 4 or 6 (for other value of r, tens place in r^2 is even). But then r^2 = 16 or 36.

Hence the amount left for Madan at the end is 6 rupees.

3. (*a*) Divide the $n + 1$ numbers 1, 11, 111, ..., 111, ...1 (all having only 1 as digits) by n. Among the $n + 1$ remainders so obtained, two must be equal as the possibilities for remainders are 0, 1, 2,...., $n - 1$ which are n in number. Thus there must be two numbers x = 11..... 1 and y = 11.....1 having say j digits and k digits respectively which leave the same remainders after division by n. We may take $j < k$. Now we see that $y - x$ is divisible by n. But $y - x$ = 11 .... 100 ... 0 where there are $k - j$ number of 1's and remaining zeros. Since n is coprime to 10, we see that n divides m = 11 ... 1, a number having only 1's as its digits.

(*b*) If p/q is any rational number ($p > 0$, $q > 0$), then we may write $q = 2^r 5^s t$, where t is coprime to 10.

Choose a number m having only 1's as its digits and is divisible by t. Consider 9 m, Which has only 9 as its digits and is still divisible by t. Let k = 9 m/t. We see that;

$$qk = 9m\, 2^r 5^s$$
$$= (10^c - 1)\, 2^r 5^s,$$

where c is the number of digits in m. Hence we can find d such that $qd = 10^b (10^c - 1)$ (multiply by a suitable power of 2 if $s > r$ and by a suitable power of 5 if $r > s$). Then

$$\frac{p}{q} = \frac{pd}{qd}$$

$$= \frac{a}{10^b(10^c - 1)}$$

where $a = pd$.

4. For P : $I = I_R + I_V = V/R + V/R_V$

$$R = \frac{V}{I}\left[\frac{R_V}{R_V - V/I}\right]$$

$$= R_{est}\left[\frac{R_V}{1 - R_{est}/R_v}\right]$$

$$\approx R_{est}\,[1 + R_{est}/R_v]$$

(neglecting higher order terms in R_{est}/R_v)

$$\delta R_P = |R_{est} - R|$$

$$= R_{est}^2 / R_V \approx \frac{R^2}{R_V}$$

Alternatively,

$$R_{est} = \frac{V}{I} = \frac{R_V R}{R_V + R}$$

$$\delta R_P = |R_{est} - R|$$

$$= R\left[\frac{R_V}{R_V + R} - 1\right] \approx \frac{R^2}{R_V}$$

For Q : $V = I(R + R_A)$

$$R = V/I - R_A$$
$$= R_{est} - R_A$$
$$\delta R_Q = |R_{est} - R| = R_A$$

If $R = \sqrt{R_A R_V}$,

then
$$\frac{\delta R_P}{\delta R_Q} = \frac{R_{est}^2}{(R_A R_V)}$$

$$= \frac{R_{est}^2}{R^2} \approx 1.$$

5. (*a*) Object is at $2f$, so the image is formed at the same distance from the lens (20 cm) to the right.

(*b*) Since light has to retrace its path, the mirror should be placed so that the previous image is at its centre of curvature. Thus the mirror must be placed 30 cm to the right of the lens.

(*c*) For the plane mirror, reflection forms an image 40 cm to the right of the lens. Using the lens formula, we see that the final image is formed at a distance of 40/3 cm to the left of the lens.

6. (*a*) $V(\theta) = mgR\,(1 - \cos\theta)$

(*b*) $mgH - mg\,R(1 - \cos\theta)$

(*c*) for H << R the body executes SHM with a time period of $\frac{1}{2\pi}\sqrt{\frac{R}{g}}$ – the time taken for it to travel from P to Q will be a quarter of this, *i.e.,* $\frac{1}{8\pi}\sqrt{\frac{R}{g}}$.

(*d*) At the lowest point, the speed is given by $\frac{1}{2}mv^2 = mgH$.

So, $$T - mg = \frac{mv^2}{R} = \frac{2mgH}{R},$$

and thus $$T = mg\left(1 + \frac{2H}{R}\right).$$

7. (*a*) $a = 3$, $b = 8$, $c = 3$, $d = 2$ and $e = 4$.

(*b*) $f = 2$, $g = 1$, $h = 1$.

(*c*) $i = 2$, $j = 1$, $k = 1$, $1 = 2$.

(*d*) 2.54 g of I_2 = 1/100 mole of I_2 = 2/100 gm atom of Cu

% Cu = (2/100) × 63.5 / 2) = 63.5%

8. Bottle A = III, Bottle B = II, Bottle C = IV, Bottle D = I

CH_2CO_2H CO_2H NH_2 NH_2

Compound with the highest solubility in distilled water : IV

9. (*a*) 2500 × 4.184 kJ= 10460 kJ;

(*b*) 342 g of sucrose produces 5600 kJ of energy. To provide 10460 kJ

we need 10460 × 342 / 5600 g = 638 g

638 g/342 g × 12 × 22.4 L = 501 L.

10. (*a*) Difference in flower colour is most likely due to environmental factors.

(*b*) Perform cross breeding between the plants from Chandigarh and those from Shimla to find out whether we get any pink flowers or flowers with any shade of color between pink and white in the F1 generation.

(*c*) Grow the plants from Chandigarh in Shimla and check whether they still produce white flowers or bear pink flowers.

11. (*a*) In experiment A, ethanol fermentation occurs producing CO_2, turning lime water milky. Since acid is not produced the dye colour does not change.

In experiment B, lactic acid fermentation takes place, which produces acid but does not produce CO_2. Hence dye colour changes to yellow but the lime water does not turn milky.

In experiment C, since the lime water turns milky, ethanol fermentation is occurring. In addition, since removal of air did not affect the reaction, the fermentation is anaerobic and yeast must be the organism in the flask.

(*b*) In RBCs, lactic acid fermentation occurs.

12. (*a*) The result of the radio-carbon dating was correct.

Reason : Vehicles running on the highway beside the house emitted carbon dioxide from the combustion of petrol or diesel, which are fossil fuels. The carbon in this carbon dioxide, coming from living material that has been converted into petroleum millions of years ago, would get assimilated into the tissues of the plant as it uses carbon dioxide from the surrounding atmosphere for photosynthesis. Therefore tissues of the plant, when used for radio-carbon dating, would show the age of the plant to be many thousands of years old.

(*b*) A simple experiment to test the validity of this explanation would be to collect seeds from the plant and grow them in a plot of land away from the highway or other sources of carbon dioxide coming from the burning of fossil fuels. Radio-carbon dating of plants growing from these seeds should show them as young plants.

YOUR SPACE

www.ingramcontent.com/pod-product-compliance
Lightning Source LLC
LaVergne TN
LVHW080544200726
843508LV00008B/1494

* 9 7 8 9 3 8 8 6 4 2 9 9 6 *